American Education

American Education

An Introduction to Social and Political Aspects

FOURTH EDITION

JOEL SPRING

Longman

New York & London

American Education: An Introduction to Social and Political Aspects. 4th edition

Longman Inc., 95 Church Street, White Plains, N.Y. 10601

Associated companies:
Longman Group Ltd., London
Longman Cheshire Pty., Melbourne
Longman Paul Pty., Auckland
Copp Clark Pitman, Toronto
Pitman Publishing Inc., New York

Executive editor: Ray O'Connell
Production editor: Camilla T. K. Palmer
Text design: Joseph DePinho
Cover design: Joseph DePinho
Director of Production: Eduardo Castillo

Library of Congress Cataloging-in-Publication Data

Spring, Joel H.
    American education: an introduction to social and political aspects/Joel Spring.—4th ed.
        p.   cm.
    Includes bibliographies and index.
    ISBN 0-8013-0251-X
    1. Education—Social aspects—United States.   2. Education—Political aspects—United
    States.   3. Educational equalization—United States.   4. Education and state—United
    States.   I. Title.
LC191.4.S684   1989   88-8083
370.19′0973—dc19   CIP

ISBN 0-8013-0251-X

94 93 92 91 90 89 9 8 7 6 5 4 3 2

Contents

Philosophy of Ed.

Preface

The fourth edition of *American Education* contains much new and revised material. The political, economic, and social factors that determine curriculum, instructions, and the popularity of particular theories of learning in American public schools are discussed in a new chapter, Chapter 3. The chapter begins with a description of how the public school curriculum in the twentieth century has reflected changing social and economic concerns. The discussion of instruction in the public schools is based on Larry Cuban's outstanding book, *How Teachers Taught,* which raises the question of why basic classroom instruction methods, despite many reform movements, have changed so little in the twentieth century. The final discussion in the chapter focuses on how changing economic and political conditions determine the popularity of particular learning theories in the public schools.

Chapters 1 and 2 now contain extended discussions of the reports of the Task Force on Teaching as a Profession, *A Nation Prepared: Teachers for the 21st Century,* and of the Holmes Group, *Tomorrow's Teachers.* A discussion of the "new immigrants" has been added to Chapter 5. Chapters on the political structure of American education and the role of the courts have been updated.

I have been convinced by recent events that my arguments in the original preface to the first edition of this book were correct. I argued then that a teaching career involves more than being an educational technician and that teachers have to be prepared for involvement in the social, political, and economic aspects of education. This argument has been made more relevant by the push by teachers' unions for teacher power and by the reforms calling for master teachers and career ladders. In fact, teachers are playing an increasing role in the determination of educational policy in local school districts, in the halls of state legislatures, and in the arena of national politics. The best example of this new role of teachers is the active and important participation of teachers in presidential and congressional elections.

I also retain my commitment to the idea that decisions about a career in education should be based on a clear understanding and knowledge of the structure and functioning of the educational system. Introductory courses in teacher education should focus on the ideological debates about the role of schooling in society, the effects of schooling on society, and the politics of education. In addition, the prospective teacher should try to understand the profession of teaching in the context of society and the educational system. Being a good teacher involves more than making decisions about methods of instruction; it includes making political, economic, and social decisions that can affect the entire society. This book's purpose is to acquaint prospective teachers with the political context in which they will work and the major social, economic, and political issues related to education.

American Education

I

THE SCHOOL
AND THE SOCIAL
STRUCTURE

1

The Purposes of Public Schooling

The public school has become one of the central and most controversial institutions of society. Parents select housing in terms of available schooling; politicians are often forced to voice their opinions on school issues; racial and religious riots take place at the schoolhouse; some parents accuse schools of not being patriotic, while others find them guilty of flag waving; some members of society argue that schools will end poverty, and others contend that they maintain poverty.

In recent years, conflicts over religious values have caused some groups to question the very existence of government-operated schools. As discussed in more detail in Chapter 10, a series of court cases in 1986 found public schools to be teaching a secular form of religion. These cases were brought to the courts by Protestant fundamentalists who believed that public schools were destroying the religious and moral values of their children. One solution proposed by these groups is for schools to teach according to the values of each individual child. Schools would select books and materials reflecting the values of each student, or parents could select a school reflecting their own values. The latter alternative, one strongly favored by fundamentalist religious groups, could result in replacement of the present system of publicly supported and privately operated schools by giving parents, instead of schools, the money to spend on their children's education.

While controversy is an integral part of the history of American schools, there is also a high level of satisfaction. This is most apparent when attitudes of American parents are compared to those of parents in other countries. For

3

instance, the 1986 report of the Task Force on Teaching as a Profession of the Carnegie Forum on Education and the Economy, *A Nation Prepared: Teachers for the 21st Century,* found that mothers in the United States expressed a higher level of satisfaction with their children's schooling than did mothers in Japan and Taiwan. The report expressed surprise at the finding because Japanese students score higher than American students on many standardized achievement tests. In the United States over 60 percent of the mothers in the sample were "very satisfied" with their children's education as compared to fewer than 20 percent of Japanese mothers, while fewer than 20 percent of American mothers were "not satisfied" as compared to 30 percent of Japanese mothers.

Such findings suggest that while conflict exists regarding the *purposes* of American education there is still considerable satisfaction in its *achievements.* It is often difficult to separate conflict over values in schools from other attitudes regarding the workings of the educational system. But at the heart of most educational controversies is a debate over public and private goals, of which the struggle over religious values is simply one aspect. The remaining sections of this chapter will examine the inherent problems and contradictions in the political, economic, and social purposes of public schooling. A review of the purposes of schooling provides a brief history of the reasons for the development of American public schools. The chapter will conclude with a discussion of how political beliefs affect the goals of schooling.

Public versus Private Goals

A great deal of confusion and conflict can occur over the difference between public and private goals in education. A parent might send his or her child to school to learn basic intellectual skills while considering moral and social training a function of the home. On the other hand, the school might assume the responsibility of producing moral, socially responsible citizens. This situation has the potential of creating conflict between the parents and the school over the content of moral and social training, and the goals that should control the education of the child.

If the school in question is a public school operated by the government, then the problem becomes even more difficult. Government-operated schools by their very nature have the responsibility of carrying out the wishes of the general public and not those of private individuals. This means that the education of a child in a public school is subordinate to the general educational goals of the government. In other words, the public school serves public purposes.

The fact that the public school serves public purposes is inherent in the very idea that governments should establish and operate educational systems; government educational systems were set up to serve public—not private— goals. How the goals were established is a political question, and will be discussed in later chapters. In general, the public goals of education have been linked to concerns about social and political stability, reform, and economic development. Therefore, parents who send their child to a public school to achieve purely intellectual goals might be frustrated and concerned about both the time spent on government goals for education and the content of those goals. Certainly, in the history of American education one of the greatest arenas of conflict has been between private moral and religious beliefs and the values taught in the public schools. Other issues have also created bitter dispute. Educating children in public schools for citizenship has always been an area of conflict, a conflict concerned with content and purpose. Similar conflicts occur over the use of public schools to pursue economic goals.

Although private goals are subordinate to government goals in public schools, they cannot simply be dismissed. It is important to understand private goals because of the potential conflict between private goals and public schools, and because of the larger issue of whether the public schools serve the interests of the individual.

One of the more recent surveys of private goals was conducted by John Goodlad for his study, *A Place Called School*. Goodlad surveyed the educational goals held by students, teachers, and parents, and divided them into social, intellectual, personal, and vocational goals. These categories differ slightly in meaning from those used in the remainder of this chapter to describe the public goals of schooling. Goodlad defines *vocational* to mean preparation for work; *social* to mean preparation for the social life of a complex society; *intellectual* to mean academic skills and knowledge; and *personal* to mean development of individual responsibility, talent, and free expression.

The most striking conclusion one reaches in looking at the results of Goodlad's survey is the difference between private and public goals. The dominant public goals for education in the twentieth century have been economic. These economic goals have included preparation for work, and controlling the labor market and economic development. In Goodlad's survey, vocational is the word closest in meaning to economic and it was chosen as the least important goal by teachers and parents. All teachers in elementary, middle, and high school grades selected vocational as the least important goal after intellectual, personal, and social goals. Parents of elementary and middle school children selected vocational goals last, and parents of high school students chose vocational as third, after intellectual and personal goals. High school students, on the other hand, selected vocational as the most important goal, whereas it was the second choice for middle school students.

Nothing gives greater evidence of the potential conflict between public and private goals than the fact that the number-one goal of teachers and parents is intellectual. Students maintain this as their number-one goal until high school, when it moves into second place after vocational. This means that the majority of parents send their children to school primarily to learn academic skills and knowledge. Although on the surface this seems reasonable and a commonsense conclusion, it is in conflict with the major public goals that have been used to justify the establishment and maintenance of public schools. In fact, parents rank personal goals as second in importance, leaving social and vocational at the bottom in relative importance.

These differences between public and private goals should be kept in mind by the reader as she or he studies the following pages. What the public official wants the school system to achieve can be entirely different from what the individual citizen wants. Also, differing attitudes and perceptions can develop about what is happening within public school systems.

The following discussion of the public goals of schooling is divided into political, social, and economic goals. In general, political goals refer to the attempts to use educational systems to mold future citizens, maintain political stability, and shape political systems; social goals include attempts to reform society, provide social stability, and give direction to social development; and economic goals involve the use of the public school system to sort and select talent for the labor market, develop human capital, and plan economic development. However, the reader should be aware that these categories often overlap. For instance, the goal of eliminating poverty through schooling can be considered both an economic and a social goal.

The Political Purposes of Schooling

The most important political goal of public schooling in modern society is the education of the future citizen. This statement can mean different things depending on the nature of the political organization. For instance, in Nazi Germany during the 1930s, schools were enlisted in a general campaign to produce citizens who would believe in the racial superiority of the German people, support fascism, and be willing to die at the command of Hitler. Racial biology and fascist political doctrines were taught in the classroom; patriotic parades and singing took place in the school yard. The lesson learned from the experience of schools in Nazi Germany is that one must carefully evaluate the citizenship-training function of public schools. Citizenship training is not necessarily good, nor can it exist apart from a general political philosophy.

In America early proposals for public systems of education reflected a variety of concerns about the establishment of a republican form of government. One of the major worries expressed immediately following the American Revolution was the source of future leadership for the new government. Since hereditary nobility and monarchy would no longer be bases for leadership, a question arose about who would be the leaders of a republican government. Revolutionary leader Benjamin Rush proposed in the late eighteenth century the establishment of a national university and a requirement that all government officials hold a degree from that institution. Rush argued that one should no more allow quacks to practice politics than one allows quacks to practice medicine. President George Washington proposed a national university before Congress as a means of training political leaders and creating a common national culture by bringing together within one institution students from all areas of the country.

One of the arguments against Washington's proposal for a national university as a training ground for political leadership was the charge of elitism. (Current criticism of reliance upon educational institutions as sources of political and social leadership makes the same charge.) Critics of Washington's proposal felt that a national university would be training leaders who would view themselves as "better" and more important than the general public. These educated leaders would not necessarily represent the interests and welfare of the general public. The hereditary aristocracy might be replaced by an aristocracy of the educated. If none but the rich had access to higher education, then the rich could use higher education as a means of perpetuating and supporting their social status.

One answer to the charge of elitism is the concept of a meritocracy. This idea permeates our existing educational institutions. A meritocracy is a social system in which all members are given an equal chance to develop their abilities and rise in the social hierarchy. In a meritocracy the school is often viewed as the key institution for training and sorting citizens. One of the earliest and most elaborate proposals for a society based on the selectivity of education was Plato's *Republic*. In Plato's utopian proposal each generation was trained in music and gymnastics, and from each generation the most talented were selected for further education as guardians. The most talented guardians were educated to be philosopher-kings. An educational system functioning in this manner, Plato believed, would result in the ruling of society by the wisdom of philosopher-kings.

One of the earliest proposals in the United States to create an educational system designed to select and promote talent into a social hierarchy was made by Thomas Jefferson in 1779 in a proposed *Bill for the More General Diffusion of Knowledge*. Jefferson's plan called for three years of free education for all free children. The most talented of these children were to be selected and educated at public expense at regional grammar schools. From this select group the most talented were to be chosen for further education. Thomas Jefferson wrote in *Notes on the State of Virginia*, "By this means twenty of the best geniuses will be raked from the rubbish annually, and be instructed, at the public expense...."

The details of Jefferson's plan are not as important as the idea, which has become ingrained in American social thought, that schooling is the best means of identifying democratic leadership. This idea assumes that the educational system is fair in its judgments and that its basis for judgment has some relationship to the role for which students are being selected.

For instance, fairness of selection in education assumes that the individual is being judged solely on talent demonstrated in school and not on other social factors such as race, religion, dress, and social class. As will be discussed in later chapters, these factors have been related to performance in school. If, for example, the educational institution tends to favor an individual from a particular religion or social class, then it would tend to select and promote that particular individual in school and, consequently, in the social hierarchy.

This situation could result in a democratic elitism in which certain groups would be favored in school, and the social power of their class perpetuated through the school. For example, if all members of society were taught to believe that the school selected fairly and only those selected by the educational system could lead society, then all members of society would accept the social hierarchy perpetuated by the educational system. Acceptance of this situation might obscure other inequalities in society. For instance, if the educational system favored those with wealth, then all members of society might come to accept differences in wealth as differences in talent as determined by educational institutions.

Another debatable issue is the assumption of a relationship between talented performance in an educational institution and performance in a social role. There might not be any necessary relationship between the skills and attitudes required for good academic performance and those required for good occupational and social performance. The best medical doctor might not be the one who received the highest grades in medical school. The best politician might not be the one who received the highest grades in political science courses. Of course, this depends on what one means by the "best doctor" or the "best politician." The important issue is whether or not one believes that the skills required to succeed in an educational institution are the best skills for a particular social role.

The differences between these approaches are reflected in the differences between Thomas Jefferson and Horace Mann, often called the father of American education. Jefferson proposed a very limited education for the general citizenry. The three years of free education to be provided to all children were to consist of training in reading, writing, and arithmetic, with reading instruction given in books on Greek, Roman, English, and American history. Jefferson did not believe that people needed to be educated to be good citizens. He believed in the guiding power of natural reason to lead the citizen to the correct political decisions. The political education of the citizen was to come from a free press; the citizen would judge between competing political ideas in newspapers. The only requirement was that the citizen know how to read.

Interestingly, while Jefferson wanted political opinions to be formed in a free marketplace of ideas, he advocated censorship of political texts at the University of Virginia. These contradictory positions reflect an inherent problem in the use of schools to teach political ideas. One is always tempted to limit political instruction to what one believes are "correct" political ideas.

Horace Mann, on the other hand, believed that a common political creed had to be instilled in all citizens. Without this political consensus a democratic society was doomed to political strife and chaos. Mann developed these ideas and his reputation as America's greatest educational leader while serving as secretary of the Massachusetts Board of Education from 1837 to 1848. Mann had begun his career as a lawyer; he dedicated his life to public schooling when, he claimed, he realized that schooling was the key to the reform of society.

Horace Mann lived during a period of great political tension and fear that the extension of suffrage would lead to violence and mob rule. Mann believed that political and social order could be maintained if all citizens accepted a common set of political values. These values were to be taught in a common public school and would provide a political consensus or framework in which democracy would function. The important thing for Mann was that all children in society attend the same type of school. This was what was meant by "common." It was a school common to all children. Within the common school, children of all religions and social classes were to share in a common education. Basic social disagreements were to vanish as rich and poor children, and children whose parents were supporters of different political parties, mingled in the schoolroom.

Within the walls of the common schoolhouse were to be taught the basic principles of a republican form of government. Mann assumed that republican principles existed that members of all political parties could agree upon and that therefore these principles could be taught without objection. In fact, he argued against the teaching of any politically controversial topic because of its potential for destroying the public school. The combination of common schooling and the teaching of a common political philosophy were to create the political consensus that would make it possible for a republican society to function. Political liberty would be possible, according to Mann's philosophy, because it would be restrained and controlled by the public school.

One of the many problems inherent in Mann's philosophy, and a problem that has plagued public schools in the United States since the nineteenth century, is the assumption of the existence of common republican principles upon which all citizens agree. Since the nineteenth century, there have been continual pressures and controversies about the political philosophy to be taught in the public schools. Conservative political groups, such as the American Legion and the Daughters of the American Revolution, have throughout the twentieth century put pressure on local public schools to avoid teaching what these organizations consider "left-wing" ideas. On the other hand, liberal organizations and particularly labor unions have attempted to influence the schools to teach their particular political doctrines.

There has also existed a tradition of strong dissent to a public system of education teaching political doctrines. As far back as the late eighteenth century, English political theorist William Godwin warned against national systems of education because they could become a means by which those who controlled the government could control the minds of future citizens. Godwin wrote in 1793, "Their views as institutors of a system of education will not fail to be analogous to their views in their political capacity: the data upon which their instructions are founded."

Another problem with Horace Mann's vision of a democratic consensus built upon the common school is that American public schooling has never been common to all children. All races, religions, and social classes have not mingled within a single common school. Racial segregation continues to exist in American public schools even after massive efforts at desegregation in the 1960s and 1970s. A variety of religious groups, including the Amish and Catholics, have maintained a tradition of parochial schools in opposition to the secularism of the public schools. Children in wealthy suburbs attend private schools, or public schools that are quite different from those in poorer school districts. Mann's dream of the common public school has never come into existence in the United States.

The way in which Horace Mann hoped to reduce tension between social groups in American society can be called a form of socialization. *Socialization* refers to the learning of habits and attitudes of social conduct. This learning primarily takes place in school through social interaction, not through the specific content taught in the classroom. For instance, in the case of the common school, a reduction of tension between groups was to be primarily a result of the intermingling of students and not of textbook learning, class recitation, or lectures by the teacher.

It has been argued that socialization in the school is one of the most powerful means of political control. The very fact of having an entire generation in an institution where they are required to cooperate and obey rules is considered by some people to be a preparation to cooperate and obey the rules of the government. Johann Fichte in Prussia in the early nineteenth century asserted that schools would prepare the individual to serve the government and country by teaching obedience to the rules of the school and developing a sense of loyalty to the school. He stated further that students would transfer their obedience to the laws of the school to obedience to the constitution of the country. What was even more important, according to Fichte, was that interaction between students, as well as loyalty and service to the school and fellow students, would prepare the individual for service to the country. The school was a miniature community in which children learned to adjust their individuality to the requirements of the community. The real work of the school, Fichte said, was in shaping this adjustment. The well-ordered government required that the citizen go beyond mere obedience to the written constitution and laws. Fichte believed the child must be adjusted to see the government as something greater than the individual, and must learn to sacrifice for the good of the social whole.

Fichte also advocated the teaching of patriotic songs, national history, and literature to increase the sense of dedication and patriotism to the state. This combination of socialization and patriotic teachings, he argued, would produce a citizen more willing and able to participate in the army and, consequently, would reduce the cost of national defense.

In the United States the combination of patriotic exercises and development of loyalty to the institution of the school began to appear in the 1890s. It was during this period of large-scale immigration from Southern and Eastern Europe that the public schools became heavily involved in what were called "Americanization" programs. Americanization involved teaching the immigrant the laws, language, and customs of the United States. Naturally, this involved the teaching of American songs and customs. With the coming of World War I, the Pledge of Allegiance, the singing of patriotic songs, participation in student government, and other patriotic exercises became a part of the American school. In addition, the development of extracurricular activities led to an emphasis on school spirit. The formation of football and basketball teams, with their accompanying trappings of cheerleaders and pep rallies, was supported with the idea that these activities improved school spirit and, consequently, service to society.

The involvement of the American public school in the teaching and development of patriotism has created problems for a democratic society with a variety of religious, ethnic, and political groups. Some religious groups object to pledging allegiance to the flag because it involves worship of a "graven image." The U.S. Supreme Court ruled in 1943 in *West Virginia State Board of Education* v. *Barnette* that expulsion of children of Jehovah's Witnesses for not saluting the flag was a violation of their constitutional rights of freedom of religion. Some teachers view patriotic exercises as contrary to the principles of a free society. In a later chapter on the rights of teachers (Chapter 10) there is a lengthy discussion of the court cases dealing with academic freedom and loyalty oaths; conflict between patriotism and students' rights are also dealt with in that chapter.

Alongside the role of patriotism in a democratic society is the question of service to the country. Is it good in a democratic society to place service to society above service to oneself? Or should the individual demand that institutions in a democratic society be designed to serve the individual?

The problems inherent in using public schools as a means of political control in a democratic society are not easily resolved. One of the central questions is who or what group should determine the kinds of political teachings and political socialization in the schools? This question leads directly to the issue of who controls American education (discussed in later chapters). It may be that the attempt to use the school as a means of creating a political meritocracy or a political consensus or a sense of patriotism is contradictory to the ideals of political liberty.

The Social Purposes of Schooling

The hope of improving society through public schooling has almost become an article of American faith. Horace Mann believed it was the key to solving all social problems. He argued that past societies had experimented with different forms of government and laws in an attempt to stop crime and that they had all failed. The answer, Mann said, was in the proper training of young children so that they would not desire or perform criminal acts. Mann even suggested with a certain amount of utopian hope that America might see the day when the training of the schoolhouse would make it no longer necessary to enforce the law.

The idea of using the school as a means of social control was first explicitly stated by American sociologist Edward Ross in the 1890s. Ross referred to education as an inexpensive form of police. He divided social control into external and internal forms. Traditionally, he argued, internal forms of control had centered on the family, the church, and the community. The family and church had worked on the child to inculcate moral values and social responsibility to ensure social stability and cohesion. In modern society, Ross declared, the family and church were being replaced by the school as the most important institution for instilling internal values. Ross saw reliance on education as a means of control becoming characteristic of American society. More and more, the school was taking the place of the church and the family. "The ebb of religion is only half a fact," Ross wrote. "The other half is the high tide of education. While the priest is leaving the civil service, the schoolmaster is coming in. As the state shakes itself loose from the church, it reaches out for the school."

One of the things heard constantly throughout the twentieth century is that the family and religion are collapsing, and thus the school must pick up the pieces. Whether these two institutions have in fact collapsed is debatable, but the argument has been used to justify the continued use of the school to solve problems.

The school has been used in a variety of ways in the twentieth century in attempts to solve social problems. For instance, the very act of requiring school attendance has been viewed as a means of reducing juvenile delinquency. The development of summer schools in the late nineteenth and early twentieth centuries was justified as a means of keeping youths off the streets. Once youths were off the streets, it was hoped that the moral and social influence of the school would keep them from future acts of crime and from the use of tobacco and alcohol. In later years, the schools would assume the burden of eliminating traffic accidents through driver training; improving family life through courses in modern living and home economics; and eliminating drug abuse, venereal disease, and a multitude of other social problems through health education.

For some twentieth-century Americans, the school became the symbol and hope for the good society. This hope is best illustrated by a story told to kindergartners in the early part of the century about two children who bring a beautiful flower from their school class to their dirty and dark tenement apartment. The mother takes the flower and puts it in a glass of water near a dirty window. She decides the flower needs more light to expose its beauty. The mother proceeds to wash the window, which allows more light into the apartment and illuminates the dirty floors, walls, and furniture. The added light sends the mother scurrying around to clean up the now-exposed dirt. In the meantime the father, who is unable to keep a steady job because of a drinking problem, returns to the aparment and is amazed to find his grim dwelling transformed into a clean and tidy home. The transformation of the apartment results in the father's wanting to spend more time at home, and less time in the tavern. The father's drinking problem is solved, he is able to maintain a steady job, and the family lives happily ever after.

This story characterizes the hope that the moral influence of the school would reach out into the homes and neighborhoods of America. One unanswered question, and a question that is inherent also in the earlier discussion of political control, is this: Whose moral and social values will permeate the American school? Horace Mann argued that there were certain moral values that all religious groups could agree upon and that these shared values would become the backbone of the moral teachings of the school. A variety of religious groups have disagreed with this idea from the time of Mann up to the present. The largest single religious group to dissent and establish its own system of schools was the Catholic church. The argument of Catholic church leaders was that all education by its very goal of shaping behavior was religious and that it was impossible for a public institution to claim that it could satisfy the needs of all religious groups. Even if the public school eliminated all religious and moral teaching, this alternative could not be accepted because education would then become irreligious.

Even more important than the question of whose social and moral values should permeate the school is the question of whether the school should be involved in attempts at social reform or improvement. One reason schools have gotten involved in so many social problems is that the school is the most available institution and the one least likely to affect other parts of the social system. For instance, alcoholism might be the product of boredom with monotonous work, deteriorating urban conditions, family traditions, or a variety of other factors in the social structure. To turn to the school to solve the problem of alcoholism through health classes is to say the problem is one of individual training and is not related to factors in the social structure. It is easier to give a health course than to change job conditions, improve urban environments, or manipulate family traditions. Of even greater importance is the fact that the school is less threatening than such direct changes. For instance, changing job conditions involves confronting the whole organization of industry and the conflicting interests of unions and business.

In other words, the school is often the safest and least controversial way of planning for social improvement. A politician in the state legislature or in the local community can call for social reform through the school and thereby give the appearance of doing good without antagonizing any community interests.

From this standpoint it can be argued that reform through the school is the most conservative means of social reform.

This has been one of the charges made against the schools' attempt to end poverty in America. In 1964 and 1965 the federal government under the leadership of President Lyndon B. Johnson launched a massive War on Poverty with the passage of the Economic Opportunity Act and the Elementary and Secondary Education Act. Both President Johnson and the congressional legislation placed primary emphasis upon the role of education in ending poverty. The theoretical support for government action came from the Council of Economic Advisers.

Within this theoretical framework education was seen as one element of a series of social factors that tended to reinforce the condition of being poor. For instance, an inadequate education restricted employment opportunities, which caused a low standard of living and, consequently, poor medical care, diet, housing, and education for the next generation. This model of poverty suggested that one could begin at any point in the set of causal relationships and move around the circle of poverty. The improvement of health conditions, for instance, would lead to fewer days lost from employment, which would mean more income. Better income would mean improved housing, medical care, diet, and education. These improved conditions would mean better jobs for those of the next generation.

The idea that the poor were locked into a circle of poverty led to the belief that a culture of poverty existed. Within this framework modern technological society had left the poor behind; and once they were caught in the circle of poverty, a culture of poverty developed that helped to perpetuate social conditions. The War on Poverty was to be a war to destroy a culture by attacking a number of social conditions. Government action was directed toward housing, diet, and health care; but greatest importance was given to education to begin the chain reaction that would end poverty.

The War on Poverty program included Head Start programs, special funding of programs in local schools for the culturally disadvantaged, job-training programs, bilingual education, minority education, and a host of other special programs. Head Start programs were based on the premise that children of the poor were culturally disadvantaged with regard to learning opportunities, when compared to the children of the middle and upper classes. Head Start programs were therefore to provide early childhood education, which would give the poor a "head start" on schooling and allow them to compete on equal terms with other children. Job-training programs were based on the assumption that the cure for teenage and adult unemployment was job training. Special reading programs were developed for the so-called "culturally disadvantaged" because it was argued that poor reading ability was the most important reason for the failure of the poor in school. Bilingual and minority education programs were developed because it was argued that public education tended to discriminate against the culture of minority groups, which resulted in the failure of these groups in school. All these programs were to contribute to the ending of poverty in the United States.

More than a decade later, poverty had not ended in the United States, and serious doubts were expressed about the role of schooling in ending it. Some argued that the War on Poverty's educational programs had never really been given a chance because of inadequate funding by the government and mismanagement by federal bureaucrats. Others insisted that better educational programs could be encouraged and that to develop them would require more time and research. Still others felt that the school could accomplish nothing because of community and family influences on the child.

Most important for our discussion of the social purposes of schooling is the charge that was made that emphasis upon education was one way of avoiding basic economic problems. The educational component of the War on Poverty assumed that if you educated the poor, they would be able to get jobs and achieve higher income levels. The one flaw in this thinking is that job training does not necessarily increase salaries. Society might always need people for menial tasks, and increased schooling might only result in educational inflation when the nature of jobs did not change but educational requirements increased.

This became one of the problems of the early 1970s when the labor market was flooded with college graduates, and scholars with doctorates were driving taxicabs and cooking in small restaurants. In this situation the occupational structure did not expand to meet the increased educational training of the labor force. The response of educational institutions was to reorganize for more specific career training and call for more limited educational aspirations. The important lesson in this situation was that the nature of the labor market was more important in determining employment than was the amount of education available to the population. In terms of social reform it seemed to indicate that education alone would not solve the problems of poverty and that more direct changes had to be made in the organization of labor and the structure of the American economic system.

In the 1980s, value conflicts resulting from the use of schools to solve social problems is most clearly evident in discussion about AIDS education. These discussions often pit those who believe in a strong moral code to control sexual behavior against those who believe in the right of free sexual activity between consenting adults. Those who believe in a strong moral code tend to support AIDS education programs that preach sexual abstinence outside of marriage and take a strong line against homosexual activities. Those at the other end of the value spectrum emphasize educational programs that teach safe sexual procedures and advocate the dispensing of condoms in public schools.

In fact, issues surrounding sex education are often the most volatile. In the 1980s, heated discussions occurred concerning the establishment in New York City of the Harvey Milk High School for homosexual teenagers. Some members of the community objected because it seemed to condone homo-sexuality, while others supported the idea because they believed homosexual teenagers needed help in establishing an identity. Similar controversies occur concerning homosexual teachers. Some people argue that homosexual teachers are not more likely to impose themselves on children than heterosexual teachers. Others fear that homosexual teachers will serve as a model for students inclined toward homosexual behavior. Those supporting gay rights believe homosexuals have as much right to teach as heterosexuals and should be role models for homosexual teenagers.

Controversy over sexual values plagues attempts to deal with such social problems as out-of-wedlock pregnancies among teenagers. In addition to unemployment, the "practical generation" is worried about the increasing number of out-of-wedlock pregnancies. According to the Guttmacher Insti-tute, in 1980 there were 1,181,000 pregnancies among women between the ages of 13 and 19—an increase from 997,000 in 1970 for the same age range. These figures reflect increased sexual activity among youth. The Guttmacher Institute reported that, in 1971, 14 percent of 15-year-old females, 26 percent of 17-year-old females, and 46 percent of 19-year-old females in metropolitan areas were sexually active. By 1979 these figures had increased to 22 percent for 15-year-olds, 48 percent for 17-year-olds, and 69 percent for 19-year-old females.

Premarital pregnancy also occurred more frequently among minority teenage females. According to Hyman Rodman, Susan Lewis, and Saralyn Griffith in their book, *The Sexual Rights of Adolescents,* a survey in 1979 found that 16.2 percent of all women between the ages of 15 and 19 became pregnant before marriage. When divided according to white and black females, the figures reveal that 13.5 percent of all white females between 15 and 19 and 30.5 percent of all black females became pregnant before marriage. It is important to understand that these percentages are almost double those reported in 1971.

Teenagers have dealt with the problem of out-of-wedlock pregnancy in a variety of ways. Many have accepted the prospect of out-of-wedlock births. In 1973 there were 205,000 out-of-wedlock births for teenagers between 13 and 19, and in 1980 this figure increased to 272,000. But the most dramatic increase was in the number of abortions. The Guttmacher Institute reports that the number of abortions for this group of female teenagers increased from 243,000 in 1973 to 460,000 in 1980.

The rapid increase in teenage pregnancy has created a major debate about sex education in the public schools. For many communities, sex education is a very explosive topic because it deals with significant moral and religious issues. Many parents believe that sex education should be a function of the family and should not be taught in the schools. When there is agreement that sex education should be taught, there is often controversy over the content.

Community controversy over sex-education courses centers on the issues of the moral content of the subject matter, contraceptives, and abortion. Some community members believe that the primary goal of a sex-education course should be to influence youth not to engage in sexual activities. Usually these members of the community do not want the schools to teach about contraceptives and abortions, because they believe that having information about them increases sexual activity. This group believes that the primary way of reducing unwanted teenage pregnancies is to convince youth to avoid intimate sexual contact.

On the other hand, some members of the community believe that a sex-education course should be designed to prepare youth for sexual activity by teaching about contraception and sexually transmitted diseases. This group usually believes that youth will continue to engage in sexual activity and that the best means of avoiding unwanted pregnancies is to provide teenagers with adequate information about contraception.

I have described the major range of opinions about sex education found in communities, but there are also other positions that can be taken. For instance, some community members might believe that sex-education courses should include discussions about improving and enhancing sexual relationships. This represents the extreme opposite position from that which supports sex education as a means of preventing sexual contact. There are also those who want sex-education classes to provide arguments against contraception and abortion.

Although community controversy can swirl around these issues, the Guttmacher Institute reports that, according to a 1982 survey by the National Opinion Research Center, 82 percent of the public approved of sex education. The Guttmacher Institute also reports a survey by the Urban Institute which found that in 200 school districts in large cities, three out of four school districts offered some sex education. A 1979 Johns Hopkins University survey found that 76 percent of a national sample of 15- to 17-year-old females stated they had received classroom instruction in human sexuality.

The effect of sex education is an important issue. Again, the Guttmacher Institute reports a survey by Johns Hopkins University which concluded that sex-education courses do not influence decisions by teenage females about whether or not to engage in sexual activities. There was also no evidence that discussion of contraception in sex-education classes was related to a decrease in sexual activity. These findings suggest that those who make the accusation that sex-education courses and discussions of contraception contribute to increased teenage sexual activity are wrong. Even more important is the finding that those who take sex-education courses are *less* likely to become pregnant. The survey found that 70 percent more black females and 60 percent more white females became pregnant if they did not have sex education courses.

Although the findings I have just described do suggest that sex education might contribute to a reduction of out-of-wedlock pregnancies there is not enough evidence to prove that school instruction will solve the problem. This leaves no apparent solution to a problem that can lead to immense personal and social tragedy. It is a personal tragedy particularly for females who must assume the emotional and economic burdens of rearing a child out of wedlock.

Out-of-wedlock pregnancy is a major social and economic problem because of the growing number of single-parent families headed by women who are living in a state of poverty. This is particularly true for minority females. According to statistics released at the 1984 Black Family Summit, cosponsored by the National Association for the Advancement of Colored People and the Urban League, almost half of all black families in 1984 were headed by women, and 70 percent of those families were classified as poor. In fact, black female-headed families have the lowest median income of all family groups in the United States.

The dream of American education as the panacea for America's social ills continues to be plagued with questions of whose social and moral values and goals should be in the schoolhouse, and whether the panacea of education is just a way of avoiding more direct and controversial approaches to social problems. These questions remain unanswered, but American educators still tend to share Horace Mann's hope that the school will be the heart and salvation of American society.

The Economic Purposes of Schooling

One of the most important arguments given for the support of mass public schooling has been that the growth of schooling increases national wealth and advances technological development. The contribution of the school to economic growth has been seen as occurring in two distinct ways. One is the socialization of the future worker into the modern organization of industry. It is contended that the school, the first formal public organization encountered by the child, provides the preparation and training needed to deal with other complex social organizations. Within this argument the school is viewed as one of the important elements in the modernizing of underdeveloped countries from traditional agricultural societies to modern industrial societies. The second way the school is supposed to help economic growth is through the sorting and training of the labor force. By "sorting" is meant the identification of individual abilities and interests and the determination of the best type of individual training and future employment.

Let us first turn to a consideration of the role of the school in preparing the individual for the modern industrial world. One of the most extensive studies on this issue was conducted in the early 1970s by a team of social scientists headed by Alex Inkeles and David Smith in rural and urban areas of Argentina, Chile, East Pakistan, India, Israel, and Nigeria. The general purpose of their study was to look closely at the interrelationship of social institutions and individual development in the making of the modern person. It was argued in the study that there is a difference between the individual existing in traditional agricultural societies and the individual living in modern industrial societies. Certain personality characteristics are required for individual participation in large-scale modern productive enterprises such as the factory and may be required for the efficient and effective operation of the organization. This particular study identified a list of characteristics of the modern person. The list included items such as openness to new experience, readiness for social change, growth of opinion, planning, efficacy, sense of time, and the valuing of a technical skill.

The school, in relationship to what the authors called their Scale of Overall Modernity, was found to be one of the major contributors to the making of the modern person. The study contended that in large-scale complex societies no single attribute of the person better predicts attitude, values, and behavior than the amount of schooling received by the individual. The authors stated that this relationship exists because the school is a *social* organization and certain consequent learning is incidental to the curriculum and formal instruction. In other words, the school modernizes through a number of processes other than formal instruction in academic subjects. The authors of the study identified these processes as generalization, exemplification, reward and punishment, and modeling.

The study declared that generalization is central to the development within the modern person of a sense of efficacy or belief that an individual can learn how to exert considerable control over the environment. The feeling that a person can advance his or her goals, the authors found, is an important attribute of the modern person. In school, persons develop this attitude when they generalize from a satisfying experience at one task or learning situation to a belief in attaining comparable success in other contexts. In other words, children learn in school to believe in their own ability to learn new things that will increase their competence to control their environments.

Exemplification was defined in the study as the incorporation within the individual of a motivational practice or general rule of a social organization. As examples of these characteristics the study gave the starting and stopping of schools at fixed times, the ordering of events within the school, and the planning of learning events. These situations, it was argued, incorporate within the individual the need for planning and maintaining a regular schedule. Put more simply, teaching a person to get to school on time is preparation for getting to work on time.

Reward, punishment, and modeling were considered as other methods used by the school to inculcate the general practices of social organizations. For instance, pupils are punished for being late, not getting their work done on time, and not obeying the general rules of the school. In modeling, the child imitates teachers or other officials of the school and adopts their behavioral patterns.

The idea of the school as socializer for an industrial society is found throughout the history of American education. One of the arguments given in the nineteenth century in support of marching, drill, and orderliness in schools was preparation for the coordination and orderliness required in the modern factory. Lining up for class as well as marching in and out of the cloakroom and to the blackboard were activities justified in terms of training for factory assembly lines.

In the 1970s the same desire to have the social organization of the school reflect the needs of the workplace was evident in a series of papers prepared by the Center for Economic Studies on the *Educational Requirements for Industrial Democracy*. These reports were part of a flood of literature that began to appear on the need to change the organization of the workplace. In part this concern was caused by a 1972 report to the U.S. Department of Health, Education, and Welfare that found that 43 percent of white-collar workers and 24 percent of blue-collar workers were dissatisfied with their jobs.

Proposals to eliminate dissatisfaction by changing work conditions all involve the problem of training workers to fit into the new organizations. The reports of the Center for Economic Studies attempt to match the changes required in work organization with changes in educational organization. For instance, allowing workers to choose their own work schedules, redesigning jobs to make them less burdensome, and increasing choices among job assignments and job rotation are linked by the reports to changes in the organization of schools that involve greater use of educational technology, differentiated staffing, and flexible school schedules.

Several important questions arise regarding the use of the school as the socialization agent for the workplace. Is it the proper role of the school to act purposely to instill certain attitudes and habits, as preparation for future employment? Such socialization might create a static society in which the worker is prepared only for existing or known work organizations. More important, whose ideas on proper preparation for work should be included in the planned socialization of work? Employers will naturally suggest the development of work attitudes and habits that will maximize their profits, but these attitudes and habits might not be in the interest of the worker. At one time, a common tenet of the Protestant ethic was that hard, steady, and faithful performance of work would result in steady promotion and increase in salary. Labor unions contended that this was an ethic designed to persuade the worker not to fight, through unionization and the strike, for higher wages and better working conditions. Like the issues of political control and social reform, the issue of socialization in the schools for the workplace calls into question whose values and attitudes will be instilled in the students.

Socialization of the future worker is one aspect of the second major economic purpose of the school, which is the training and sorting of the labor supply. The development of this purpose of schooling is directly related to the development of vocational education and vocational guidance. Vocational guidance as a function of schooling developed in the United States in the early part of the twentieth century as part of a general reform movement to create a more efficient society. It was argued that one of the most inefficient aspects of society was the distribution and selection of human resources. Strikes and worker dissatisfaction were seen as resulting from people being in jobs that did not interest them and for which they had no aptitude. In addition, human resources were not being fully developed to meet the needs of the labor market.

The early emphasis in vocational guidance, and certainly one of its lasting purposes, was the identification of student interests and abilities and the matching of those interests and abilities with an educational program that would lead to a suitable vocation. The vocational guidance counselor was envisioned as the link between school and industry. The counselor would determine the needs of industry in terms of labor shortages and surpluses. This information would be used in the development of educational programs and the vocational counseling of students.

This general goal for vocational guidance counselors has never been achieved because of the difficulty of training enough people to staff all the junior and senior high schools in the country with counselors who possess expertise in labor-market analysis, work analysis, testing, educational programming, and psychology. Also, predicting the future needs of the labor market is very difficult and not easily adapted to educational programming. In addition, within the profession of counseling a tension developed between counseling for improvement of psychological problems and interpersonal relations, and counseling for vocations. During the depression of the 1930s, as the job market retreated, counselors got more and more involved in student psychological problems. During the 1950s the National Manpower Council and the Carnegie Corporation placed pressure on the federal government to support training of guidance people that would emphasize vocational guidance and labor-market analysis. It was believed that guidance had to get out of therapy and back into manpower planning.

During the 1970s vocational guidance expanded its role in manpower planning and vocational training as it became part of career education. Career education was born in the early 1970s as a response to apparent dissatisfaction with the educational system and the large numbers of unemployed college graduates. Career education brought together vocational guidance and vocational education and attempted to resolve one of the major controversies in vocational education.

This traditional controversy has centered on whether vocational education should provide the future worker with a broad set of skills and knowledge or whether it should prepare the worker for a specific vocation. The controversy originated at the beginning of the twentieth century when unions were suspicious that vocational education would destroy apprenticeship programs. Unions worked hard both to assure their involvement in vocational education and to assure that vocational education should be training for broad sets of skills and not narrow specialization. In educational ranks there was controversy about whether vocational education should be located in specialized institutions or in a general high school. The National Education Association in 1918 supported the development of comprehensive high schools with both college preparatory and vocational programs. It was felt that comprehensive high schools, with all students under one roof, would contribute to a sense of national community and that separate institutions would separate people and cause a breakdown of society.

During the late 1950s the role of vocational guidance in a comprehensive high school was reiterated in a widely circulated report by James Conant on *The American High School Today*. The 1959 report, written for the Carnegie Corporation, called for the consolidation of small high schools so that a greater variety of subjects could be offered within one comprehensive school. The courses of study within the school were to be more closely geared to the future vocational destination of the student. Conant argued that the heart of the school had to be the vocational guidance person, who would measure skills and interests and arrange an educational program that would provide the student with marketable skills. Educational administrators were to maintain contact with the local employment situation and assess educational needs in terms of the local labor market. Conant even made the recommendation, which never became a reality, that all high school graduates be given a wallet-size record of their subjects and grades, which could be presented on demand to any employer.

In 1971 and 1972, in response to unemployment problems and the supposed breakdown of American education, the U.S. Office of Education initiated conferences and projects in career education. Like a fast-moving brush fire, career education entered the public schools of the United States. Within one year the Office of Education could claim the participation of 750,000 young people.

Career education places vocational guidance at the center of academic planning and learning. During the elementary and junior high school years, career education is to be a subject-matter field that acquaints students with the world of work and the varieties of occupations available. After studying and preparing for an occupational choice in these early grades, the student upon entering high school is to begin preparing for entry either directly into an occupational career or into higher education. Career education as a subject-matter field means learning about all the different occupations available in the labor market and the interests and abilities associated with these occupations. In other words, career education or vocational guidance, like science and arithmetic, is something to be studied as a formal subject.

The process of acquainting the student with a variety of occupations supposedly answers the charge that vocational education at the public-school level restricts future vocational choice by segregating students in a particular educational program. In addition, under a policy of career education other school subjects are made more relevant because the student supposedly is able to see the relationship between present learning and a future occupation.

A question central to career education (and to the political and social purposes of schooling) is whether career education should be a function of public schooling. For instance, a realistic problem in career education is the school's ability to acquaint students with all possible occupations and at the same time teach the required subjects. The curriculum of the public school is extremely cluttered. One proposal suggests that subjects such as reading, writing, and social studies be taught using career-education material. But this would mean that a student's contact with other literature, and with conflicting economic, political, and social ideas would be greatly reduced.

It is also questionable whether social scientists have developed the necessary methods for accurately predicting future labor needs and rapidly organizing vocational training material to meet these needs. Even if the available methodology were to make this possible, would it be desirable? Using the school as a key element in controlling the labor market assumes that the best economy is planned and managed, and that the existing economic system is the best. This assumption contradicts the traditional laissez-faire economics of the United States, which is based on the premise that the best economic system is one controlled by the natural forces of the free marketplace. Critics of the existing economic system could argue that career education would be an educational system designed to maintain the power of the existing economic structure.

Also, career education does not change the nature of the labor market; it only eases the transition from school to the existing occupational structure. It does not mean that workers will receive higher pay or better working conditions. All that career education can promise is the hope that less time will be spent finding a job and that the entry-level job will be related to an individual's interests and abilities. The danger lies in viewing career education as a way to solve basic economic problems in the United States.

The National Reports and The Economic Demands of the 1980s

A series of reports issued in the 1980s called upon the schools to solve problems in international trade. In 1983 the federal government's National Commission on Excellence in Education issued a report, *A Nation At Risk,* that declared: "If only to keep and improve on the slim competitive edge we still retain in world markets, we must rededicate ourselves to the reform of the educational system for the benefit of all." In language designed to frighten the reader into supporting more money for public education, the commission warned, "If an unfriendly foreign power had attempted to impose on America the mediocre educational performance that exists today, we might well have viewed it as an act of war."

Also in 1983, the Task Force on Education for Economic Growth established by the Education Commission of the States issued its report, *Action for Excellence*, which linked improved schooling to economic development. The task force primarily was composed of state governors and heads of American corporations. The report of the task force warned of America's declining position in world markets as a result of increased productivity and efficiency of foreign industry. The answer to these problems, according to the report, was improved schooling to make the American labor force more efficient. The task force stated, "It is the thesis of this report that our future success as a nation—our national defense, our social stability and well-being and our national prosperity—will depend on our ability to improve education and training for millions of individual citizens."

A somewhat more radical approach was taken in 1986 by the Carnegie Forum on Education and the Economy in the report of its Task Force on Teaching as a Profession, *A Nation Prepared: Teachers for the 21st Century*. The report directly tied the reform of the teaching profession to the goals of international economic competition. The report prefaced its executive summary of these proposed changes in the teaching profession, which will be discussed in detail in Chapter 2, with the statement, "America's ability in world markets is eroding. The productivity growth of our competitors outdistances our own."

Unlike the other reports, the Carnegie Forum report argued that the problem is not the failure of schools, but their organizational goal of educating students for an economy requiring routine skills. The report states, "Much of our system of elementary and secondary education evolved in the context of an economy based on mass production. It emphasized development of the routinized skills necessary for routinized work." Consequently, the report argues, American schools developed under an administrative structure that emphasized the teaching of routine basic skills from textbooks. Within the context of these economic goals a large bureaucracy emerged to keep the system operating smoothly. According to the Carnegie report, "The design of the bureaucracy was modeled on the factories in which many of the school's graduates would work."

From this perspective, meeting the threat of international trade required restructuring the educational system to meet the new economic reality that the United States can no longer compete with other nations in the production of goods requiring routine industrial skills. The report on the teaching profession gives this ominous description: "At a modern factory outside Seoul, Korean workers produce home video recorders sold under many name brands in the American market. They work seven days a week (with two days off a year), twelve hours a day. They earn $3,000 a year."

To compete with this type of foreign competition, the report argues, would require a major reduction in wage scales and standard of living in the United States. Avoiding this situation, the Carnegie Forum maintains, requires shifting from an economy based on mass production to a knowledge-based economy. This means America should "provide to the many the same quality of education presently reserved for the fortunate few."

A surprising thing about *A Nation Prepared: Teachers for the 21st Century* is the acceptance by a rather conservative group of a radical interpretation of American educational history. Schools, the report suggests, primarily developed in the twentieth century to socialize and educate most students for routine and repetitive mass production jobs, and reserved real intellectual development in the public schools to the children of the elite. The report calls for a restructuring of the educational system to provide an "elite" education for all children, but the actual nature of a "knowledge-based" economy is never described. The report implies that all American workers will be engaged in some knowledge-based enterprise. A knowledge-based economy could mean, however, that one group of workers would develop new products in biotechnology, electronics, health care, and other post-industrial sectors, while the rest of the population would function as service workers for this intellectual class.

A Nation Prepared, as discussed in Chapter 2, is having a significant impact on the reform of teaching. Many of the other reports stressing problems of international trade want more rigorous academic requirements, particularly in mathematics and the sciences. Like the demand in the 1950s for schools to produce more scientists and engineers to win the military race with the Soviet Union, the hope in the 1980s was for the schools to produce more scientists and engineers to increase American productivity. In addition, in the 1980s American industry has been concerned with the quality of workers directly entering employment after leaving high school. There have been complaints from industry about the low level of academic skills of these young workers and their lack of socialization to the workplace.

The concerns of American industry with productivity and the quality of public-school students is directly related to changes that have taken place in the economic system in recent decades. In fact, this set of circumstances provides an excellent example of the relationship between changes in economic conditions and changes in educational policy. To understand these changes, we must first examine the economic conditions of the 1970s and 1980s and the resulting actions by American business leaders and educational policymakers.

The 1970s were a period of relatively high unemployment, particularly among youth, slowly increasing productivity, and dwindling capital investment by American industry. The high unemployment figures during this period were caused by the entry into the labor market of a large number of youths of the baby boom. There was no decrease in labor demand during this period. In other words, unemployment was not caused by a decline in available jobs but by an increase in the numbers seeking employment. This flooding of the labor market, or cohort overcrowding, resulted in a decline in wages, particularly for entry-level occupations.

The response of American business to a labor surplus and declining wages was to become more labor intensive and to decrease capital outlays. For instance, a company might choose to add work shifts to increase production as opposed to investing in new equipment. These changes in labor use and capital investment led to a slowing of the rate of increase in productivity in American industry. Productivity is simply defined as the level of output divided by the amount of labor used to produce it within a certain period of time. The increased use of labor naturally led to a productivity problem within the boundaries of this formula.

What happened in the 1980s is almost the exact opposite of the trends of the 1970s. With the bust of the baby boom in the 1980s there are now fewer young people entering the labor market. One set of figures shows that the average number of new workers entering the labor force in the 1970s was approximately 2.5 million and that, by the late 1980s, this number would decline to approximately 1.5 million workers. Another estimate has set the figures for the decade of the 1980s at a 14 percent decline in the number of persons 14 to 24 years old and a 20 percent decline in high school enrollments and graduates.

The response of business and industry to the baby boom bust has been twofold. On the one hand there has been a major concern with the decrease of qualified employees for entry-level jobs. This dwindling pool of workers threatens to drive up wages. In response to this situation, business has increased its involvement in the schools, in order to improve the education of those students who in the 1970s would have been marginal and unemployed. This is reflected in adopt-a-school programs, Jobs for America's Graduates, local alliances between business and schools, and increased emphasis on career preparation. Michael Timpane in his study for the Carnegie Corporation, *Corporations and Public Education,* detailed the extent of these new cooperative programs and argued that the basic reason for them was the growing shortage of entry-level workers. He stated, "For the first time in a generation there will probably be, in several urban locations, an absolute shortage of labor supply for entry-level positions. Urban employers already report great difficulty in locating qualified employees for entry-level positions."

On the other hand, American business is faced with delayed capital investments and declining productivity. The response has been a call by both business and political leaders for greater technological development to meet international competition. With regard to educational policy this has meant a call for increased graduation requirements in mathematics and science, and other academic fields. It is hoped that these new requirements would lead America to victory in the world's technological competition.

Not all of the reports issued in the 1980s place as much stress on economic concerns as do *A Nation At Risk* and *Action for Excellence.* For instance, the report of the Carnegie Foundation for the Advancement of Teaching, *High School,* authored by Ernest Boyer, gave recognition to economic problems, but tried to deflect public criticism from the schools. The report rejected the use of the schools as a scapegoat for economic problems as confusing the symptoms with the disease. The report also tried to temper concerns with economic productivity with a recognition of other important educational goals. Boyer wrote,

> Clearly, education and the security of the nation are interlocked. National interests must be served. But where in all of this are students? Where is the recognition that education is to enrich the living of individuals? Where is the love of learning and where is the commitment to achieve equality and opportunity for all?

While the Carnegie Foundation report, *High School,* tried to soften the criticism of the schools, it did not reject the idea of linkages between the schools and the economy, nor did it reject the idea of greater business involvement in the schools. In fact, an entire chapter is devoted to lauding those relationships. But what is different from the other reports is an emphasis on the idea that the public high school, and by inference all levels of public schools, must be saved to maintain the school's role in assuring the safety of the present organization of social and political institutions. The report stated, "A deep erosion of confidence in our schools, coupled with disturbing evidence that at least some of the skepticism is justified, has made revitalizing the American high school an urgent matter."

Some of the reports about education issued in the 1980s avoided dealing with problems of international trade, and stressed equality of educational opportunity as a means of enhancing equality of opportunity. For instance, the 1983 College Board report, *Academic Preparation For College,* stressed that the improvement of the quality of secondary education was necessary "to fulfill our national promise of equal access to higher education." The report warned that inadequately prepared high school students were being limited in their choice of colleges and were often forced to drop out of college. The economy was not completely neglected in the report. "In the years ahead," the College Board stated, "our economy will need an increasing number of well-educated people."

Another report that made equality of educational opportunity a central focus is Mortimer Adler's *The Paideia Proposal.* Adler argued that the key to equality of educational opportunity is the elimination of vocational education and the adoption of a single curriculum for all students. He argued that it is undemocratic to divide students into separate curricula and that equality of educational opportunity should literally mean that all students receive an equal education. Improvement in the economy and increasing equality of educational opportunity, Adler argued, cannot be accomplished by training students for immediate industrial needs. In Adler's opinion, the goal of schooling should be lifelong learning. Vocational training or learning should take place after secondary school, when the individual has gained the skills to learn and to adapt to a changing labor market. According to Adler, this would also decrease the tendency to give children of the poor one type of education and children of the rich another type of education.

A Nation at Risk, Action for Excellence, High School, Academic Preparation for College, and *The Paideia Proposal* are five of approximately nine reports issued on education in the early 1980s. All of these reports reflect concerns with equality of opportunity or declining economic conditions. It is in the context of these concerns and goals for American education that the reports advocate major changes in the public schools. These proposals range from changing the curriculum to improving the quality of teachers to extending the school year and day.

A review of these proposals demonstrates the close relationship between national policy goals and the educational system. They give evidence of the importance of understanding the goals of American education as a means of understanding the functioning of the public schools. As government institutions, public schools have traditionally been shaped to meet public goals. And, in the case of the 1980s, these changes have taken place against a background of concern about the national economy.

A number of the reports call for an extension of the school day and the school year as a means of improving the academic quality of school graduates. For instance, *A Nation at Risk* urges that "school districts and State legislatures should strongly consider 7-hour school days as well as a 200 to 220 day school year." *Action for Excellence* recommends that "states should increase the duration and the intensity of academic learning." Along with these recommendations to improve student learning are demands for better discipline and more homework. As a result of these reports many state legislatures began to consider laws for extending the school day and year.

Also, most of the reports sought some means of improving the quality of the teaching profession. These recommendations usually involve more selectivity in recruiting teachers, better education of teachers, and changing the career patterns and methods of paying teachers. These issues will be discussed in more detail in Chapter 2. What is important to understand in the context of this chapter is that the reports contribute to debates occurring in state legislatures about the career patterns of teachers. The result has been the creation of new methods of compensation, which in many states has created a minor revolution in the profession of teaching (see Chapter 2 for a discussion of these changes).

The reports sought changes in academic requirements in the public schools. *A Nation at Risk* recommends that state and local high school graduation requirements be strengthened and that all students be required to complete what the report calls the "Five New Basics." These new basics are

1. four years of English
2. three years of social studies
3. three years of mathematics

4. three years of science
5. one-half year of computer science

The Carnegie Foundation's *High School* recommended a more broadly based core of common learning. This report proposes:

	Academic Units
Language, 5 units	
Basic English: Writing	1
Speech	$\frac{1}{2}$
Literature	1
Foreign Language	2
Arts	$\frac{1}{2}$
History, $2\frac{1}{2}$ units	
U.S. History	1
Western Civilization	1
Non-Western Studies	$\frac{1}{2}$
Civics, 1 unit	1
Science, 2 units	
Physical Science	1
Biological Science	1
Mathematics	2
Technology	$\frac{1}{2}$
Health	$\frac{1}{2}$
Seminar on work	$\frac{1}{2}$
Senior independent project	$\frac{1}{2}$

Action for Excellence simply urges that "states and local school systems... launch energetic efforts to strengthen the curriculum from kindergarten through high school." The report states, "If the needs of our society and of industry for skilled and well-educated people are to be met, courses not only in mathematics and science, but in all disciplines, must be enlivened and improved." As mentioned previously, this report was issued by a task force composed of state governors and heads of leading corporations. Apparently, from the actions of many of these governors, they were influenced by the report and sought changes in the academic requirements in their particular states (the political activities of governors will be discussed in more detail in Chapter 7).

Both the College Board's *Academic Preparation for College* and Mortimer Adler's *The Paideia Proposal* provide general outlines for changing the curriculum. Neither report gives specific course titles and content. *Academic Preparation for College* outlines the knowledge and skills that students would "need in order to have a fair chance of getting full value from their college education." *The Paideia Proposal* emphasizes a common curriculum for all students that would include discussion of the great writings of the world.

The importance of these proposals for this chapter is not their details, but the fact that they were presented in the context of concern about an economic crisis. In other words, they were justified by their contribution to economic improvement and equality of educational opportunity. As I will discuss in Chapter 2, the reports had a major effect on the profession of teaching. Whether the changes would actually improve America's position in world trade has never been proven, but the effect of the discussion is to give impetus to the reform of the educational system.

Liberals, Neo-Conservatives, and Critical Theorists

Educational goals are directly related to political beliefs. This is true because schools play an important role in providing access to jobs, determining social equality and inequality, and distributing knowledge about the political system. What one believes about the proper role of government in regulating the economy and providing social justice is almost always reflected in one's beliefs about the purposes of schooling.

To illustrate the relationship between political beliefs and the goals of schooling, I am going to examine three distinct political philosophies, not because these are the *only* political philosophies affecting education, but because of their current impact on American schools. These are the liberal, neo-conservative, and critical theorist positions.

In general, liberal beliefs have their greatest impact on the educational platforms of the Democratic party, while neo-conservatives are influential in the Republican party. (Given the confused nature of American party politics and the lack of ideological clarity of the major parties, many different political beliefs, of course, creep into the discussions of each party. But it can be said with some certainty that liberal beliefs are dominant in the Democratic party and neo-conservative beliefs are dominant in the Republican party.) Critical theory is a recent movement among American intellectuals; its impact on American politics, at least at the time of the writing of this book, cannot be clearly discerned. As a set of political beliefs, the major impact of critical theory is in academic discussions about educational policies.

Let us begin by discussing the relationship between liberal political beliefs and political policies. Twentieth-century liberalism is characterized by a belief in the positive role of government in assuring social justice and regulating the economy. While believing in private ownership of the means of production, liberals argue that the government should manage and regulate the economy to protect against economic depressions and assure that corporations work for the public good. Also, liberals are characterized by a belief that government should take an active role in protecting the rights of minorities and in assuring equal opportunity in the economic system.

Liberal educational concerns are a direct reflection of these political beliefs. Liberals tend to favor strong government intervention to assure equal opportunity for minorities and the poor. They support federal funds for educational programs to help the disadvantaged. In keeping with their belief in positive government intervention, liberals favor federal programs that support special educational programs for the disadvantaged and the minorities, and federal intervention to protect minority rights. In general, liberals favor a curriculum designed to meet individual needs. Often this has meant having the schools offer a variety of educational programs that students can select according to individual needs and goals. The individualization of the curriculum reflects a general concern with humanpower planning that is designed to match educational programs with labor market needs. Also, in keeping with concerns with the rights of minorities, liberals tend to favor educational programs that recognize minority languages and cultures.

In contrast to liberals, neo-conservatives believe in the "negative state"— that is, an absence of government control—with a free market as the primary regulator of the economic system. Consequently, neo-conservatives want to minimize government regulation and interference in the economy. While recognizing the importance of minority rights, neo-conservatives believe that minority rights are best protected by the courts with minimum government intervention. In fact, neo-conservatives argue that most government programs primarily benefit government bureaucrats and provide only minimum aid to the poor and minority groups. Neo-conservatives argue that the best hope for the poor and minority groups is through self-advancement in a free-market economic system. While neo-conservatives would minimize government intervention in the economy, they tend to support laws to regulate personal morality.

In keeping with their philosophy of the negative state and in contrast to liberals, neo-conservatives oppose federal support and regulation of public schools. During the Reagan years of the 1980s, neo-conservatives supported a reduction of the federal role in education and an increased role for state and local governments. Neo-conservatives are critical of education programs designed to meet individual differences and want all students to study the same core curriculum. Reflecting their concern with morality, neo-conservatives believe that a core curriculum will teach moral values and will be a source of educational excellence. Neo-conservatives argue that the needs of the labor market can best be met through school-business partnerships, where school leaders learn the employment needs of the business community. Also, neo-conservatives believe that the best hope for minority and immigrant groups is to learn English and to be socialized into American culture. Consequently, neo-conservatives oppose educational programs that emphasize minority languages and cultures.

Critical theorists find fault with both liberal and neo-conservative positions on the economy and education. From the perspective of critical theorists, the debate about the positive versus the negative state is really a debate about different forms of economic exploitation. On the one hand, they argue, large corporations use government regulation as a means of maintaining economic monopolies. Within this framework, government intervention and regulation can sometimes be a means of increasing the advantages of business in the marketplace. On the other hand, critical theorists argue, corporations demand less government intervention and regulation of the economy when the actions of government are hurting profits.

For critical theorists the key to economic and social justice is democratic struggle. While recognizing that some forms of government regulation and intervention are to the advantage of ruling elites, critical theorists believe that economic and social justice can be achieved by democratic movements working through government. For critical theorists, history is the continuous expansion of political, economic, and social rights as a result of struggle against oppression. In other words, their view of history is optimistic and hopeful, but this optimism and hope depends on people continuing to fight against oppression and economic exploitation.

Given this optimistic view of history, critical theorists emphasize an education for democratic empowerment, which simply means giving students the knowledge and skills they need to struggle for a continued expansion of political, economic, and social rights. Of utmost importance is making students aware that they have the power to affect the course of history and that history is the struggle for human rights. Critical theorists accept the importance of government regulation and intervention to protect equality of educational opportunity. In fact, they would argue that equality of educational opportunity is one of the achievements of the civil rights movement in the United States in the 1950s and 1960s.

The educational concerns of critical theorists can be understood by comparing their ideas regarding a core curriculum with those of neo-conservatives. Neo-conservatives want a core curriculum as a means of teaching a common moral code to maintain social order and as a means of improving academic standards and intellectual skills. Critical theorists, however, might instead support a core curriculum organized to teach students that they have the power to shape history and that gives students the skills and knowledge to participate in shaping that history.

The consideration of liberal, neo-conservative, and critical theorist positions on education is meant to show the relationship between political values and educational goals. Often, this relationship is related to the types of political knowledge taught in schools. For instance, in the 1970s there was an actual decline in the teaching of history, government, and social studies as a backlash to the extremely political student demonstrations of the late 1960s and early 1970s.

Lee H. Ehman, in his summary of research on political socialization in the spring 1980 *Review of Educational Research,* found agreement among research studies that there was a steady decline during the 1970s in the political knowledge held by American youth. Ralph W. Tyler reported in the January 1981 *Phi Delta Kappan* that international tests given on knowledge of students' political systems and on citizenship found that among students who had completed secondary school, test scores were lowest in Ireland and the United States. In the same issue of the *Kappan,* Mary Tubbs and James A. Beane reported in their survey of changes in the American high school that the "teaching of social issues, student involvement in community service, and student involvement in curriculum planning have all decreased in frequency since 1974." In addition, they noted a marked increase in the teaching of career and vocational education.

It is important to understand that the decline in the teaching of social issues, history, and government, and the increase in vocational and career education were the result of conscious political decisions made by educational planners. The curriculum of a school cannot cover every phase of knowledge and training. Decisions have to be made about what to include and what to exclude. These political decisions can have a tremendous effect on the culture of a society.

Readers of this text who graduated from secondary school within the last ten years might ask themselves what effects their apparent lack of political knowledge has had on their lives and on their ability to understand and debate the issues raised in this chapter. One possible result of the education provided in American schools in the last decade is an apolitical citizenry—a citizenry so apolitical that it not only lacks political knowledge and sophistication but is not even aware of the existence of major political issues surrounding institutions like schooling. Readers who find that this is personally true should begin to consider the political purposes of education that caused their apolitical stance.

The political, social, and economic purposes of schooling are the major reasons public schools have received wide support and have become one of the major social institutions of the twentieth century. In the United States the political reasons for supporting schooling have been the schools' promise to establish a democratic community held together by a consensus of political values. Good education is supposed to be the backbone of good government. Yet this promise has constantly encountered the question of whose political values and ideas will guide the school. The reality of democratic politics is not consensus but a struggle for power.

The social purposes of schooling have been supported by the schools' promise of a society free from crime, poverty, and other social ills. Yet reliance on the school for these results has frequently been a method of avoiding the basic issues. Education as the hope of tomorrow is one way of avoiding the problems of the present.

The school as a "sorter" for the economy prepares students for an existing labor market. Again, this avoids direct confrontation with the fact that the economic conditions surrounding the existing labor market have caused unemployment.

One of the major questions implied throughout this chapter has been, who controls the educational system? The answer to this question determines the political, social, and economic values taught in the school system. For example, the school could become an instrument for control by one social class, economic group, or government institution. Even if a totalitarian power controlled the educational system, there would be some hope. All learning carries with it the potential of learning things not prescribed in the curriculum. All modern societies need to educate people, simply to maintain their present complex technologies. For a totalitarian educational system, the inherent contradiction is that knowledge can lead one to question the system and seek fundamental changes.

Exercises

This chapter has focused on the major political, social, and economic purposes of education. Throughout the chapter questions have been raised about these purposes and about the continuing problems they cause for public education in the United States. In a discussion group or in essay form present your ideas on the following issues:

1. Who or what group should determine the political teachings and political socialization in public schools?
2. Should public schools be used to create a political meritocracy?
3. What citizenship training should public schools provide in a democratic society?
4. Who or what group should determine the moral and social values to be taught in public schools?
5. What social probelms do you think the schools are best able to solve?
6. What do you think should be the relationship between the school and social reform in a democratic society?
7. What do you think should be the relationship between the school and the economic system?
8. Should the focus of public schooling be on career education, or should occupational choice and training be a direct function of the labor market?

Suggested Readings and Works Cited in Chapter

Adler, Mortimer J. *The Paideia Proposal*. New York: Macmillan, 1982. This educational proposal calls for the elimination of tracking and the requirement of a single curriculum for all students.

Berlowitz, Marvin J., and Frank E. Chapman. *The United States Educational System:*

Marxist Approaches. Minneapolis: Marxist Educational Press, 1980. This collection of articles provides an introduction to Marxist interpretations of the education system in the United States.

Boyer, Ernest L. *High School*. New York: Harper & Row, 1983. This is the report on secondary education in the United States of the Carnegie Foundation for the Advancement of Teaching.

The College Board. *Academic Preparation for College*. New York: The College Board, 1983. These are the general recommendations of the College Board for the preparation of high school students for college.

Conant, James. *The American High School Today*. New York: McGraw-Hill, 1959. A major study of the conditions and goals of the American high school. This book had an important impact on shaping the future direction of the high school.

Cremin, Lawrence. *The Republic and the School*. New York: Teachers College Press, 1957. A good selection of Horace Mann's Writings taken from his reports to the Massachusetts Board of Education. A good introduction to the social and political purposes of American education.

Ehman, Lee H. "The American School in the Political Socialization Process," *Review of Educational Research* 50 (Spring 1980): 99–119. A summary of studies on the political socialization of American school children.

Goodlad, John I. *A Place Called School*. New York: McGraw-Hill Book Company, 1984. A detailed study of what actually happens in American schools. Goodlad uses a great deal of data to analyze the functioning of the American educational system.

Inkeles, Alex, and David Smith. *Becoming Modern: Individual Change in Six Developing Countries*. Cambridge, Mass.: Harvard University Press, 1974. An important study of modernization in underdeveloped countries and its relationship to social institutions including the school.

Katz, Michael. *The Irony of Early School Reform*. Boston: Beacon Press, 1968. An important study of the early relationship between social reform and education.

Lazerson, Marvin, and W. Norton Grubb. *American Education and Vocationalism: A Documentary History 1870–1970*. New York: Teachers College Press, 1974. A good collection of documents dealing with vocational education and the relationship between the school and the economy.

Lee, Gordon. *Crusade Against Ignorance: Thomas Jefferson on Education*. New York: Teachers College Press, 1961. A collection of statements by Jefferson on education with a good introductory essay.

Levin, Henry. *Educational Requirements for Industrial Democracy*. Menlo Park, Calif.: Portola Institute, 1974. An attempt to change the methods of school socialization to meet the requirements of work reforms.

The National Commission on Excellence in Education. *A Nation at Risk*. Washington, D.C.: U.S. Government Printing Office, 1983. The report and recommendations of this commission had a major impact on discussions about the American school.

Perkinson, Henry. *The Imperfect Panacea: American Faith in Education, 1865–1965*. New York: Random House, 1968. A study of attempts to use the school to solve major social problems in the United States.

Rodman, Hyman et al. *The Sexual Rights of Adolescents*. New York: Columbia University Press, 1984. This book provides information on the legal, social, and psychological aspects of adolescent sexuality.

Task Force on Education for Economic Growth. *Action for Excellence*. Denver:

Education Commission of the States, 1983. Recommendations that were made by a task force composed primarily of state governors and leading business people.

Task Force on Teaching as a Profession. *A Nation Prepared: Teachers for the 21st Century.* New York: Carnegie Corporation of New York, 1986. Important report calling for restructuring of the teaching profession and the establishment of a national teacher certification board.

Timpane, Michael. *Corporations and Public Education.* Report distributed by Teachers College, Columbia University, 1981. This was a study conducted for the Carnegie Corporation on the growing links between public schools and business.

Tyler, Ralph W. "The U.S. vs. the World: A Comparison of Educational Performance," *Phi Delta Kappan,* January 1981. This article provides a summary of the data collected by the International Association for the Evaluation of Educational Achievement.

2

The Profession of Teaching

In the 1980s, teacher shortages, combined with concerns about international trade, ushered in a decade of reform in the structure of the teaching profession, the role of teachers in schools, teacher certification standards, and teacher education. A flood of reports, the most important issued in 1986 by the Carnegie Corporation and titled *A Nation Prepared: Teachers for the 21st Century,* link the improvement of schools and the economy with the reform of teaching.

The report of the National Commission on Excellence in Education, *A Nation at Risk,* argued "that not enough of the academically able students are being attracted to teaching; that teacher preparation programs need substantial improvement; that the professional working life of teachers is on the whole unacceptable; and that a serious shortage of teachers exists in key fields." As discussed in Chapter 1, a major concern of *A Nation at Risk* was the improvement through public schooling of America's industrial and technological development in relationship to other competing nations. It was for this reason that the report decried a shortage of teachers in mathematics and science, and the poor academic quality of teachers.

Action for Excellence, the report of the Task Force .on Education for Economic Growth, also complained of shortages of science and mathematics teachers, low teacher salaries, and lack of rewards for superior teachers. This report was significant because at least half of the task force members were governors. And it is state legislation that has the greatest impact on the certification, recruitment, and training of teachers.

Action for Excellence argued that one of the causes for the crisis in teaching was social progress, which has provided greater opportunities for women and minorities. In the words of the report, "In former years, when women and minorities suffered greater job discrimination than today, teaching was often their major opportunity for work at a professional level. Today, however, job opportunities are broadening for women and minorities; teaching can no longer monopolize their talents." As will be discussed later in this chapter, the traditional low pay and status of teaching can be directly linked to the traditional exploitation of women.

Some of the reports issued in the early 1980s linked the problem of teachers with working conditions in the schools. These reports recognized the importance of salary, career improvement, and improved training, but also argued that many people avoided or left teaching because of the conditions of teaching. In *High School,* the report of the Carnegie Foundation for the Advancement of Teaching, Ernest Boyer portrays teachers as working in hostile environments where overcrowded classrooms, unreasonable class loads, lack of professional surroundings, and a hierarchical administrative structure sap teachers of their enthusiasm and desire to remain in teaching. Certainly, one of the most poignant portraits is English teacher Horace Smith in Theodore Sizer's *Horace's Compromise,* the first report from *A Study of High Schools,* cosponsored by the National Association of Secondary School Principals and the Commission on Educational Issues of the National Association of Independent Schools. Both Boyer and Sizer believe that internal reforms in schooling are a necessary condition for improving the quality of teachers.

As discussed in Chapter 1, the report of the Carnegie Forum on Education and the Economy, *A Nation Prepared: Teachers for the 21st Century,* linked the reform of the teaching profession to a change in the goals of American education from serving an economy based on mass production to one based on knowledge industries. To achieve this restructuring of the American economic system, the report states, "the key to success lies in creating a profession equal to the task—a profession possessed of well-educated teachers prepared to assume new powers and responsibilities to redesign schools for the future." As will be discussed in more detail later in this chapter, the report recommended sweeping changes in teacher education, certification, and roles within schools.

The criticisms and recommendations of the previously mentioned reports will be discussed in more detail throughout this chapter. The reports were catalysts for attempts to solve long-standing complaints about teaching. State legislatures developed new plans for ending the careerless nature of teaching and improving the quality of teachers. New approaches have been taken to increase the dignity of the profession of teaching.

This chapter covers these issues by examining the rewards and dissatisfactions of teaching, the pay structure and career pattern in teaching, the problems in the professionalization of teaching, and teacher education. Both the history of the teaching profession and current concerns about teachers will be integrated into a discussion of these topics.

The Rewards and Dissatisfactions of Teaching

Although the proposed reforms of the teaching profession emphasize salaries and status, actual studies of teacher satisfaction consistently suggest that interacting with students provides the greatest reward for teachers. The issue of teacher salaries and status are more clearly highlighted in comparisons between American and Japanese teachers. A 1987 report prepared for the United States Office of Education, *Japanese Education Today,* states that in general Japanese educators have a much higher status in their society than educators in the United States. For instance, elementary school principals in Japan have a higher status than department heads of large corporations, public accountants, and authors. And, suprisingly when one thinks of the United States, elementary school teachers in Japanese society have a higher status than "civil and mechanical engineers, white collar employees in large firms, and municipal department heads." University professors were ranked above physicians and just below court judges and presidents of large corporations.

According to the report, a Japanese high-school teacher with a bachelor's degree had a starting salary 15 percent higher than that of a starting white-collar worker with a similar degree and 12 percent higher than the starting salary of an engineer. The report states, "First-year teacher salaries are generally higher than those of other professions such as businessmen, engineers, pharmacists, etc."

In contrast, *A Nation Prepared: Teachers for the 21st Century* reports that the median weekly income of American teachers was slightly below that of mail carriers and slightly above that of plumbers. Ranking above American teachers in median weekly earnings were attorneys, engineers, chemists, systems analysts, and accountants.

These contrasts paint a grim picture of the economic and social status of American teachers, but the most important issue for job satisfaction remains interaction with students. A major complaint about the organization of American schools is that the organization itself interferes with the relationship between students and teachers. For example, Dan Lortie, whose study *Schoolteacher: A Sociological Study* is the most complete report on the social world of the teacher, surveyed teachers in Dade County, Florida, and found that the reward from teaching identified most often by teachers was "knowing that I have reached students and they have learned."

For the purposes of his study, Lortie divided teacher rewards into extrinsic, psychic, and ancillary. Extrinsic rewards are those associated with salary and community status. Psychic rewards are associated with the psychological satisfaction derived from the job. Ancillary rewards refer to security of position, summer vacation time, and freedom from competition.

Of the more than 5,800 teachers included in Lortie's survey, over 76 percent gave top priority to the psychic rewards of teaching. Only 11.9 percent selected extrinsic rewards, and 11.7 percent chose ancillary rewards. The choice given teachers with regard to psychic rewards ranged from the "knowing that I have reached students..." statement to "chance to associate with other teachers." "Knowing that I have reached students..." was selected by 86.1 percent of the teachers as the most important psychic reward. The second choice, "chance to associate with children or young people," was selected by 8 percent of the teachers in the survey.

An aspect of psychic rewards that Lortie did not include in this particular survey, but to which he has given reference throughout his study of American schoolteachers, is the psychic reward experienced by teachers through the exercise of creative autonomy in the classroom. It has been estimated that teachers make over two hundred decisions an hour in their classrooms. These decisions range from curricular and teaching problems to behavioral problems.

Compared to the routine of some factory and office jobs, the autonomy and creative decision making required of teachers attracts many individuals to the profession. This particular psychic reward has also led to conflict when administrators and other agencies outside the classroom have attempted to control the behavior of teachers. This threat to the independence of teachers may be one of the reasons for the rapid growth of teacher unions.

The ancillary rewards of teaching are also attractive to many individuals. The most popular ancillary reward is the time for extended vacations and travel provided by the long summer vacation and other school holidays. Second to vacation time is the security of income and position. In most states teacher tenure laws provide a security not often found in other jobs. Of course, school closings and financial crises can threaten this security for many younger teachers.

John Goodlad, in *A Place Called School,* provides a somewhat different picture than Lortie's. In Goodlad's sample 57 percent of the major reasons for teaching centered around the desire to teach, while only 15 percent of the reasons were related to liking children. Because of the differences between questions asked by Goodlad and Lortie in their surveys, it is difficult to compare their results. The desire to teach can be considered a desire to interact with students. But, on the other hand, the desire to teach does reflect a greater concern with subject matter as opposed to simply interacting with students. Goodlad also found a higher level of satisfaction among teachers than one would have suspected from the current criticism of the profession. In his sample, 74 percent felt their "career expectations had been fulfilled," and 69 percent said they would again "select education as a career."

Goodlad found that "personal frustration and dissatisfaction in the teaching situation" was the major reason teachers left teaching. Conflicts with fellow teachers, administrators, and students ranked low as reasons for leaving the profession. Even low pay was not given as a major reason except insofar as it was related to a general sense of dissatisfaction. Goodlad argued that even though interest in money was not a major reason given by teachers for entering the career of teaching, it was given as the second reason for leaving it. Goodlad writes:

We might speculate that, anticipating rewards intrinsic to the work, teachers begin with a willingness to forego high salaries. However, when confronted with the frustration of these expectations, the fact that they sometimes are paid less than the bus drivers who bring their students to school may become a considerable source of dissatisfaction as well.

As mentioned in the introduction to this chapter, Ernest Boyer and Theodore Sizer provide vivid portraits of the types of frustrations encountered in the school. Certainly, Theodore Sizer's description of a day in the life of high school English teacher Horace Smith is one of the finest pieces of educational literature. Sizer provides sympathetic insight into the life of a 28-year veteran of teaching who still cares about his work but is constantly forced to compromise his instructional ideals with the realities of public school teaching.

Sizer assures the reader that Horace's compromises are not the result of unusually poor working conditions. In fact, the reader is often reminded that Horace Smith teaches in a suburban school where conditions are far superior to those faced by teachers in central city school systems. Sizer is also realistic. He recognizes that all jobs involve compromises between ideals and realities. But, he feels, the compromises required in teaching require more than ordinary adjustments to the realities of work. The compromises required in teaching not only shatter ideals but cheat students of opportunities to learn.

Horace Smith is proud and committed to his job. His day begins at 5:45 A.M. with a brief breakfast and a 40-minute drive, bringing him to school by 7:00. He heads directly for the teachers' lounge, where he enjoys a cup of coffee and a cigarette before the beginning of his 7:30 class. The teachers' lounge is portrayed as a warm setting in which there is the smell of old cigarette smoke and a continual card game being played by groups of teachers during their off hours. It is the one haven in the school where teachers can meet and share daily events and professional concerns.

His three junior-level classes for the day are reading *Romeo and Juliet*. As a veteran teacher who has spent many years teaching *Romeo and Juliet,* he moves his classes quickly through the drama, anticipating their difficulties and avoiding distracting issues. His second-bell class is excused for an assembly, which allows him to return to his coffee cup in the teachers' lounge. His fourth-bell class is a senior advance-placement class that is studying *Ulysses.* On this particular day, 13 of the 18 seniors are attending a United Nations week at a local college. Sizer describes Horace's annoyance at losing the teaching days but also his feeling of gratefulness at being able to avoid teaching, thus allowing his students time to read. In addition to his 5 classes, Horace has a preparation period and a lunch hour.

The final bell ends the school day at 2:00 P.M. After conversations with students, he collects his papers, leaves his classroom at 2:30, and goes to the auditorium. Horace is faculty adviser to the stage crew, for which he earns an extra $800 a year. For that small amount he puts in about 4 hours a week—

and many more hours than that in the 10 days before a performance. After stopping in the auditorium he drives to his brother-in-law's liquor store where he works behind the counter in the stockroom from shortly after 4:00 P.M. until 6:30. His salary from the school system is $27,300, and the work at the liquor store adds another $8,000.

He eats dinner at 7:45 and then spends an hour grading papers. This is followed by several phone calls from sick students wanting assignments and students wanting to talk about the upcoming stage production. Finally, Horace ends his day by drifting off to sleep after the 11:00 news.

Horace's compromises are in the shortcuts he must take in order to deal with his busy day. He knows that he should be assigning his students a weekly essay of a page or two. But with a total of 120 students (central-city teachers often have more than 170 students) he is realistic and only assigns one or two paragraphs. Even with these short assignments, he estimates that grading and writing comments will take 15 to 20 minutes of his time per student. This still involves roughly 30 hours of grading. Again, Horace is realistic about his time and takes shortcuts in grading to reduce the time per student to 5 minutes. This means that even with reducing the assignment from a short theme to one or two paragraphs, and cutting corners while grading, Horace still must devote 10 hours a week to grading.

He must also take shortcuts in class preparations. He has taught some of his classes before, whereas others require more preparation. But even when classes are studying the same material, the differences among students require separate lesson plans. Horace recognizes that he should spend many more hours on preparation but again compromises and spends only about 10 minutes per class on preparation.

His shortcuts in grading and preparation, along with his teaching, administration, and extracurricular drama work give him a 42-hour work week. If he didn't cut corners there would be another 20 hours of grading and possibly another 6 hours for preparation, which would mean a 68-hour week. On top of this is the time spent by Horace in his brother-in-law's liquor store trying to add to his inadequate salary. And, of course, there are the 3 full days he spends during Christmas vacation writing letters of reference for his students.

Lost in all these commitments is the time that should be used for reading professional journals and new literature, and to do those things that renew the life of the mind. As Sizer describes the situation, Horace hides his bitterness toward the critics who demand from teachers more scholarship and intellectual involvement. And, in the end, the students are as cheated as Horace's ideals.

In *High School,* Ernest Boyer provides similar descriptions of teachers who are overwhelmed by course loads and are forced to seek outside employment to add to their meager salaries. In many ways, Boyer paints an even grimmer picture of a high-school teacher's life. His teachers have five to six classes a day with three different levels in a course. The different levels mean that more of the teachers' time is required in order to review subject matter and prepare for class. In addition, many teachers are assigned classes for which they have had no training. For instance, a social studies teacher might be assigned a science or mathematics course, which means endless hours of preparation. Added to this is the time spent on grading papers, preparing lesson plans, and counseling students.

Boyer found that a great deal of a teacher's time is spent on clerical and administrative chores. Many of these extra duties are nothing but babysitting and security tasks such as supervising hallways, lunchrooms, and student activities. Boyer found widespread complaints about clerical chores resulting from endless requests from both the school administration and the central administration of the school district. Also, teachers must keep elaborate student attendance records and send written reports to school counselors.

A great deal of a teacher's time is spent counseling students. Boyer gives the average pupil-to-counselor ratio in the United States as 319 to 1. This means there is little hope for the average student to find a counselor who has enough time to deal to any great extent with personal, academic, and career problems. This means students often turn to teachers for help. This creates a bind for many teachers because the better and more popular teachers often have the greatest demands on their time.

A feeling of isolation among teachers was also found in the high schools visited by Boyer. Teachers spend very little time in the company of other adults. Contact with other adults usually occurs only at lunch time or during preparation periods in the faculty lounge. This situation gives teachers few opportunities to discuss common problems, professional issues, and intellectual topics with other teachers. *working conditions*

Teachers are also frequently without a permanent classroom, which means they are without their own desk: most move from room to room carrying all their material. Many schools, particularly in central cities, are poorly maintained and have dirty windows and floors. In addition, there is often a shortage of school materials, and teachers dip into their own pockets to buy supplies.

For Boyer, a teacher's working conditions are made even more intolerable *lack of* by a lack of public recognition and reward. Boyer argues, using the previously *regard* mentioned research by Dan Lortie, that the primary satisfaction for teachers comes from psychic rewards. But he finds little evidence of these rewards in high schools of the 1980s. First, students have a negative attitude toward school. Boyers cites statistics that in 1980, 73 percent of high school teachers stated that student attitudes toward learning had a negative effect on teacher satisfaction from teaching. Second, there is a lack of respect from other adults outside of teaching. The teachers Boyer interviewed reported a subtle disrespect for teachers by many adults. A number of teachers even avoid mentioning to other adults the nature of their occupation. One teacher, who works as a meat cutter during the summer, was told by a fellow butcher who discovered he was a teacher, "Man, that's a dead-end job. You must be a real dummy."

Although Sizer and Boyer spent their time analyzing the life of the high school teacher, many of their conclusions can also apply to elementary school teachers. Elementary school teachers also feel time pressure in their class preparations and grading. They also feel the grim climate of isolation from adults, poor physical environment, and lack of community respect. They also must seek extracurricular school and summer employment to fill the gap left by inadequate salaries.

The descriptions by Sizer and Boyer provide some understanding of the phenomenon of "teacher burnout." This condition has as its symptoms periods of depression and an extreme dissatisfaction with teaching, to the point of finding it difficult to get up in the morning and go to work. It can be the cause of excessive fatigue resulting from depression and stress. Teacher burnout does not always result from the same circumstances. For instance, a salesperson for a book publishing firm recently came to my office and, after discussing the texts her company had for sale, she told me, "I quit teaching last year to take this job. I am a product of teacher burnout. I just couldn't face those students again." She had taught in a wealthy suburban district with comparatively good working conditions and few disciplinary problems. Another "burnout" case was a teachers' union leader in an inner-city school who declared, half in jest, "I warn all teachers to take an extra pair of underwear to school because of the fear caused by student violence."

One way of understanding teacher burnout is to consider it in terms of Lortie's survey of rewards. If the primary rewards of teaching are psychic, what happens when those psychic rewards are withdrawn? Except for the flexibility of schedules and long vacations, there is little left in a low-salaried, careerless profession. In terms of Lortie's survey, if a student resists learning and does not care about school, then the major satisfaction in teaching no longer exists. When this lack of reward is combined with threats of student violence and problems of student discipline, it seems reasonable for teachers to "burn out" and either become bitter or quit teaching.

"Burnout" is not a phenomenon peculiar to teaching. People in other occupations also become frustrated and bored and seek career changes. What is distinctive about teacher burnout is that it may be intrinsic to the educational system. Students are not rewarded by the system for demonstrating a joy of learning. The educational structure is built on accumulating course credits and years of instruction in order to get a degree or pass on to another level of instruction. Classes filled with students who are there because the law requires their presence or because they want a degree do not constitute ideal educational circumstances. Teachers are often trying to figure out how to make students learn, while students are trying to figure how to get by with the minimum of effort. This situation cannot maximize teachers' psychic rewards.

In recent years the satisfaction teachers have gained from autonomous decision making and creativity has been threatened by expanding bureaucratic structures and attempts to control teacher behavior in the classroom. These changes may have led to greater unionization by teachers as they have attempted to restore their autonomy and ability to influence educational policy.

The growth of bureaucratic structures in education can be illustrated as follows: Consider the expansion in the twentieth century of the hierarchical administrative staff in education. According to the *Digest of Education Statistics,* in 1919–20 there was a single supervisor or principal for every 31 teachers, librarians, and other nonsupervisory instructional staff. During the 1920s, educational administration began to professionalize and expand so that by 1929–30 there was a principal or supervisor for every 22 teachers, librarians, and other nonsupervisory instructional staff. This trend continued so that by 1973–74 the ratio was 1 to 16.

As teachers experienced an expanding bureaucratic structure they also found their schools and school districts becoming larger. The 1940s saw a major national effort to reduce the number of school districts and increase the size of schools. Reducing the number of school districts was achieved by consolidating existing districts into larger units. The general purpose of school consolidation was to provide more services to students. It was argued that the larger the school district, the more opportunity there was to provide specialized programs that could not be offered in smaller districts.

The major school consolidations occurred from the 1940s to the mid-1970s, when the number of school districts was decreased from 101,000 to 16,300—a dramatic reduction of 83.8 percent in 30 years. By the late 1970s the rate of decline in the number of districts had slowed to 250 consolidations a year.

At the same time that school districts were consolidating, the numbers of administrative staff, instructional staff, and students were increasing. The combination of school district consolidation and more complex hierarchical administrative structures resulted in increasing the distance between the leaders of a school district and the classroom teacher. For example, it became much more difficult for a teacher to have direct contact with a superintendent and school board members. Yet this sort of contact between a teacher and administrative leaders can often result in the teacher's having some influence over educational policy.

As teachers found themselves working in larger bureaucratic structures they increasingly turned to unionization as a means of influencing educational policy. (Chapter 9 discusses in detail the organization and objectives of teacher unions.) It should be noted that there is no way to prove that expanded bureaucratic structures caused teachers to form and join unions. All that can be argued is that teacher unions provided a formal organizational mechanism by which teachers could influence educational policy. Teacher unions are concerned not only with salaries and benefits but with a wide variety of issues including curriculum content and textbooks.

Joining a union and/or a professional organization can be a means by which a teacher can increase his or her sense of self-worth and also influence educational policy. Every area of teaching has some organization that publishes journals dealing with developments in curriculum and teaching methods and that attempts to influence school policy at state and national levels. Usually the professional organization has an annual national convention at which policies affecting the particular teaching field are discussed and formulated. For instance, the National Council of Teachers of English has spent many sessions and has devoted many pages of its journal to the vital issue of censorship. In a similar manner, professional organizations in the social studies, mathematics, science, vocational education, art, physical education, and other fields work actively to spread new knowledge among their members and protect the interests of the profession.

Professional organizations and unions can be an important means by which teachers can increase their rewards from teaching. Obviously unions provide a possible means of increasing external and ancillary rewards. Professional organizations in particular subject-matter areas can provide increased psychic rewards by enhancing a teacher's sense of control and autonomy.

The knowledge gained through active participation in a professional organization can also be a means by which a teacher can counter the increasing intrusion of bureaucratic structures in the classroom. It is important to understand that this intrusion is not inherently wrong. A problem arises because the intrusion can reduce the important psychic rewards from teaching by limiting the autonomy and creative decision making of teachers. When there are no significant increases in salaries and few external rewards, this intrusion can seriously contribute to teacher burnout and to an increased number of teachers changing careers.

Dan Lortie argues that the best protection teachers have against the loss of autonomy is through claims of expert knowledge. This means that the more knowledge teachers have of their subject matter, methods of teaching, and educational policy, the better they are able to protect their power in and control over the classroom. From this standpoint, active participation in a professional organization and keeping abreast with new knowledge in the field are the best means teachers have of assuring personal satisfaction from their work.

The Professionalization of Teaching

A much-discussed issue in education for over a century is whether teaching is a profession. One of the difficulties in resolving this issue is that *professionalism* can be defined in a variety of ways. For example, some people argue that teaching is not a profession because teachers do not control entrance into the field; nor do they control teaching practices, salaries, and working conditions. Arguments such as these often compare teaching to the medical profession. Medical doctors through their professional organizations control medical-school education, licensing, medical practice, working conditions, and fees. If this comparison defines professionalism, teaching is not a profession. Professional teacher organizations do not have the power that professional medical organizations have.

But defined in narrower terms, teaching is a profession. For the purposes of this text, *profession* is defined as an occupation requiring expert knowledge that justifies a monopoly of services granted by government licensing. The ability to gain a government license is dependent on the applicant's demonstrating this expert knowledge, either by passing an examination or by completing special training courses in an educational institution. In the teaching profession this usually means graduation from a college or university, and a claim to expert knowledge based on courses taken in departments or colleges of education. Teacher licenses are usually granted by the government on the basis of fulfilling certain educational requirements. In a growing number of states there is the added requirement of passing a state examination.

The term *profession* also involves a set of ethical standards based on service to the client of the profession. In other words, a teacher's primary ethical responsibility must be to the client, namely, the student. (In a similar manner, doctors and lawyers must serve their patients and clients.) If a teacher's primary responsibility is to serve the student, then the teacher must assume responsibility for maintaining the knowledge and skills that can provide the student with the best possible education. In addition, the teacher must be willing to defend and fight for teaching conditions that enhance learning opportunities.

There is a difference between ideal definitions and reality. Some doctors and lawyers are more interested in increasing their incomes than serving their clients. And some teachers lose sight of the fact that their primary responsibility is to serve students. This can easily happen in school systems where teachers are bombarded with administrative tasks and recordkeeping. Every teacher facing five classes of forty students thinks primarily in terms of how to make the job manageable. When teachers have to struggle to survive, they can often forget where their primary service should be directed. In a school where a heavy emphasis is placed on discipline, a teacher may lose sight of the fact that the primary goal of an educational institution is to teach students and not to maintain orderly classrooms.

The other reality facing teachers at present is the low status of their profession compared with other professions. This low status is rooted in historical conditions that have reduced both economic rewards and the status of the teaching profession. One can argue that those responsible for the mind of the child and its future development, such as teachers, should receive compensation comparable to those responsible for the body of the child, such as doctors. This argument can be made even more forcefully for educational specialists—reading specialist, special-education teachers, and teachers with other specialized training. When one considers the number of years of training needed to acquire this specialization, the gap in salary between educational specialists and other professionals is out of proportion to the differences in their training.

It is important for teachers to understand how education became professionalized so that they can participate in changes that may enhance the status of the teaching profession. The present conditions surrounding the profession of education are not the result of historical accident but of certain policies and developments. Teachers can serve their students and increase their own external and psychic rewards by working to enhance their professional status.

The first step in the professionalization of education in the United States was the establishment in 1839 of a teacher training institution in Lexington, Massachusetts. Called a *normal school,* this institution was designed primarily to train teachers for the elementary grades. The establishment of the school gave recognition to the fact that certain teaching skills can be *taught* to prospective teachers. The normal school emphasized not only subject matter but also methods of teaching.

A major problem in the early professionalization of teaching was that it accompanied the increasing recruitment of women into teaching. Women in the nineteenth century were inexpensive and stable members of the work force; they were second-class citizens in both the political and economic arenas. Willard S. Elsbree, in *The American Teacher: Evolution of a Profession in a Democracy,* quotes the Boston Board of Education in 1841 as it discusses why there should be an increased number of women in teaching. States the board:

> As a class, they [women] never look forward, as young men almost invariably do, to a period of legal emancipation from parental control, when they are to break away from the domestic circle and go abroad into the world, to build up a fortune for themselves; and hence, the sphere of hope and of effort is narrower, and the whole forces of the mind are more readily concentrated upon present duties.

Horace Mann, a common-school leader and the person mainly responsible for the founding of the first normal school, wrote in 1846: "Reason and experience have long since demonstrated that children under ten or twelve years of age can be more genially taught and more successfully governed by a female than by a male teacher." He went on to state that as more and more schools experimented with the use of female teachers, opposition to their entry into teaching would decrease. Elsbree reports that from the 1830s up to the Civil War, increasing numbers of women entered teaching through training in the normal schools. And the Civil War, with its demands for manpower in the military, completed the evolution of elementary school teaching from a male occupation to a primarily female occupation. For example, Elsbree states that in Indiana the number of male teachers in all grades dropped from 80 percent in 1859 to 58 percent in 1864; in Ohio the number of male teachers went from 52 percent in 1862 to 41 percent in 1864.

The second-class citizenship of women in the nineteenth century made it possible to keep teaching salaries low and contributed to the continuing low status of teaching as it became professionalized. In many school systems male teachers received higher salaries than female teachers. In the twentieth century, in spite of the struggle by women teachers for equal salaries, the low status of the profession continued because of changes in teacher–certification laws.

Nineteenth-century teachers were usually certified by taking an examination administered by the employing school system or the county board of education. Licensing, or the granting of certificates to teach, was based primarily on examination and not on the number of education courses taken. Elsbree reports that in 1898 only four states had centralized certification or licensing at the state level. The rest of the states gave the certification power to local districts and counties. By 1933 forty-two states had centralized licensing at the state level; the primary requirement for gaining a teacher certificate was the completion of a certain number of courses in teacher education and other fields.

The centralization of certification and the dependence on teacher-education courses led to a rapid expansion of normal schools and colleges of education in the early part of the twentieth century. State certification laws and expanded training in education completed the professionalization of teaching. Since 1933 this pattern of professionalization has continued, with the elimination of most normal schools and the expansion of college and university departments of education. Course requirements in most states have generally increased and there has been a greater monitoring of teacher education programs. By the 1970s some states had added state teaching examinations as part of the certification requirement.

One would assume that with the increased professionalization of teaching there would have been an increase in the status of teachers. The problem was that as teaching became more professionalized, its status was linked to the status of its professional training.

On some college campuses, taking courses in education is viewed as a form of "intellectual slumming." Dan Lortie in his previously mentioned study found teachers referring to their education courses as "Mickey Mouse" courses, and he never found a teacher who complained that education courses were too difficult. The status of the education faculty also is often not as high as that of other faculty members. In *To Be A Phoenix: The Education Professoriate,* Theodore Sizer and Arthur Powell (at the time dean and associate dean, respectively, of the Harvard School of Education) portray the professor of education as a "gentle, unintellectual, saccharine, and well-meaning... bumbling doctor of undiagnosable ills, harmless if morosely defensive. He is either a mechanic... or he is the flatulent promoter of irrelevant trivia."

Some authors argue that the status of the education professoriate is a result of the recruitment that occurred when education faculties expanded in the early part of the century. Many faculty members were recruited directly from teaching or public-school administration. They often lacked the academic and scholarly background of other faculties on college campuses. Once on campus they tended to concentrate only on problems dealing directly with classroom practice rather than with a broader concept of learning in a modern society. The narrow focus of education faculties has often contributed to the low academic status of departments of education.

It is difficult to pinpoint exact reasons for the low status of the education professoriate, but the consequences of that status are evident. Obviously, the lack of prestige of training in education contributes to the low prestige of the profession and probably influences the relatively poor economic rewards received by teachers as compared with other professionals. A claim to rigorous training and specialized knowledge is one of the most important ingredients in maintaining the status of a profession.

In addition to the effect of lack of rigorous training on status and income, this lack also affects psychic rewards. Dan Lortie found that teachers not only consider education courses "Mickey Mouse," but also do not perceive their preparation as conveying anything special. There is no sense of shared ordeal among teachers as there is among graduates of medical and law schools. Many teachers do not feel honored by having graduated from college or university departments of education.

How much the lack of prestige in the training and the lack of shared ordeal contribute to teacher burnout is difficult to measure. On the surface, one would feel that a teacher who had negative feelings about his or her training, who gained little status from that training, and who taught in a world of decreasing psychic rewards, would be prone to burnout.

It is evident from the previous discussion that an important way of increasing economic and psychic rewards for teachers is to upgrade the quality of professional training. Higher academic standards, requiring more rigorous training and more selectivity among applicants for teacher education, will help increase teacher rewards and status. They will create among teachers the sense of shared ordeal and the sense of shared technical culture.

From the standpoint of upgrading the status of the teaching profession, it is essential for teachers to become involved in influencing and controlling teacher education. An important function of a professional is to participate in the quality and training of those entering the field. For many years, teachers have failed to fully realize the importance of this involvement to their economic and psychological well-being. Becoming a professional means continuous study of and interest in new knowledge in the field, in addition to a concern for and involvement in the training of new entrants into the profession.

In recent years, the reform movement in teaching is attempting to increase professionalism by creating career ladders and new professional roles. In addition, teachers are gaining greater control over the certification process for entering the profession. This is a key element in the development of a profession. The next two sections will discuss career ladders, the role of master teachers, and the important efforts by the Carnegie Forum on Education and the Economy to restructure the teaching profession. All of these are important efforts in the continuing professionalization of teaching.

Career Ladders and Master Teachers

In the 1980s a flood of proposals and legislation for master-teacher plans and career ladders appeared in response to the problems of the American school teacher. One of the issues addressed by these plans is the "careerless" nature of teaching. What is meant by "careerless" is the lack of advancement possibilities in teaching, except for leaving the classroom and taking an administrative position in education. Other careers usually hold out the hope of advancement within the organization or through individual entrepreneurial skills. An office worker can move through the hierarchy of the organization, and a professional can attempt to increase income through his or her own ability.

Traditionally, when teachers entered the classroom there was no possibility of advancement except to leave the classroom and be trained as an administrator—or to get out of the education profession completely. Most teachers could not increase their income by superior teaching or service. In fact, merit pay is often opposed by teachers because of its potential abuse.

Career ladders and master-teacher plans attempt to correct the problem of the careerless nature of teaching and the lack of rewards for superior teaching by providing diferent career levels. One way of understanding this idea is to compare it to university teaching. Traditionally, universities hire new faculty members as assistant professors. After a period of five to seven years the faculty member applies for tenure and a position as an associate professor. Once promoted to associate professor, the faculty member might be promoted to professor if he or she demonstrates superior qualities in teaching or scholarship. Each advancement in rank provides increased recognition and rewards.

The same basic idea underlies proposals for career ladders and master-teacher plans. For instance, a teacher might be hired as an apprentice teacher and after a number of years of receiving satisfactory evaluations be promoted to the rank of regular teacher and receive tenure. Later, if the teacher is considered superior, that teacher might be promoted to master teacher. It is important for the reader to understand that this example is only a simple example. Some proposals are more complex and involve added duties for the master teacher. These will be discussed later in the text.

In addition to overcoming the problem of the careerless nature of teaching, master-teacher and career-ladder proposals are supposed to solve the problems inherent in traditional methods of compensating teachers. The traditional salary schedule for teachers allows for increases in pay with each year of service and for added academic degrees from universities. Under a traditional pay plan all beginning certified teachers with a bachelor's degree receive the same base salary. For each year of service after the first year, salaries increase by a fixed percentage. Under this method of payment a teacher receives an automatic salary increase with each year of service. In addition, a teacher can increase his or her salary by earning more college credits. Usually, the earning of a master's degree results in an increase in salary in addition to the automatic yearly increase. Also, there are usually increases for earning an additional 15 hours beyond the master's degree and for earning a doctoral degree.

One of the major complaints about the traditional method of compensation is that it is not based on the ability of teachers to teach. This became a heated issue in the early 1980s when everyone admitted that teachers were underpaid but many felt that salaries should be increased only for superior teachers. This is the reason for proposals for career ladders and master teachers. These plans are considered as replacements for the traditional salary schedule.

Another plan for providing additional compensation without changing the traditional salary schedule is that of merit pay. With merit pay, superior teachers would be identified and would receive an additional salary increase over their automatic yearly increase in salary. But merit-pay plans have been bitterly resisted by teachers because of the problem of setting criteria for superior teaching. This is also an issue with career ladders and master-teacher proposals. Teachers fear that school administrators would use merit pay to reward only personal favorites and those who are compliant with administrative orders. There is also the real difficulty of defining and evaluating superior teaching.

Some of the recent proposals for changing the nature of the career of teaching and the methods of compensation have also attempted to redefine the role of teacher. For instance, one of the major recommendations of the National Commission on Excellence in Education in its report, *A Nation at Risk*, is for school boards to adopt an 11-month contract. Traditionally, teachers are paid for 9 or 10 months of work. The longer contract would mean increased responsibilities. The additional time would be used, in the words of the report, "for curriculum and professional development, programs for students with special needs, and a more adequate level of teaching."

In its plan for career ladders and master teachers the commission proposes a recasting of the role of the teacher. The report recommends that "school boards, administrators, and teachers should cooperate to develop career ladders for teachers that distinguish among the beginning instructor, the experienced teacher, and the master teacher." Of importance to changing the role of the teacher, the report recommends that "master teachers should be involved in designing teacher preparation programs and in supervising teachers during their probationary years." This recommendation would add new responsibilities to the role of teaching. Traditionally, teachers have been confined to classrooms, extracurricular activities, policing chores, and committees established by the school principal. Supervision of new teachers introduces a role traditionally assumed by the administration. It adds an administrative function to the role of teaching. Participation in the design of teacher preparation programs adds another dimension to the role of teaching.

One can criticize these additional responsibilities and an extension of the teaching contract as not providing an actual increase in compensation but only additional pay for additional work. It would, however, be possible to have the category of master teacher include additional compensation without adding extra work. In the university system, promotion from assistant to associate or full professor does not entail any additional responsibilities. Similar criticisms can be made of the extended contract year. Why not just increase salaries without requiring additional months of work?

In its report by Ernest Boyer, *High School,* the Carnegie Foundation for the Advancement of Teaching also proposes a career ladder with the addition of new responsibilities to the role of teacher. Boyer recommends that the beginning teacher be identified as an *associate teacher* and work under the guidance of a senior teacher. The associate teacher would have a full load of classes, with continuous assessment by a senior teacher. After two years of teaching, the associate teacher's performance would be reviewed through statements by students and supervising teachers, accumulated comments on teaching skills, and observations by other school personnel. A satisfactory review would mean promotion to *full teacher* status.

The final step in promotion would be to the rank of *senior teacher.* This would be similar to what other plans call master teacher. To become a senior teacher, the teacher would have to teach three years as a full teacher and be recommended by a panel of senior teachers. If the teacher did not gain the rank of senior teacher he or she would continue to hold the rank of full teacher. A senior teacher in this plan would assume the additional responsibility of supervising associate teachers. Promotion to each new professional rank would involve a major increase in salary.

High School also contains other proposals for increasing salaries. It recommends a two-week Teacher Professional Development Term to be added to the school year, for the purpose of improving instruction and expanding knowledge. Teachers would receive additional compensation for this time. Also, Boyer recommends that every five years teachers should be able to receive extra pay through a Summer Study Term. And finally, the report recommended a travel fund for teachers so that they can attend professional meetings and have contact with others in their field.

The actual changes in teacher compensation and in the establishment of career ladders are occurring at the level of state government. The national report that has directly influenced the actions of governors and state legislatures is the previously mentioned *Action for Excellence,* written by the Task Force on Education for Economic Growth of the Education Commission of the States. The report complains that "in every state...teachers are paid according to rigid salary schedules based primarily on training and years of experience. No state, to our knowledge, has a system for rewarding exceptional teachers for their superior performance." To solve this problem the report recommended that "states should create 'career ladders' for teachers."

This simple recommendation reflected the interests of Governor Lamar Alexander of Tennessee, who was one of the major participants on the task force. In fact, Governor Alexander is a pioneer in the development of state plans for career ladders for teachers. In 1983 he proposed a bill to the Tennessee legislature for a career ladder for teachers. The bill ran into heavy opposition from teachers' organizations, which were concerned about methods of evaluation and the consequences for teachers already covered by the state's existing certification program. In February 1984 the legislature finally passed the bill after a compromise had been reached with the state teachers' organization. At the time of its passage it was hailed as the most ambitious program of its type ever put into law.

The Tennessee legislation established five levels in the career ladder, with additional compensation ranging from $500 to $7,000 per year. The first level is for new teachers on probationary status who receive state certification after receiving positive evaluations. Teachers who receive certification become apprentice teachers for three years and receive a yearly supplement of $500. Apprentice teachers are evaluated each year and by the third year must receive tenure and be promoted to Career Level One teachers or lose their jobs. Career Level One teachers are certified at this level for five years and receive an annual supplement of $1,000. Teachers at this career level assume the additional duties of supervising student teachers and probationary teachers.

It is possible under this plan that a teacher might remain at Career Level One for his or her entire teaching career. Promotion to Career Level Two requires evaluation by the state, using Career Level Three teachers from outside the district of the teacher being evaluated. If the teacher is promoted to Level Two, he or she receives an annual pay supplement of $2,000 for a 10-month contract and $4,000 for an 11-month contract. Career Level Two teachers are given the additional responsibilities of working with remedial and gifted students, along with supervising apprentice teachers. The evaluation procedure for Level Three is similar to that for Level Two. Level Three teachers receive an additional $3,000 for a 10-month contract, $5,000 for an 11-month contract, and $7,000 for a 12-month contract. In addition to the duties added for Level Two teachers, Level Three teachers also conduct evaluations of teachers who are on other career levels.

The Tennessee plan might become a model for other states. Politically, the issue depends on the reactions of local teacher organizations. In Tennessee, teacher organizations were satisfied with an agreement that allows a teacher currently entering the career ladder to withdraw at any time and work under the regular certification system. This provides protection for teachers who might lose their jobs as the career ladder becomes the only system of certification.

Of primary concern in all of these proposals is the method of teacher evaluation and who should conduct the evaluations. Traditionally, evaluation of teachers has been conducted by school administrators. Teachers have complained for years about this system and have argued that if teachers are truly professionals they should be evaluated by their peers. The Tennessee legislation incorporates this idea by using Level Three teachers for evaluation. Also, most master-teacher proposals give senior teachers the added duty of participating in teacher evaluations.

The issue of method of evaluation is more complex. The debate on this issue ranges across several dimensions. First is the problem of whether teachers should be evaluated on the basis of their performance in the classroom or the performance of their students. The difficulty of using student performance is the range of abilities existing among students and between classes of students. Some students, because of a variety of factors including family background and intelligence, might learn faster than other students. It would be unfair to evaluate a teacher of students with rapid learning abilities against a teacher of students with slow learning abilities. Also, most evaluations of students are conducted by using standardized tests. Systems using student performance as a means of teacher evaluation run the danger of teachers directing their efforts mainly toward preparing students to do well on performance tests.

If teacher performance becomes the basis for evaluation, then there will be a set of problems arising from the need to define good teaching. Historically, there has been an almost continuous debate dating from the nineteenth century over whether teaching is an art or a science. Obviously one's position on this issue would be reflected in the teaching qualities one would consider in evaluation. In recent years there has been a debate between those who believe that good teaching is composed of measurable competencies, and those who believe that good teaching is a product of experience that is displayed in reaction to a variety of classroom situations.

The debate over methods of evaluation and who should do the evaluating will probably continue to dominate discussions about merit pay, career ladders, and master-teacher proposals. But whatever the outcomes of these discussions, the resulting changes in the structure of teacher compensation and promotion will have a lasting effect on the profession. These changes might end the long-standing criticism that teaching is a careerless profession. Whether or not they will end teacher burnout will probably depend on other reforms in the working conditions of teachers. A method must be found to save the "Horace Smiths" of teaching from having to make endless compromises in their professional endeavors.

A Nation Prepared: Teachers for the 21st Century

In 1986, the Task Force on Teaching as a Profession, working under the auspices of the Carnegie Forum on Education and the Economy, made far-reaching proposals for changing the basic structure of the teaching profession. Its recommendations include the establishment of a national certification board, a complete reorganization of the administrative structure of schools, the creation of a new position called *lead teachers*, and reorganization of teacher education.

As discussed in Chapter 1, the task force report, *A Nation Prepared: Teachers for the 21st Century,* is premised on the belief that America can no longer compete in mass-production goods in world markets. Consequently, the report argues, the nation must shift its economy to emphasize knowledge-based industries. In this context, the schools must stop teaching repetitive skills needed in mass production and start teaching all students higher order thinking. According to the report, the old educational requirements needed for a mass production economy could be packaged in texts, and teachers could be trained to use those texts. A knowledge-based economy, according to the report, requires students who are intellectually prepared to deal with a nonroutine world and unexpected events. The report argues that the training of students in higher order skills requires abandoning traditional textbook teaching and developing new teaching strategies. These new teaching strategies require a teacher who no longer uses routine teaching methods, but constantly adapts to different learning situations. This is why, at least in the eyes of the Carnegie Forum, the key to changing the schools to meet the requirements of a knowledge-based economy is the reform of the profession of teaching.

The report describes the teacher needed for a knowledge-based economy as one who is highly creative and has the ability to constantly learn as new knowledge become available. In the words of the report, these new teachers "must think for themselves if they are to help others think for themselves, be able to act independently and collaborate with others, and render critical judgement. They must be people whose knowledge is wide-ranging and whose understanding runs deep."

The Carnegie Forum believes the teacher shortage of the 1980s and 1990s provides an ideal opportunity to change the profession of teaching and, as a result, adapt the schools to the requirements of a knowledge-based economy. The report's figures show that in 1985 the demand for teachers was roughly equal to the supply of teachers. After 1985 and into the 1990s, the report projects an increasing demand and a decreasing supply.

It is important to understand the reasons for this projected shortage of teachers because it provides insight into the challenging demographic patterns in teaching. One reason for the projected increased demand for teachers is increasing teacher retirements. When the baby boom ended in the 1970s and classrooms were closed because of decreasing student enrollments, school systems stopped hiring many new teachers and fired many young teachers. Consequently, the average age of teachers increased. Between 1976 and 1984, the number of teachers with fifteen years of experience increased from 27 percent to 44 percent. During the same period, the number of teachers under 34 years of age declined from 53 percent to 37 percent. Because of retirements from the more experienced teachers, some school districts will be replacing over half their teachers between 1986 and the early 1990s. Adding to the problem of teacher retirements is an increase in school populations as the children of baby boom parents enter school.

As a result of these factors, the Carnegie Forum projects an increase in annual demand of from 115,000 new teachers in 1981 to 215,000 by 1992. From 1986 to 1992 it is estimated that 1.3 million new teachers will be hired in American schools.

The problem of demand is intensified by the fact that more job opportunities are available now to women and minorities. Women, who we have previously noted traditionally dominated the ranks of teaching, are now finding more rewarding opportunities in other careers. For instance, in 1966 the intended occupation of almost 40 percent of freshmen women in college was education, while less than 5 percent intended to enter business. By 1976 the percentages were about equal, and after that year more women began to select business over education as a career. By 1985, more than 20 percent of freshment women planned a career in business, while less than 10 percent planned to be teachers. In addition, the number of minority teachers is declining.

Besides the issue of supply, the Carnegie Forum is also interested in the quality of future teachers. If a knowledge-based economy requires a more intellectual teacher than a mass-production economy, then the academic qualifications of teachers must increase. Traditionally, education students have been academically poorer than other college students. And, according to the report, the academic qualifications of teachers dropped dramatically between 1973 and 1983. In 1973, the average verbal score on the Scholastic Aptitude Test (SAT) for college-bound high school seniors was slightly more than 440, while the average score for those intending to major in education was less than 420. By 1983, the average score for those intending to enter education programs dropped to less than 400, while the average score for all college-bound seniors dropped to 430. In addition, the number of potential teachers graduating from high school academic programs has been declining. In 1974, 25 percent graduated from general high school programs and in 1982 this increased to 34 percent. And in 1974, 7 percent of education majors graduated from high school vocational programs; by 1982 the figure was 8 percent.

Therefore, while the teacher shortage offers the opportunity for changing the profession by hiring large numbers of new teachers, there is the potential for a decrease in the academic qualifications of teachers. The problem for the Carnegie Forum is attracting students to careers in education and assuring that these new students have high academic qualifications.

The Task Force on Teaching as a Profession recognizes that higher salaries are important in attracting better qualified people into teaching, but also suggests that changing working conditions is of equal importance. In the words of the report, "the conditions under which teachers work are increasingly intolerable to people who qualify for jobs in the upper tiers of the American work force, the people who must now be attracted to teaching."

The report suggests that the factorylike organization and bureaucratic structures that developed when schools were serving a society based on mass production are no longer suitable for a truly professional teaching force. The task force argues that true professionals act with a great deal of autonomy and intellectual independence. In fact, it is the lack of autonomy in present bureaucratic structures that causes many teachers to abandon their careers. The report claims that the current bureaucratic organization of schools exercises control over most teacher behaviors. Textbooks and curriculum guides define teacher actions in the classroom. A hierarchy of supervisors and outside experts determines methods of instruction.

In contrast to this traditional bureaucratic model of control, the task force proposes a radical restructuring of the school environment. A major element in the task force's proposal is to replace the traditional hierarchical model of school organization with a collegial model of professionals working together to make decisions. In other words, the proposal envisions committees of teachers making the major decisions about curricula and instruction and about the administration of schools. The collegial model could mean the elimination of the role of school principal. While the report recognizes that it might be possible for a collegial model to function with a nonteaching principal in charge of a school, it also suggests other alternatives to school organization.

A suggested model, and one strongly opposed by school administrators, is to put a committee of Lead Teachers in charge of the school. (How a teacher becomes a Lead Teacher will be discussed shortly in reference to certification standards.) This committee of Lead Teachers might then hire administrators to take care of routine business, reversing the traditional process of administrators hiring teachers. In addition, the report advocates greater control of educational budgets and regulations at the school site, and a deregulation of state control. Higher salaries and collegial working relations, the task force suggests, will attract more academically prepared people to teaching and keep them in the teaching force for longer periods of time.

The Carnegie Forum also proposes to improve the quality of teachers by the establishment of a national certification board. The report makes a clear distinction between the current licensing of teachers by individual states and national certification by a professionally controlled board. The task force argues that licenses are issued by states to ensure that prospective teachers meet the minimum standards established by state laws, and to signify that the holder is not a danger to public safety and the safety of a client.

A profession issues a certificate, however, also to indicate that the holder meets the standards established by the profession itself. The purpose of a national certification board, then, is to establish standards for the profession of teaching and to certify that individuals meet these standards. The task force plan establishes two levels of certification. The first, a General Teacher's Certificate, would indicate a high level of competence as determined by the board. The second, an Advanced Teacher's Certificate, would identify holders as Lead Teachers, who would then assume major administrative roles in the schools.

Initially, the national certification board is to be composed of from 33 to 63 members and, in keeping with the goal of professional control, two-thirds of the membership is to be drawn from the teaching profession. During the original planning, a struggle occurred between the two major teachers' unions. Obviously, each union wanted as many places on the board as possible for its own members. The agreement to establish the first board in May 1987 states that equal numbers from leadership positions in each union would comprise one-third of the teacher membership on the board, another third would come from teachers' disciplinary organizations, and the final third from teachers identified as having outstanding records of accomplishment. After this initial membership selection, all future teacher members of the board will be selected by current board members. In addition to the two-thirds membership made up of teachers, the rest of the board is to be selected from the general public and from other educators, including elected state officials, college deans, school board members, parents, professors, and business and industrial leaders.

The national certification board, composed primarily of teachers, has the difficult tasks of establishing standards for teaching and creating a means of determining who meets those standards. The first task is particularly difficult because there is little agreement on the best means of instruction. The task force report assumes an agreed-upon body of scientific research about good teaching. In fact, as we shall see in Chapter 3, methods of instruction are usually a reflection of political values and beliefs about the best way to organize society. In other words, selecting a method of instruction involves value judgments. Researchers disagree not only about the methods but also about the outcomes of various instructional methods. Part of the problem is the lack of agreement among educational researchers on a psychological model for interpreting human behavior.

Under the Carnegie Forum plan, states would license teachers according to their laws, and the national board would certify teachers according to its standards. Those identified by the board as Lead Teachers would assume major responsibility in the management of local schools. The practice of certification could give the national board considerable power for establishing standards for teaching and evaluation, as will be discussed in the next section of this chapter, and these standards could affect teacher education programs.

Since the national certification board is not attached to any branch of government, recognition of the board's certificates will be voluntary. The hope is that the board's standards will be so high and the certificate so prestigious that local school systems will want to hire only those teachers certified by the board.

While the Carnegie Forum on Education and the Economy primarily stresses changing the educational system from one serving a mass-production economy to one serving a knowledge-based economy, it also is concerned with protecting democratic ideals, avoiding the creation of an economic underclass, and recruiting more minority teachers. The task force report proposes no specific educational reforms for protecting democratic ideals beyond improving the teaching profession, but it does state that "a passive electorate that derives much of its knowledge from television is too easily manipulated. School must provide a deeper understanding necessary for a self-governing citizenry." The report recommends the teaching of a shared cultural and intellectual tradition.

Without stating specific solutions, the report worries about a growing class of permanently unemployed people. From the task force's perspective, this problem will be heightened by the creation of a knowledge-based economy. The report argues that in the past people could stay ahead by working hard. This would no longer be possible in a knowledge-based economy that requires an eagerness to win in international economic competition. As the report points out, "A heavily technology-based economy will be unable to invest vast sums to maintain people who cannot contribute to the nation's productivity."

One factor considered important in avoiding a permanent underclass is the recruitment of more teachers from minority groups. From the standpoint of the task force, this is both a matter of justice and is vital for the education of minority children. According to the figures in the task force report, 90 percent of the increase in the number of children living in poverty will be babies born to single black and Hispanic women. In contrast, only 5 percent of the teaching force will be black by 1990, and only 7 percent of Hispanics will complete college. Qualified minority college students tend to be attracted to careers other than teaching. According to the figures offered by the Carnegie Forum, only 3 percent of black college-bound high school seniors intend to enter education while 11 percent choose engineering, 15 percent the sciences, 16 percent computer science, and 21 percent business. The remainder of black high-school seniors choose health, medicine, biological science, and arts and humanities. The same pattern exists for Mexican-Americans and Puerto Ricans, with 5 percent of Mexican-American college-bound seniors and 4 percent of Puerto Rican seniors choosing education. Consequently, a major goal of the task force is to recruit more minority students to teaching. To accomplish that, of course, education must be competitive in terms of status and income with other college majors.

A Nation Prepared: Teachers for the 21st Century contains many debatable arguments in its justification for the establishment of a national certification board. First, the report is based on the argument that schooling must be changed to meet the requirements of a knowledge-based economy. Its authors assume that all future workers will be using higher order intellectual skills at the workplace. In fact, this might not be the case. It is possible that only a few workers will be required to use higher order intellectual skills, while the majority will be working in factories, fast-food chains, and other service industries using robotic and high-technology machinery that will require few intellectual skills. In fact, with modern technology using color-coded or picture-coded operating buttons, the future factory or service worker might not even need to know how to read or add.

A national certification board and the increased professional status for teachers also are a threat to the traditional school bureaucracy. Proposed administrative roles for teachers threaten the power of school administrators. An indication of this conflict is the claim in the May 27, 1987, issue of *Education Week* by June Gabler, superintendent of schools in Fort Dodge, Iowa, and president of the American Association of School Administrators, that the national certification board is "an attempted takeover of American schools by the teacher unions... The American people value education as the bedrock of our free and democratic society and we don't believe they want to turn their public educational system over to teacher unions."

As the profession of teaching evolves, there will be continued debate over the role of teachers controlling schools, the standards that should define teaching as a profession, the context and methods for evaluating teachers, and, as discussed in the next section, the content and organization of teacher education.

Teacher Education

Teacher education, like other aspects of public schooling, became a target of major criticism in the 1980s. In its report, *A Nation at Risk,* the National Commission on Excellence in Education complained that too many "teachers are being drawn from the bottom quarter of graduating high school and college students." The report was also concerned with the large number of required courses in educational methods, and the fact that, nationally, elementary-school teacher candidates spent 41 percent of their course time in education courses.

Consider the logic of certain educational requirements that must be met before a person becomes a teacher. It is logical that teachers know the subject matter they are to teach, the psychological and physical natures of those they plan to teach, the political and social structures of the institutions in which they will be teaching, the methods by which people learn, and the best methods for teaching particular subject matter.

Most teacher-education programs include all of the above components. An introductory course on American education or educational foundations provides the future teacher with an understanding of the political and social contexts in which he or she will be working. Courses in educational psychology, human development, and theories of learning provide the prospective teacher with an understanding of the individuals to be taught. In addition, courses in methods of instruction prepare a would-be teacher to teach in particular subject-matter areas. General education requirements are designed to ensure that a teacher knows his or her subject matter well.

Teaching not only requires knowing the subject matter, the learner, and the political and social context of learning; it also involves skills that can be improved through actual practice. All teacher-education programs have some form of practice teaching that allows experienced teachers to aid prospective teachers in gaining teaching skills. Some teacher-education programs require observation periods before actual practice teaching. Other programs provide clinical experiences before or during practice teaching.

Although most teacher educators would agree that the preceding combination of knowledge and skill development should form the basic components of a teacher-education program, there are disagreements about the actual content of each component, the proportion of time that should be devoted to each area, and the additional knowledge and skills necessary for teaching. There are also general disagreements about the whole process of teacher training.

For instance, there can be major disagreements in particular fields of study. Usually the content of a course reflects the training and intellectual beliefs of the faculty member who is teaching the course. A wide variety of theories of learning can be taught in a course in educational psychology. A faculty member may attempt to cover all theories, but there is the inevitable human tendency to stress the theory one thinks is most correct. In a similar manner, courses in methods of teaching can encompass a variety of schools of thought about which is the best method. These are different schools of thought about what is the best method of teaching English, social studies, science, mathematics, and so on.

Students in teacher-education programs and practicing teachers should become aware of these differences and begin to participate in influencing the direction of knowledge in their particular fields of interest. Certainly one of the best ways to begin to do this is to read the professional journals. As mentioned previously, every subject-matter area has its own organization and journal; these provide the best starting point for an investigation of a field of study.

Some important issues related to teacher education are not specific to a particular field of teaching. A major controversy in the twentieth century has been the balance between a general or liberal education and professional training. Although this debate goes back to the early days of professionalization in the nineteenth century, it has come into sharper focus over the last three decades. During the 1950s public schools came under attack for the quality of education they provided. A major charge was that public schools were controlled by professional educators who had lost contact with traditional academic disciplines. The result, it was argued, was poor academic performance by students and an atmosphere of anti-intellectualism in the schools. Of central concern, and the focus of a number of books, was the education of teachers. It was argued that the majority of university faculty had abandoned teacher education to the education faculty and that teacher education had been overwhelmed by professional-training courses. What was needed, claimed the critics, was the involvement of a community of scholars in teacher education and to place greater stress on academic training in the subject matter to be taught, with less emphasis on professional and technical training.

The result of that controversy was the development in the 1950s and 1960s of five-year programs in teacher education. The basic idea of these programs was for teachers to receive a solid academic training in a four-year college program before beginning technical training in methods of teaching. Some colleges instituted a Master of Arts in Teaching (MAT) program, which the prospective teacher could enter after completing a regular liberal arts degree program. Some states made teacher training a fifth-year program to be taken after completion of other college requirements. The goal in both cases was to ensure that professional training requirements did not interfere with an education that would give the teacher a firm grasp of subject-matter material.

There is another dimension to the tension between the technical and the liberal aspects in teacher education. Many teachers and teacher educators argue that teaching is primarily an art to be developed, as opposed to a set of skills that can be taught. Within the framework of this argument, courses in education would be kept at a minimum with a primary emphasis on academic training and general intellectual development of the teacher. This issue became very heated in the 1970s with the development of the concept of performance-based teacher education (PBTE).

PBTE resulted from the rapid development of behavioral psychology, computer sciences, and systems analysis during the 1960s and 1970s. PBTE attempted to identify those behavioral skills most closely related to student achievement. The skills had to be measurable and had to be stated in terms of specific behavioral objectives. For teacher training, this meant that a teacher had to be taught what these skills are, and had to demonstrate a competence in their use before being certified to teach.

A major objection to PBTE was that being a good teacher is not a simple matter of learning some specific skills; teaching is an art that has to be developed by the individual. PBTE, it was felt, was too mechanical and imposed a false sense of being "scientific" on the "art" of teaching. It assumed that human interaction could be reduced to measurable scientific terms.

Despite these objections, some states adopted forms of PBTE as part of their certification process. By the early 1980s, PBTE-type programs came under heavy criticism because of the lack of agreement among researchers about the teaching skills that are related to student achievement. With no agreement and no convincing evidence that particular skills are related to student achievement, it has been difficult to construct a list of specific behavioral objectives for PBTE that can be accepted by all scholars.

By the 1980s a general concern developed that teacher education could not be improved given its present institutional structure. For instance, B. Othanel Smith, in the October 1980 lead article of the *Phi Delta Kappan,* argued that the variety of colleges of education, and the conflicts within departments and colleges of education, made it impossible for significant reform in teacher education to be a product of those institutions. Smith considered the hodge-podge of existing teacher education programs as a major hindrance in creating a truly "professional" teacher education program. As mentioned previously in this chapter, this issue is important not only because reforms in the institutional structure of teacher education can improve the quality of teaching, but also because they can increase the status and rewards of the profession for teachers.

Smith has proposed that leaders of professional organizations and colleges of education should work toward organizing a national commission on teacher education that would formulate plans and lobby in state legislatures for new legislation regarding teacher education. Two important aspects of this proposal are related to the politics of teacher education. The first is that the proposals suggest a centralization of policy making and a national uniformity in teacher education. In other words, the proposal is based on the assumption that a "hodgepodge" of approaches to teacher education is wrong. This assumption can be countered with an argument that no one yet knows the best way to train teachers and that a maximum amount of variety may be a means of promoting program innovation. Second, the proposal relies on a centralized national commission that would lobby state legislatures to change teacher-education requirements. This approach would closely tie teacher education to the political process. (In later chapters there is an expanded discussion of the politics of education.) Smith's proposed changes would assure the politicalization of teacher education and force teachers interested in changing professional education to work at state and national levels of government.

The increased politicalization of teacher education that would result from Smith's proposal is immediately evident in the response to his article by educational leaders. The executive director of the National School Boards Association said that Smith's proposed national commission did not go far enough and should include members of local school boards interested in teacher education. This response reflects a reality of the politics of education. Everyone and every organization in education is interested in influencing policy. This often leads to conflict as each group attempts to protect its own membership.

Concern over special-interest needs is also evident in the response of the director of professional development of the National Education Association. While the NEA applauded the idea of reform in teacher education, it doubted the feasibility of reaching a consensus because of conflicting interests among different groups in education. From this perspective, the proposed national commission could become a major center for political struggle among interest groups.

Smith's proposal for a national commission reflects a general trend toward greater centralization of teacher education and certification at the state level. One possible national trend can be seen in changes that took place in Georgia in the latter part of the 1970s. After they complete their college work, candidates for state licensing to teach in Georgia must pass an examination covering the specific curriculum area in which they plan to teach. When the test was first given, state officials in Georgia claimed that 20 percent of the college graduates who took it failed.

Statewide testing under the Georgia plan is designed to determine if potential teachers know the subjects they are planning to teach. To further determine if individuals know how to teach, they are put on three years' probation after they pass the subject-matter test, during which time they are required to demonstrate an ability to teach in the classroom. Information about candidate performance for those three years is collected; if the teaching is found to be satisfactory, the individual is given a certificate to teach.

Other states are adopting variations of the Georgia plan, with some planning tests covering knowledge of pedagogy. On the surface, these plans would seem to strengthen the teaching profession and provide an element of rigor that would enhance the professional status of teachers. But, as with all plans, there are problems. The first problem is that teachers are still not in control of the certification process. One of the distinguishing features of a professional is the ability to exert some control over entrance into the profession. With control centralized at the state level, teachers' organizations must compete with other organizations for influence over the certification process. As with Smith's proposal for a national commission, this could mean a greater politicalization of teacher education as different factions battle to influence state standards.

As states turn to an examination system as a means of certification, the political struggle becomes extremely important. The results of that struggle can have grave consequences for both colleges and elementary and secondary schools. For instance, take the issue of statewide testing of knowledge of subject matter. It is important to understand that knowledge is not neutral. In any discipline, competing factions claim to have the "right" interpretation or framework for understanding the subject. This is particularly true in subject areas like history, political science, sociology, economics, and psychology. It can even be true in the "hard" sciences and mathematics.

The important question regarding statewide testing is this: Who will determine the content and interpretation of the subject-matter area covered by the test? Tests by their nature can cover only part of a subject. There has to be some selection of the most important items to be covered on any examination. In addition, there has to be some value judgment regarding the correct answers to specific questions.

The issue of correct answers is particularly important if the examination is given in the form of multiple-choice questions. Multiple-choice examinations can be the most value-laden form of testing because the answers are determined solely by the authors of the examination. A student's response is limited by the specific choices on the examination and the interpretation by the author of the test as to what is the correct answer. For instance, consider the issue of inflation. Not only do economists disagree about the causes of inflation, but thinking about how to interpret the causes of inflation has shifted rapidly throughout the twentieth century. Even if you brought the leading economists in one state together, and they all agreed on important questions and the answers to those questions, there would still be the issue of whether their thinking represents the "right" thinking in the field. Those identified as "leading economists" might be no more than "established economists" in their field; younger scholars might be preparing newer theories that would replace those held at present by the leaders. This situation is true in almost every field of academic study.

The issue becomes more important when one considers the potential consequences of a statewide examination on subject matter. First, there would probably be a tendency for colleges to teach for the examination. After all, colleges would be embarrassed if large numbers of their students failed the examination. Also, teacher candidates would want to be taught in terms of passing the examination. In other words, the content of the state examination could have a powerful influence on the content of courses in colleges and universities.

Second, if colleges begin to teach in terms of preparing students to pass a state examination, then what a college graduate knows about a field will be determined by the examination. This means that when that individual teaches, the content of his or her teaching will be strongly influenced by the state examination. This would not be a problem if knowledge were neutral and all people agreed upon what knowledge has most worth. But that is not the case, and state examinations could have a stultifying effect on the development of knowledge.

The same problem exists with any statewide evaluation of teacher performance. Educators do not agree about what makes a good teacher or about how to evaluate teaching. There are several schools of thought. Within any college of education one can find as many ideas about what constitutes good teaching as there are professors of education. What items are to be used in the evaluation of teaching performance or on examinations in pedagogy, and how answers are to be determined, is very important.

Issues involved in the control of content of evaluation are extremely important as greater centralization of teacher education occurs. It is also important to understand that this trend is the result of an attempt to improve the quality of teaching in the schools and create higher professional standards, which will result in higher status and greater rewards for teachers.

The flood of education reports that appeared in 1983 and 1984 recommended reforms that included increased selectivity of teacher-education candidates, more emphasis on general academic training, and incentives to attract more qualified candidates to teacher-education programs. *A Nation at Risk* recommended simply that "persons preparing to teach should be required to meet high educational standards, to demonstrate an aptitude for teaching, and to demonstrate competence in an academic discipline." In addition, the report urged that colleges of education be judged on the basis of the performance of their candidates and that grants and loans should be made available to attract outstanding students to teaching. These general recommendations were not accompanied by any specific plans for action.

The report of the Task Force on Education for Economic Growth, *Action for Excellence,* was also general in its recommendations. This report was intended to serve as a guide for governors in planning the educational policies of their particular states. The report called for financial aid to attract the most able people to teaching. More important, the report stated that the improvement of the academic knowledge of teachers and their teaching skills would require "a substantially restructured and renewed curriculum for teacher training, which would include the management and application of technology." In a general plea for action, the report called upon governors to improve the academic quality of teacher-education curriculum.

The Carnegie Foundation for the Advancement of Teaching's report, *High School,* provided more specific recommendations for carrying out the general improvement of teacher education. The author of the report, Ernest Boyer, recommended that the first two years of college training be devoted to the study of a core of common learning. The responsibility for this core curriculum would be in the hands of the liberal arts faculty. Admission to a teacher-education program would occur in the junior year of college, and admission would require a "B" average or better plus strong recommendations from two professors. The teacher-education program would be three years long, with the first two years (the student's junior and senior years) devoted to completing a major in an academic discipline and to classroom observation.

After studying a core curriculum and completing an academic major the prospective teacher would take teacher-education courses. Boyer is aware of the criticism directed at education courses. He writes, "While many speak disparagingly of teacher education courses, we conclude there is important information uniquely relevant to teachers." Boyer believes that four areas of study should be part of the teacher-education curriculum. The first area is what the report calls "schooling in America." This course would be devoted to the history of education and current issues in education. The other three areas would deal with "learning theory and research," "teaching of writing," and "the use of technology." Boyer writes that "all teacher education students should study theories of learning, the ways teachers teach and students learn, and examine also the findings of current psychological and physiological research bearing on these themes." Boyer's emphasis on prospective teachers learning to teach writing reflects the general concern of the report with language instruction. The report argues that writing is not only an essential skill for self-expression but is also an important means of teaching critical thinking. Boyer believes that all teachers should be prepared to teach students how to write better. Also, prospective teachers should study educational technology, including computers, as a means of significantly improving class-room instruction.

In addition to the course work, Boyer recommends that the fifth year include classroom observation and practice teaching. He recognizes that teaching ability is dependent upon the type of experience that can only be gained in practice and in working with other experienced teachers, which is why he believes that practice teaching should be done with a team of teachers. The report also recommends that fifth-year teacher-education students should meet with outstanding arts and sciences "scholar-teachers" in a series of common learning seminars to "relate the knowledge of their fields to a contemporary political or social theme." Boyer expresses the hope that this seminar will help prospective teachers to relate to other disciplines and be able to teach a common core of learning to students in the schools.

A Nation Prepared: Teachers for the 21st Century, discussed in detail in the previous section, links raising standards in teacher education to increasing the status of teaching and, as a result, attracting more capable students to education programs. Basic to the report's program of restructuring teacher education is the replacement of undergraduate programs in education with graduate programs in education. While the report states that the national certification board will not establish national standards for teacher education, the authors do admit that their proposed evaluation techniques and standards for certification will have a significant effect on teacher education.

In general, *A Nation Prepared* advocates an undergraduate program devoted to a broad liberal education and a thorough study of the subject or subjects the student plans to teach. In keeping with the general trend toward a core curriculum, the report recommends an undergraduate curriculum that would provide rigorous study of history, government, science, literature, and the arts. The authors argue that elementary teachers need the same strong academic background as high school teachers because they have equal re-sponsibility in imparting our common culture and heritage.

Professional courses in education would be provided at the graduate level in a master-in-teaching degree program, to give teachers information about techniques of teaching, research on teaching, human development, and different learning styles. In addition, teachers seeking advanced certification would study philosophy of education, policies in education, and techniques of measurement.

The ideal two-year master-in-teaching degree program as outlined by the report would begin with a semester of courses on methods of instruction. During the second semester, students would perform an internship in teaching at a school with a diverse student population while taking several other graduate courses in education. In the following summer, students would take a full load of courses building on the teaching experience of the internship. Finally, students would spend the second year in residence at a school working under the guidance of a Lead Teacher.

The recommendations of the Task Force on Teaching as a Profession are guided by a medical model. The second year of graduate work in education places the student in residence at school, as a medical student spends a year in residence in a hospital. In fact, the report recommends the identification of *clinical schools* that would be analogous to teaching hospitals. These clinical schools would be models of the type of collegial environment advocated by the report.

Also recommending abolishment of the undergraduate education degree is the 1986 Holmes Group report, *Tomorrow's Teachers*. Originally organized in 1983 as a coalition of 23 deans from major research institutions in education, the Holmes Group expanded by 1987 to include representatives of 94 leading universities. Unlike the Carnegie task force, the Holmes Group gives little attention to the relationship between economic problems and changing educational goals. Its basic premise is that new knowledge about teaching practices requires changing teacher education and the organization of schools. This new knowledge about methods of instruction is drawn from advances in what is called cognitive psychology. Cognitive psychology stresses the importance of how the mind processes information and makes decisions about future action. This approach to learning and teaching is very different from the forms of behavioral psychology that dominated education in the 1970s.

Within the framework of behavioral psychology, student learning and teaching is managed by specific behavioral objectives that are listed in lesson plans. (A more complete discussion of this psychology and methods of instruction will be given in Chapter 3.) In reality, according to followers of cognitive psychology, it is difficult for a teacher to follow a lesson plan based on specific objectives because of the constantly changing conditions within a classroom. For instance, some unexpected event might occur with a student or some train of thought might develop that is more important than any written objectives.

Real teaching, according to cognitive psychology and the Holmes report, is the product of continual decisions being made by the teacher based on his or her knowledge of the subject matter and the processing of information about what is occurring in the classroom. The emphasis on teacher thinking and decision making results in a call for changes in teacher education, the organization of the profession, and the environment of the school that are similar to the changes advocated by the Carnegie task force.

Based on the psychological model of teacher as decision maker, the Holmes report argues that teachers must be treated as professionals who can and should exercise independent judgment in the classroom. This means abandoning the traditional business model used in school governance and replacing it with a model giving greater power of self-management to teachers.

In addition, the Holmes Group, like the Carnegie task force, proposes replacing the careerless quality of the teaching profession with a career ladder that would begin with novice *Instructors* at the bottom, *Professional Teachers* in the middle, and *Career Professionals* at the top. Professional Teachers would be selected by examination and the fulfillment of education requirements from the ranks of Instructors. Career Professionals would be selected by peer review and examination, and would participate in administrative decisions in the school.

The Holmes Group calls for the elimination of the undergraduate degree in teacher education. It advocates a strong undergraduate education in the subject matter areas each individual plans to teach. Graduate training in education, the report proposes, should focus on subject-matter-oriented studies of teaching and learning that integrate research on cognitive psychology.

Exercises

1. Interview teachers regarding the rewards and dissatisfactions they gain from teaching. Compare their remarks with what you want from a career.
2. Investigate the organization and publications of a professional educational group in a particular subject matter. What are current educational issues within the organization?
3. Design an ideal program of teacher education. Compare that program to the one currently offered by your college.
4. List what you think should be the requirements for gaining teacher certification. Compare your list with the requirements in your state.

Suggested Readings and Works Cited in Chapter

Boyer, Ernest L. *High School*. New York: Harper & Row, 1983. This study conducted for the Carnegie Foundation for the Advancement of Teaching contains important descriptions of the work life of teachers and recommendations for the reform of teaching.

Borrowman, Merle. *The Liberal and Technical in Teacher Education: A Historical Survey of American Thought.* New York: Teachers College, 1956. This is the classic study of the debates that have surrounded the development of teacher education in the United States. The book provides the best introduction to the history and issues regarding teacher education.

Elsbree, Willard. *The American Teacher: Evolution of a Profession in a Democracy.* New York: American Book Company, 1939. Still the best history of the profession of teaching in the United States. Unfortunately it traces the professionalization of teaching only to the 1930s.

Goodlad, John. *A Place Called School.* New York: McGraw-Hill, 1984. This detailed study of American schools contains surveys and recommendations about the profession of teaching.

Holmes Group, *Tomorrow's Teachers.* East Lansing, Michigan: Holmes Group, 1986. Report on restructuring teacher education and the profession issued by an organization composed of leading research institutions in education.

Lortie, Dan. *Schoolteacher: A Sociological Study.* Chicago: University of Chicago Press, 1975. The most complete study of the social interactions and world of the American teacher.

The National Commission on Excellence in Education. *A Nation at Risk.* Washington, D.C.: U.S. Government Printing Office, 1983. This important report contains recommendations for improving the quality of teachers and teacher education.

Phi Delta Kappan Special Issue: Reform in Teacher Education, October 1980. Articles by a wide range of authors on issues in teacher education.

Powell, Arthur and Sizer, Theodore. "Changing Conceptions of the Professor of Education," in *To Be a Phoenix: The Education Professoriate,* ed. James Counelis. Bloomington: Phi Delta Kappa, 1969.

Sizer, Theodore. *Horace's Compromise: The Dilemma of the American High School.* Boston: Houghton Mifflin, 1984. This study of the American high school contains important insights into the problems encountered by teachers.

Task Force on Education for Economic Growth. *Action for Excellence.* Denver: Education Commission of the States, 1983. This report by governors and corporate leaders contains recommendations that have influenced the actions of state governments regarding teachers.

Task Force on Teaching as a Profession. *A Nation Prepared: Teachers for the 21st Century.* New York: Carnegie Corporation of New York, 1986. Important report calling for the restructuring of the teacher profession and the establishment of a national certification board.

United States Office of Education. *Japanese Education Today.* Washington, D.C., 1987.

3

The Politics of Curriculum, Instruction, and Theories of Learning

Often what teachers teach, how they teach, and the psychological theories they use in the classroom are determined by political and economic conditions and the structure and organization of the school. To gain a critical perspective and to be able to participate in decisions about content and methods of instruction it is important for teachers to understand the effects of these organizational, economic, and political factors.

In this chapter I will review the major trends in curriculum, methods of instruction, and theories of learning in American schools in the twentieth century and will relate these trends to larger social and political issues. For instance, curriculum, or what is taught in schools, is primarily determined by the general goals of schooling. As discussed in Chapter 1, American schools are constantly affected by changing educational goals. As these goals change, so does the curriculum. For example, human capital goals might result in a curriculum that emphasizes vocational instruction. Concern with educating democratic citizens might result in more courses in history and government.

Methods of instruction, or how the curriculum is taught in schools, are primarily determined by the organization of the school. Larry Cuban reached this conclusion in *How Teachers Taught: Constancy and Change in American Classrooms 1890–1980.* Cuban finds that despite constant attempts in the twentieth century to change methods of instruction in the schools, actual classroom practices remain the same. Constancy exists in classroom teaching, he concludes, because of the effect of school organization and educational goals on teachers working in classrooms.

The popularity of particular psychological theories is also affected by general educational goals. Some psychological theories are popular during times of concern with student discipline and educating for specific occupations, while other theories become popular during periods of concern with independent and creative thinking by students.

Curriculum

In *The Struggle for the American Curriculum 1893–1958,* Herbert M. Kliebard identifies four types of curricula that have vied for dominance in American public schools. Each of these curricula receive support from issues generated by particular social, economic, and political factors. The curricular struggle Kliebard portrays continues into the late 1980s. Kliebard's four curriculum categories are:

1. social efficiency
2. humanism
3. social meliorism
4. developmentalism

Each of these categories is complex when considered in the context of the development of American education. Simply defined, a curriculum based on ideas of *social efficiency* is designed to teach subjects that will prepare the student to participate in the economic system. Often, social-efficiency curricula emphasize vocational subjects and are associated with the educational goals of human capital as discussed in Chapter 1. In general, social-efficiency ideas have the greatest influence over the curricula of American public schools.

In sharp contrast to the advocate of social efficiency, the *humanist* wants the curriculum to introduce students to the cultural traditions of society. A humanist spurns the idea of a vocational curriculum and favors the development of general intellectual skills. Often the humanist wants the curriculum to be organized around standard academic subjects like literature, history, foreign languages, the arts, and science.

The *social meliorist* wants the curriculum to bring about social improvement and change. Social meliorism reflects the reform element in American education. At the most extreme, the social meliorist will ask for courses to solve each new social problem. Sometimes this means the education of students to bring about general political and economic changes. But more often it means the advocacy of courses to solve problems such as alcoholism, drug abuse, AIDS, and traffic accidents.

In many ways, *developmentalism* is the most radical of the four curriculum types. The developmentalist wants the curriculum organized around the psychological development of the child. This means a curriculum focused on the needs of the individual child as opposed to the focus of social-efficiency educators, humanists, and social meliorists respectively on economic needs, the passing on of culture, and social reform. Of the four curriculum types, developmentalism has had the least influence on the public-school curriculum. The child-centered curriculum of developmentalists is often rejected by supporters of the other types of curricula for being anti-intellectual and failing to provide the student with the necessary skills to function in society and the world of work.

Historically, one type of curriculum achieves prominence over another in the public schools as a result of changing political and economic conditions. For instance, in the 1980s humanism receives support because of the perception that a lack of intellectual skills among public-school graduates is responsible for America's declining position in world trade. Humanists in the 1980s advocate that all students be required to take a core curriculum emphasizing traditional academic subjects. In the 1970s, however, concerns with unemployment and student unrest resulted in an emphasis on a social-efficiency curriculum which evaluated the worth of each course according to its contribution to a person's future career. Vocational education and career education were the central focus of the social-efficiency education of the 1970s.

The tension between humanists and advocates of social efficiency can be traced to the early part of the twentieth century. Humanists fought against the onslaught of social efficiency by trying to preserve the teaching of Greek and Latin in the schools. They argued, in the tradition of the liberal arts, that the purpose of education should be the training of the mind and, as a result of that training, the development of character. For humanists, the study of classical languages, literature, and history would give students the mental tools and character to be moral and successful.

Social-efficiency educators in the early twentieth century, however, argued that the school should provide individualized training based on a person's future destination in the labor force. The worth of all public school courses, they argued, should be judged by their contribution to a person's social worth in the world of work. Therefore, social-efficiency educators called for abandoning the long-standing tradition of teaching Latin and Greek for more vocational courses.

In their enthusiasm for the practical, social-efficiency educators went so far as to advocate that particular courses be geared to a student's future work. For example, they asked why a prospective mechanic or bricklayer should be taught Shakespeare, when the intended occupation required only minimal language skills. Instead, they proposed that occupations should be analyzed to determine their specific academic requirements, and courses could then be organized around those requirements. Future bricklayers, then, would be taught only the English, arithmetic, and science actually needed for that occupation.

By the 1920s, the battle lines were clearly drawn between the humanists and social-efficiency advocates. Neither side could claim victory, but the social-efficiency philosophy did replace many of the traditional humanist components of the curriculum. In the 1930s, a new group of humanists working under the label of *essentialists* reacted against the overly specialized curriculum of the social-efficiency advocates and declared the need for a common-core curriculum. While essentialists did not base their proposals for a core curriculum on a traditional classical education, they emphasized the importance of teaching a common cultural tradition. Unlike earlier humanists who looked to the past, essentialists examined the cultural requirements of the present.

While the humanist argument for a core curriculum was being modified by the practical outlook of the essentialists of the 1930s, social meliorists were calling for major transformations in the public-school curriculum. Since the early days of the common-school movement of the 1830s and 1840s, public schools had been viewed as a source of social change and improvement. The depression of the 1930s sparked widespread concern with social and economic conditions. Many Americans began to believe that the only hope lay in basic changes in the economic organization of the society.

Influenced by these arguments, a group of educators calling themselves *social reconstructionists* called for the teaching of subjects that would prepare the individual to be an active participant in the economic transformation of society. Often this meant a stress on social studies courses designed to give students the skills to analyze political and economic conditions.

The radicalism of the social reconstructionist position created tension with more conservative elements of society, best exemplified by the conservative attacks on one of the most popular social studies series in the history of American education. The series, authored by social reconstructionist educator Harold Rugg, was first published in 1929 and sold 1,317,960 copies by 1939. The series contained 8 volumes for grades from junior high school to high school. The controversial parts of the series included pictures contrasting the lives of the rich and poor, attempts to eradicate prejudice against immigrants, discussions of racism, and a declaration that America was entering an age of social planning. Attacks against the series of books were led by conservative organizations like the American Association of Manufacturers, the American Legion, the Daughters of Colonial Wars, and conservative publications like the business journal *Forbes*. These virulent attacks and the patriotism associated with the outbreak of World War II eventually forced the series off the market in the 1940s. Besides being an example of social reconstructionist philosophy, the history of Harold Rugg's books highlights the problem of freedom of ideas in American schools.

The postwar period of the late 1940s shifted the concern of American educators from the economic problems of the depression to the international problems of the cold war between the United States and the Soviet Union. The rhetoric of the cold war tended to dominate curriculum discussions from the 1940s into the 1960s. The result was a strange amalgam of humanist and social-efficiency ideas. Social-efficiency ideas were present in the call for more courses in mathematics and science to train students to be engineers, scientists, and mathematicians in order to win the military race with the Soviet Union. In addition, there was a call for the teaching of more and a greater variety of foreign languages so that the United States could compete with the Soviet Union for influence in other countries. The common rhetoric of the period was that American schools needed to meet humanpower needs or the United States would succumb to the power of the communist threat.

Humanists joined the chorus of those arguing that the schools needed to meet the humanpower needs of the cold war by stressing the importance of academic rigor and the teaching of intellectual skills. Within the concerns of the cold war, the humanist stress on intellectual skills was complemented by the social-efficiency demand to produce highly trained workers for the war machine. Humanists declared American public schools anti-intellectual and called on academic scholars to gain control of the public-school curriculum.

By the 1960s, the cold war concerns of educators gave way to the pressures of the civil rights movement and fears of increasing poverty. Again, social meliorists were prominent in calls for changes in the curriculum that would prepare minorities and poor people for more equal participation in the economy. For social meliorists of the 1960s, a major goal of education became the elimination of poverty and racism. Discussions of new science and math courses gave way to proposals for compensatory education and Head Start courses. These changes in the curriculum were designed to provide the children of the poor with equal access to education by improving their basic skills. Combined with desegregation, these curriculum changes were to end poverty and racism.

In the late 1960s, the social unrest sparked by the Vietnam War dimmed the hopes of social meliorists. Campus protests and disruptions alarmed conservatives and created demands for the restoration of law and order. Republicans attacked the curriculum changes of the social meliorists as unproven social experimentation. War protestors, however, linked antiwar activities with greater demands for cultural freedom. Included in these demands was greater educational freedom for students to pursue their own interests. In addition, the financial cost of the war and energy problems in the 1970s caused unemployment and economic stagnation.

Thus in the late 1960s and early 1970s, a confused period of curriculum change occurred with conservatives demanding more discipline in the schools, cultural and antiwar protestors demanding more freedom in the schools, and social-efficiency advocates demanding that the curriculum change to solve the problems of unemployment and economic stagnation. The final result in the 1970s was that conservatives and social-efficiency advocates joined forces to emphasize, as a solution to both discipline and economic problems, career-education courses, expanded vocational offerings, and closer linkages between the curriculum and the needs of the labor market.

By and large, those seeking greater educational freedom established private alternative schools outside the organization of the public schools. While a number of reasons might be given for the short life of these schools, certainly financial problems made it difficult for them to compete with public schools.

It is important to understand that the private alternative schools established in the 1960s and 1970s were part of a long tradition of efforts to organize a curriculum based on student choice and interest. In most cases this tradition flourished in private schools. A major difficulty in organizing a student-centered curriculum in a public school is that the public school exists to serve the interests of society in general. This means, as we have discussed, that the public school curriculum is primarily determined by constantly shifting social, economic, and political goals.

The attempt to create a child-centered curriculum is part of the developmentalist tradition of adjusting the curriculum to the child's nature. The assumption is that the source of motivation, interest, and learning is within the nature of the child. Education, therefore, involves providing the opportunity for children to learn as their interests and desires unfold. Some educators in this tradition argue that a child passes through different stages of development and that the curriculum should be adjusted for each developmental stage.

The private alternative schools of the late 1960s and early 1970s were often called *free schools* because children were given freedom to learn according to their own needs and interests. They were identified with the English school Summerhill, established in the 1920s by A. S. Neill. Neill believed that aggression was primarily a product of the repression of a child's free development. Authority and discipline, according to Neill, rather than making a child socially responsible, often created a personality that was destructive and aggressive. At Summerhill children were given complete freedom to determine what they studied and how they lived. The only restriction was that they not interfere with the freedom of others. Neill believed that a free school educated individuals who would strive for a free and peaceful world.

Summerhill was one of many alternative schools in the 1920s. In the United States a variety of schools appeared in the early part of the twentieth century devoted to freedom of learning and natural development. The Modern School opened in New Jersey before World War I and lasted into the 1950s. It was dedicated to a nonauthoritarian education where the children determined their own learning. The Walden School was opened in the 1920s by Margaret Naumberg, who believed that the individuality of the child developed through the study and practice of art. The politically radical Manumit School opened during the same period based on the idea that children should manage their education in the same manner as workers organized in unions. Labor-management contracts defined the relationship between students and teachers.

The educational philosopher most often associated with the development of curricula based on student self-interests is John Dewey. It is difficult to measure the impact of Dewey on American education. Certainly his ideas on learning and curriculum have been widely discussed since the beginning of the century. However, there is little evidence that his ideas caused significant changes in the public schools.

Dewey evaluated the impact of the child-centered education movement on the public schools in a *Time* magazine article in 1952. On the positive side, he said the movement made teachers more aware of the growing human being and personal relations and that the "older gross manifestations...of education by fear and repression...have, generally speaking, been eliminated...." On the negative side, while these grosser forms disappeared, Dewey argues, the "fundamental authoritarianism of the old education persists in various modified forms." Indeed, he found little cooperative and democratic learning in American schools.

A problem in discussing Dewey's impact is the complexity of his thinking and the varying interpretations that can be made of his writings. Consequently, Dewey's ideas have been attacked as anti-intellectual and catering too much to the whims of children, as politically radical, and as promoting group conformity.

Probably the two most controversial aspects of Dewey's thinking, and the source of his ideas on curriculum organization, are the beliefs that all knowledge has a social origin and that the interests of the child are the primary sources of learning. Of course, the conviction that all knowledge has a social origin is rejected by religious groups who believe that God is the source of knowledge. This is one reason many religious groups have attacked Dewey's ideas. Dewey argues that all knowledge and ideas, including ideas about social organizations and morality, are relative to the social situations that produced them. Principles of morality and the organization of society, according to Dewey, must constantly change to adapt to new problems and social situations.

Therefore, the curriculum should be organized, Dewey argues, so that the child learns that knowledge has a social origin and is socially useful. Rather than the teacher acting as if knowledge fell out of the sky, the teacher is to guide the student to an understanding of the historical and social conditions that produced particular knowledge. For instance, arithmetic can be taught as an abstract set of rules or it can be taught in situations where students learn its social usefulness such as counting other children or objects for a particular purpose.

In keeping with the belief that standards of social conduct and of institutions must constantly adapt to changing situations Dewey believes schools must adapt to the needs of the modern world. One of the primary problems in the modern industrial and urban world, he states, is the need for a sense of cooperation. He argues that in the modern world the stress on individual economic competition needs to be replaced with economic co-operation. Since modern industry and urban life are not fostering cooperation, Dewey maintains, the school needs to change and become the center for teaching cooperation. For instance, Dewey replaced individual classroom desks with group tables on the belief that individual desks promoted individual economic competition while working at tables promoted cooperation.

Dewey rejects the idea that children are primarily motivated to learn by rewards and punishments. He argues that the source of individual action is not stimulation from an outside reward or punishment, but originates in individual interests and desires.

Dewey's beliefs result in a curriculum based on student interests and designed to teach the social origins of knowledge and cooperation. In this curriculum, teachers guide student interests to sources of knowledge. In addition, knowledge is taught as a whole and not in isolated fragments. Cooperative group activity is the method of learning. Thus, a student or students might express an interest in milk. The teacher would guide the students to sources about the production, chemistry, and distribution of milk. Groups of students might visit the local dairy and develop a group project on milk for the classroom. In the process of this group study of milk, students might learn chemistry, economics, arithmetic, social history, and cooperation. While Dewey did not agree with many of the experiments in child centered-curricula, his name is most often associated with the movement.

Financial pressures, the decline of a protest culture, and attacks by conservatives contributed to the demise of most private alternative schools by the middle of the 1970s. Within the public schools, social-efficiency advocates dominated and the curriculum was increasingly oriented toward educating for specific careers. Vocational offerings expanded and students were encouraged to choose, based on their future goals, from a wide variety of courses.

In the 1980s, international trade problems have caused a sharp reaction to the social-efficiency curriculum of the 1970s. In what seems like a replay of the 1950s, critics argue that the curriculum did not develop the intellectual skills needed to compete in the development of new technology. Humanists, such as Mortimer Adler and Secretary of Education William Bennett, advocate a core curriculum where all students develop intellectual skills through the study of important historical documents and literature. In general, critics argue that the vocational orientation of the 1970s needs to be replaced with an academic orientation.

The constant changes in the American public school curriculum are primarily the result of constantly changing political and economic needs. As long as the public school serves public purposes, its curriculum will constantly change. The shifting patterns of the public school curriculum primarily involve humanists concerned with maintaining cultural traditions and intellectual skills; social-efficiency advocates wanting the schools to serve the economic needs of society; and social meliorists wanting the curriculum organized to promote social reform. Often, the public-school curriculum is a blend of all three curricular patterns with one or more dominating as a result of the particular political and economic conditions of the time.

Instruction

While the curriculum of the public schools shifts with changing political and economic goals, the actual methods of instruction, despite attempts at reform, remain relatively constant. In *How Teachers Taught: Constancy and Change in American Classrooms 1890–1980,* Larry Cuban details the factors that made public-school instruction primarily teacher-centered as opposed to student-centered.

Cuban, for the purposes of his history of instruction, defines *teacher-centered instruction* as occurring when teacher talk dominates the classroom, instruction is primarily given to the whole class as opposed to small groups or individuals, the teacher determines the use of classroom time, and the classroom is arranged in rows of desks facing the front of the room. On the other hand, Cuban describes the opposing *student-centered* tradition as occurring when student discussion of learning tasks is equal to or greater than teacher talk, instruction is individual or in small groups, students participate in determining the rules of the classroom, and instructional materials are available for students to use individually or in groups.

Cuban portrays the history of instruction as attempts by advocates of student-centered instruction to change, with modest success, the entrenched patterns of teacher-centered instruction. At the beginning of the century, the physical conditions of schools influenced patterns of instruction. Urban classrooms were constructed for 40 to 60 students with bolted-down desks in rows facing the front of the room. The classroom organization was standardized between the 1890s and the 1920s by the architect for the New York Board of Education, C. B. J. Snyder, who according to Larry Cuban designed the standardized classroom based on a prescribed number of permanent desks ranging from 40 to 48 for each school grade. In addition, teachers were poorly trained and often had to cover 10 different subjects daily using textbooks and curricula prescribed by the central administration. The result on teachers of large classes, arranged classrooms, prescribed textbooks and curricula, and many preparations for teaching, Cuban argues, was the continued reliance on teacher-centered instruction and textbooks as sources of knowledge. In addition to the physical and working conditions of teaching, social-efficiency ideas reinforced patterns of teacher-centered instruction. During the early part of the twentieth century, school administrators developed a mania for bureaucratic efficiency. Viewing the schools as factories, they stressed standardization and uniformity of instruction. Efficiency administrators compared themselves to factory managers, where power flowed from the top of the organization to the bottom. This meant that just as they believed administrators should control and dominate teachers, teachers should dominate and control students.

While working conditions and ideas of social efficiency reinforced patterns of teacher-centered instruction in the early twentieth century, advocates of student-centered instruction, led by John Dewey, began to press their reforms on the public schools. But, by and large, most of these instructional reforms were unable to penetrate the organizational structure of the public schools and received their greatest acceptance in private schools.

Cuban describes a number of attempts before 1940 to introduce student-centered instruction in public schools with the results being only minor and affecting only a few teachers. For instance, the New York City school system began in 1934 to experiment with what was called an *activity program,* which stressed teachers and students working together to select subject matter and learning activities, and a focus on the needs and interests of the students. In addition, classroom schedules were to be flexible with the standard teacher-dominated recitation being replaced by excursions, research, dramatization, and sharing. Controlled discipline was to be replaced by self-control. In 1942, after eight years of attempted instructional reform, it was estimated that only 25 percent of all city elementary schools incorporated activity methods in some classrooms. In a survey of New York teachers in the same year, 93 percent said they preferred conventional forms of instruction.

Between 1920 and 1940, Denver public schools were widely hailed as leaders of student-centered instructional reform. Under the leadership of four superintendents dedicated to the implementation of student-centered instruction, the school district emphasized teacher-constructed curricula, an activity program like that of the New York schools, and the project method. The *project method* involves students learning through the development of individual or group projects. In evaluating the effects of these reforms on high school teaching, Cuban found that only 20 percent of the classrooms during this period had extensive student-centered instruction.

In general, Cuban concludes, reforms based on student-centered instruction between 1920 and 1940 did not significantly change the instructional methods of American teachers because of the structure and organization of the schools. The primary method of instruction remained that of the teacher standing in front of the room, talking to the whole class, and questioning students who mainly listened to the teacher talk. Teachers retained control of subject matter and manner of instruction.

While these standard practices remained, student-centered reforms, according to Cuban, did loosen up the atmosphere of the classroom. More student movement in the classroom was permitted, desks became movable, and there was less formal recitation characterized by students rising and speaking by their desks.

Following World War II, student-centered instruction came under attack as causing a deterioration of the academic standards considered necessary for winning the cold war with the Soviet Union. Advocates of student-centered instruction, including John Dewey, were accused by the extreme political right of being communists trying to undermine the country by destroying discipline and academic standards in the classroom. Even more moderate observers claimed that the schools were made anti-intellectual by student-centered instructional methods. Consequently, advocates of student-centered instructional reforms made a hasty retreat and did not appear on the scene again until the late 1960s.

As described in the last section on curriculum the late 1960s witnessed the growth of alternative schools based on differing forms of student-centered instruction. In the public schools, the major attempt to introduce student-centered instruction came in the form of the open classroom. Originally developed in England, the *open classroom* captured the imagination of many American educators in the 1960s and early 1970s. A flood of newspaper and journal articles and experiments in public school systems seemed to indicate that this instructional method would become a standard part of public-school systems. Indeed, many schools built during this period incorporated the principles of the open classroom into their design.

Like other forms of student-centered instruction, the open classroom emphasized active as opposed to passive learning, and student-directed learning as opposed to teacher-determined instruction. Classrooms were to be large open spaces divided into interest areas or learning centers. Each learning center was to contain a variety of learning materials. Students were to plan their own learning and move from interest station to interest station.

The open classroom movement quickly ended by the middle of the 1970s with demands for student discipline and an emphasis on basic subjects. Competency-based instruction replaced the open classroom movement. In the framework of *competency-based instruction,* teachers develop specific instructional objectives, develop methods to achieve those objectives, and measure the achievement of those objectives. Students learn discrete skills in incremental steps using preplanned instructional packages. The emphasis on measurement contributed to the rise in the importance of standardized testing. Often, this meant the standardized test had a controlling influence over the actions of the teacher and students.

Larry Cuban cites a number of examples of the organizational difficulties encountered in the introduction of student-centered learning in the 1960s and 1970s. For instance, consider the 1968 staff bulletin from the central administration of the New York public school system, which told teachers that students must during recitation raise their hands, they must ask permission to go to the bathroom, and they must regularly clean their desks under the supervision of a teacher. According to Cuban, one New York teacher during this period stated that students were whipped into shape by sitting at their desks for long hours and by using textbooks and notebooks to study formally organized lessons. Silence and good behavior were the standards of classroom conduct.

Cuban identifies three major reasons for the lack of significant change in instructional methods in American public-school classrooms in the twentieth century. The first is that public schools exist to serve larger social purposes and to instill behaviors required by the prevailing economic system. This produces teaching practices that emphasize uniformity, authority, and other traits required by bureaucratic organizations. Student-centered instruction, on the other hand, develops traits of individual choice and expression that run counter to the demands of society on the public schools.

The second reason for the persistence of teacher-centered practices, according to Cuban, is the organizational structure of the public school. In most situations, teachers are expected to maintain control, use a textbook, and teach from a prescribed curriculum. Class size and structure inhibit the use of student-centered activities. Teachers find it convenient under these circumstances to have students seated according to a seating chart, to have students raise their hands and wait their turn before speaking, and to allow student movement only with the permission of the teacher. It is also most convenient for the teacher to instruct with lectures, seatwork, and homework using textbooks. Student-centered instruction, on the other hand, does not fit the organizational and structural requirements of the public schools, is inconvenient for the teacher, and creates more work.

The third reason for the lack of change in instructional practices is the culture of teaching. According to Cuban, teachers are socialized to be conservative and resistant to change. In many cases their teaching is modeled on that of the teachers they had in school and on the teachers who supervised their student teaching. This modeling tends to perpetuate standard methods of instruction.

In addition, Cuban argues that teacher beliefs and administrative ineptness contribute to a failure to change. Those teachers who believed in student-centered instruction did change their classroom practices, but large groups of teachers continued to believe in traditional methods. When attempts to implement student-centered instruction did occur, school administrators, Cuban argues, failed to adequately carry through with their plans.

For all these reasons, classroom instruction has changed little in the twentieth century. Classroom practices did soften with the introduction of movable chairs, the decline of the requirement that students stand by their desks when speaking, and the growth of informality between teachers and students. But, by and large, teachers continue to instruct from textbooks using planned lessons and students remain passive learners.

Theories of Learning

Like curriculum and instruction, the popularity of particular theories of learning in American education is primarily a function of social and economic conditions. Given the wide range of theories about human behavior available throughout the twentieth century, the fact that one theory is chosen over another theory for emphasis in the public schools has more to do with it meeting institutional and organizational needs than with the possible inherent validity of the theory. In other words, since there is no general agreement among psychologists about the correct theory for describing human behavior and learning, then the acceptance or selection of a psychological theory to use in an organization has more to do with the needs of the organization than the "truth" of the theory.

In American education, three theories of learning (behavioral, developmental, and cognitive) have vied for dominance in the classroom. Of these three, behavioral psychology has historically best served the interests of the public schools. As discussed in the previous section on instruction, classroom teaching remains teacher-centered despite years of educational reform. One reason for the popularity of behavioral psychology in American schools is that it justifies the teacher-centered classroom and the general authoritarian model of public-school administration.

Stated simply, *behavioral psychologists* believe that human learning is primarily a result of rewards reinforcing human actions. For instance, if children are given approval (reward) for correctly adding two plus two, then they will tend to remember (learn) that particular mathematical operation. This approach to learning supports teacher-centered instruction because the teacher is made a manager of a reward system designed to shape student behavior. In fact, as will be discussed later in this section, behavioral psychology is used to justify the traditional classroom practices of drill and repetition.

Traditionally, *developmental psychology* is associated with forms of student-centered instruction. The general belief of developmental psychologists is that teaching should be based on the natural development of the child. This approach does not necessarily mean a rejection of teacher-centered instruction. Historically, developmental psychologists believe that learning arises from the desires and interests of the individual as opposed to behavioral psychology's emphasis on the control of individual behavior through the manipulation of a reward system. The student-centered open-classroom movement discussed in the previous section received its theoretical justification from the work of developmental psychologist Jean Piaget, for example, while the teacher-centered competency-based movement that displaced the open classroom was based on theories of behavioral psychology.

Cognitive psychology gained popularity in American education during the 1980s, when concern about the international technological competition with Japan and West Germany created a demand for a renewed emphasis on intellectual skills in the public schools. Cognitive psychology also provided theoretical justification for the demands (as discussed in Chapter 2) that teachers be permitted to act as independent professionals in their schools and classrooms, as opposed to being managed by public-school administrators. Simply stated, cognitive psychology stresses the importance of the mind as a processor of information. Learning is a product of the strategies and decisions made about information received. In other words, the most important factor in classroom learning is not a reward system, nor the desires of individual students, but the manner in which the individual student's mind processes information and makes decisions about its use.

The same is true of teacher behavior in the classroom. The cognitive approach stresses the ability of the teacher to make correct decisions about student learning in a constantly changing classroom situation, as opposed to the behavioral approach emphasizing the teacher's ability to establish specific behavioral objectives for learning and to manipulate student behavior through a reward system to achieve those specific objectives.

Of these three theories of learning, behavioral psychology received the strongest support in American schools in the early twentieth century. Edward Thorndike (1874–1949) was an early advocate of behavioral approaches to learning and was a founder of the field of educational psychology. Thorndike studied psychology at Harvard University during the 1890s with William James, author of the two-volume *Principles of Psychology,* which is a classic work in the history of American psychology describing behavioral theories. In these volumes, James describes a child learning not to touch fire by reaching for the flame of a candle. As James describes the learning process, the flame stimulates the child to reach out; the burn he or she then receives causes the child in the future to associate fire with pain. For James, learning is the process of stimulation, response, and reinforcement.

Under the influence of James's work, Thorndike developed several general laws of learning. These theories gained wide popularity in educational psychology in the early twentieth century and provided a justification for traditional classroom practices. Thorndike argued that a connection or bond is made in the human mind between a response and a reaction to that response (reinforcement). In his first law of learning, called the *Law of Exercise,* he argued that these connections could be made stronger through classroom drill. His Law of Exercise states that "other things being equal, the oftener or more emphatically a given response is connected with a certain situation, the more likely it is to be made to that situation in the future." Thorndike gave as an example a child responding "six" to the question, "How many are four and two?" If the child repeats the answer enough times, Thorndike suggests, the answer will be permanently connected in the child's mind. Thorndike states this law more briefly: "Other things being equal, exercise strengthens the bond between situation and response."

Thorndike's second law of learning, the *Law of Effect,* states, "The greater the satisfyingness of the state of affairs which accompanies or follows a given response to a certain situation, the more likely that response is to be made to that situation in the future." For instance, in the example of the child responding "six" to the question, "How many are four and two?" the correct answer would be strengthened if the child were rewarded with candy or a smile.

These two laws of learning justify the traditional classroom practices of drill and reward. Thorndike emphasized teacher-centered instruction in his argument that "using psychological terms, the art of teaching may be defined as the art of giving and withholding stimuli with the result of producing and preventing certain responses."

In addition, Thorndike was one of the early advocates of standardized testing as the tool for determining whether or not teachers achieved their instructional objectives. Thorndike believed that testing is the key to the good society. Accepting the educational goals of social-efficiency advocates, Thorndike believed that through proper testing of an individual's intelligence and abilities it could be determined where that individual should be placed in the labor market. Educational programs were to be designed based on test results and labor-market needs. For Thorndike, the ideal society is where individual ability is matched with occupational requirements. Within this framework, the school, through the use of tests, becomes the main sorter of human resources to meet the needs of society.

In more recent times, the leading advocate of behavioral psychology has been B. F. Skinner. Skinner based his early work on the conditioning of pigeons to perform particular operations, a process called *operant conditioning*. Skinner argues that human actions are determined by a system of rewards. Rewards and not punishment, according to Skinner, reinforce patterns of human behavior. Skinner dismisses the idea of free will and argues that all human action is determined by the rewards received from the environment.

In the 1950s, Skinner developed the first programmed learning machines based on the principles of operant conditioning. For Skinner, the best method of instruction is to divide each learning situation into the smallest units of behavior or specific behavioral objectives. Each specific behavioral objective is taught through a system of rewards. Of course, each specific objective is related to the other objectives in achieving the general goal. Thus, the teaching machine presents the student with specific exercises and rewards correct answers with the opportunity to move on to the learning of the next specific behavior.

Like many other psychologists, B. F. Skinner developed his own view of an ideal society, which he expressed in his novel of the 1940s, *Walden II*. Rejecting free will, Skinner envisioned an ideal society managed by behavioral engineers who would scientifically design a culture that would make people feel happy. Within the framework of this novel and Skinner's other writings, the ideal teacher is a behavioral engineer shaping human action toward an established objective.

Behavioral theories became extremely popular in American schools in the 1970s as part of the conservative support of a social-efficiency curriculum and the backlash against the open classroom. Teachers were requested to write long lists of specific behavioral objectives, explain how they would achieve those objectives, and develop instruments for measuring the achievement of those objectives. Many classrooms used "token economies" where student behavior was rewarded by a "token." These tokens might be candy, actual money, or points that allowed the student to participate in some other activity.

The popularity of behavioral psychology in the public schools is a result of its tendency to justify teacher-centered instruction and also, as was the case in the 1970s, to assert the authority of the school over the student. After the protests resulting from the Vietnam War, some political and educational leaders demanded law and order in the schools. Behavioral psychology filled the bill because it defines the student as an object whose behavior is to be manipulated in the classroom. The rejection of free will by behaviorists justifies control and manipulation of student behavior. But, as I will discuss later, the concern in the 1970s with law and order gave way to problems of international trade in the 1980s, and the popularity of behavioral psychology predictably decreased while that of cognitive psychology increased.

Unlike behavioral psychologists, developmental psychologists rely on an understanding of the internal nature of the individual to explain the process of learning. Jean Jacques Rousseau's famous book *Emile* was an early statement of learning based on human development. Rousseau's influence extended into the twentieth century in the work of the famous developmental psychologist Jean Piaget.

In *Emile,* Rousseau argues that instruction should be related to stages of human development. For instance, he claims the young child is primarily focused on self-preservation. A sense of social relationships begins to develop before adolescence and reaches full development only during early youth. Consequently, according to Rousseau, the education of the child should center on concrete and practical experiences, and the early adolescent should be introduced to the interdependence of society through social education.

The most revolutionary aspect of Rousseau's pedagogical proposal was that of a natural education. Following what he believed to be the natural development of the child, he argued that early education should be based not on abstract teaching but on practical experiences. For instance, children should learn about maps and geography by exploring the countryside, not through studying maps while sitting in the classroom. Rousseau proposed that Emile not be taught how to read until the child saw the social usefulness of reading and asked to be taught. This occurred when Emile was unable to read invitations. For Rousseau, the young child needs to learn by doing rather than by sitting in the dull warmth of a schoolroom reading texts.

Rousseau's *Emile* is a classic text in the movement for student-centered instruction and in the history of developmental psychology. In the early twentieth century, G. Stanley Hall, an American, described human development occurring in stages similar to those proposed by Rousseau. In one of the first studies of adolescent psychology, *Adolescence* (1904), Hall argues that the development of the individual parallels the development of the race. For example, the young child, according to Hall, is in a period of growth similar to that of civilization during its tribal period. Like Rousseau, Hall believed that adolescence represents the birth of the social individual. For Hall, adolescence is a crucial period of development because, he believed, it corresponds to the development of modern civilization.

Both Rousseau and Hall argue that it is the developing sexual drives of adolescence that create the social person. From Hall's perspective, channeling the sexual drives of adolescence is key to the development of civilization. Painting a highly romantic portrait of adolescence, Hall argues that adolescent sexual drives can lead the individual either down the path of depravity and destruction or to a life dedicated to the service of others. For Hall, the most important thing for the progress of civilization is to channel the sexual drives of youth into social service. This, he argues, can be accomplished by the creation of organizations and institutions that direct sexual drives into service to others. Of course, the most important of these organizations is the high school.

Hall's most important impact on American schools is the idea that different stages of human development require different types of education. Based on this reasoning, junior high schools were established in the early part of the twentieth century. Also, it was argued that elementary school education needed to be more child-oriented and concerned with learning from experience and high school education more abstract and book-oriented.

The romantic view of adolescence transformed the American high school from a purely academic institution to an institution concerned with social development. The stated purpose of high school social activities like clubs, auditorium events, pep rallies, building school spirit, student government, and athletics was to capture the sexual drives of adolescence for the social good.

In the early twentieth century, this view of adolescent development fit easily into arguments for a social-efficiency curriculum. Social-efficiency educators not only wanted the schools to educate individuals to fit into particular slots in the labor market, but also to cooperate with others in modern specialized organizations. Nothing better captures this attitude than the phrase "team spirit." Team spirit meant corporate spirit.

Capturing the sexual drives of adolescence for social service involved, according to social-efficiency educators, channeling those drives into team spirit. In the high school this meant building school spirit, which later in life was to translate into team or corporate spirit. Nothing better exemplifies this than the development of football and basketball in the 1920s as the most important high school social events. Not only were these team games to socially educate the players, but also they were to socially educate student spectators. Both sports exemplified the modern corporation in their requirements of specialization and cooperation. For student spectators, organized cheers and pep rallies were to create school spirit. The cheerleaders added obvious sexual overtones to these attempts to build school and team spirit.

Therefore, developmental psychology, as exemplified by G. Stanley Hall in the early twentieth century, contributed to the idea that education should be adjusted to the developmental stage of the individual and that the social activities of educational institutions, particularly high schools, should be expanded. Also, advocates of student-centered education in the 1920s called for adapting instruction to the natural development of the child. This argument often justified the teaching of young children through activities and experience or, in the language of the time, learning by doing.

Some child-centered educators such as the previously discussed A. S. Neill at Summerhill relied on Freudian ideas to justify the freedom given to children. Neill argues that aggression is a product of the repression of the natural drives of adolescence and childhood. Freedom for children to determine their own education and manner of living, according to Neill, would eliminate aggressive behavior later in life and bring about world peace.

Developmentalists like Hall and Freudians like Neill share a common belief that education should be based on the internal nature of the individual and not on the manipulation of a reward system as advocated by behaviorists. In other words, developmentalists believe in an internal structure that determines how a person acquires knowledge.

Jean Piaget, working at the Rousseau Institute in Switzerland in the middle of the twentieth century, refined the relationship between stages of development and learning. His work influenced the development of open-classroom instruction in the 1960s and 1970s. Piaget divides developmental stages according to schemas or intellectual structures by which the individual interacts with the world. For instance, children are born in the *sensorimotor* stage in which they primarily interact with the world through reflexes. The next stage, *preoperational* (ages 2 to 7), is characterized first by imitation and play and later by intuitive thought. A favorite example used for describing this stage of development is that of a child filling two glasses of the same size with equal numbers of beads and then transferring the beads from one of the glasses to a taller glass. The child is then asked which glass has the most beads. Usually, according to Piaget, the child will choose the taller glass because his or her thinking is focused on one aspect, height. Piaget characterizes 7- to 11-year-olds as being in the stage of *concrete operational* thought because they can begin to engage in complex mental acts using concrete objects. In the *formal operation* stage (ages 11 to 16), the individual develops the processes of formal thinking.

What is important about Piaget's theory for our discussion is the support it gives for student-centered instruction. Like most advocates of student-centered instruction, Piaget argues that students should initiate their own learning activities and that learning should be spontaneous. The reason, according to Piaget, is that the child will initiate a process of learning that is best matched to his or her stage of intellectual development. In other words, students intuitively know what they are best able to learn. While engaged in learning, according to Piaget, the student needs to be active and to learn through experience.

The role of the teacher in Piaget's framework is to create environments that students can use to initiate learning experiences and discover logical relationships. Within the context of the open-classroom movement, discussed in the section on instruction, teachers organize interest areas or learning stations adapted to the developmental stage of the students. Children are to spontaneously choose a learning station based on their particular needs. Teachers are never to give students answers, but are simply to guide them through learning activities.

Piaget's ideas remain attractive to early-childhood educators, but the open-classroom movement died in the public schools with the conservative reaction of the late 1970s. Why were Piaget's ideas lost in the new wave of behaviorism of the 1970s? One reason was the association of student-centered types of instruction with the rebellions and demonstrations of the 1960s and early 1970s. The conservative reaction sought to restablish authority in the classroom, and authority was provided by behavioral theories. Also, the social-efficiency concern with education for employment and basic skills left little room for the free and independent thinking promoted by Piagetians. Social-efficiency educators advocated teaching the development of good work habits, proper dress for work, and job skills.

The acceptance of behavioral theories has waned in the 1980s with increasing concern about international competition with Japan and West Germany, and with the rise of the political power of teachers' unions. Concern with international trade has placed a premium on the development of intellectual skills needed to develop new technologies. Teachers' unions have demanded a more independent and professional role for teachers in schools, which has meant an opposition to theories that make administrators the managers of teacher behaviors.

The theories of the developing field of cognitive psychology have proved most useful to those concerned with developing intellectual skills in students and with a more independent role for teachers in the classroom. In general, cognitive psychology is concerned with strategies used by the mind to process information. In *The Mind's New Science: A History of the Cognitive Revolution,* Howard Gardner identifies a variety of sources for the development of cognitive psychology, including the work of Piaget, experiments in artificial intelligence, developments in linguistic theory, new discoveries in neuro-science, and theoretical work in philosophy. All of these factors, according to Gardner, have helped create a theoretical perspective that rejects the behaviorist notion that the source of all learning and behavior is the environment and argues instead that the mind determines what and how things are learned.

The arguments of cognitive psychology have found their way into the major reform reports of the 1980s. Both the Holmes Group's report, *Tomorrow's Teachers,* and the Carnegie Forum's report, *A Nation Prepared: Teachers for the 21st Century,* justify their proposals in the framework of cognitive psychology. As discussed in detail in Chapter 2, real teaching is considered in these reports as the product of continual decisions being made by the teacher based on his or her knowledge of the subject matter and the processing of information about what is occurring in the classroom. This argument suggests that the teacher should act as an independent professional and not as a person who is managed from above. In addition, the stress is on developing intellectual skills and learning strategies in students. The Carnegie Forum report, using arguments from cognitive psychology, specifically calls for the abandonment of teacher-centered and textbook-centered instruction.

Conclusion

As stated at the beginning of the chapter, my purpose in this discussion is to make you aware of the effect of political and economic factors and of school organization and working conditions on the curriculum, methods of instruction, and theories of learning popular in the public schools. After this discussion, you can begin to understand why public schools fall victim to constantly changing educational fads and reforms. The political and economic factors affecting schools are constantly changing and making new demands on education. But even as these factors attempt to change schooling, the basic organizational structure of the school, as Larry Cuban argues, tends to make some things constant.

Suggested Readings and Works Cited in Chapter

Cuban, Larry. *How Teachers Taught: Constancy and Change in American Classrooms 1890–1980*. White Plains, N.Y.: Longman, 1984. A study of how teachers actually taught in classrooms in American public schools.

Dworkin, Martin, ed. *Dewey on Education*. New York: Teachers College University Press, 1959. A collection of Dewey's writings including Dewey's 1952 statement on the effect of progressive education on the public schools as quoted in this chapter.

Gardner, Howard. *The Mind's New Science: A History of the Cognitive Revolution*. New York: Basic Books, 1985. A history of cognitive psychology that investigates the contribution of philosophy, psychology, artificial intelligence, linguistics, anthropology, and neuroscience.

Hall, G. Stanley. *Adolescence*. Englewood Cliffs, N.J.: Prentice-Hall, 1904. The classic text in adolescent psychology, which had a major influence on the organization of the modern high school.

James, William. *Principles of Psychology*. New York: Dover, 1950. The early source of most of the intellectual traditions in American psychology.

Joncich, Geraldine, ed. *Psychology and the Science of Education: Selected Writings of Edward L. Thorndike*. New York: Teachers College Press, 1962. A collection of

Thorndike's important writings, including the educational laws quoted in this chapter.

Joyce, Bruce, and Weil, Marsha. *Models of Teaching*. Englewood Cliffs, N.J.: Prentice-Hall, 1986. This is now a classic text describing different models of instruction. Included is a discussion of instructional models based on Jean Piaget and B. F. Skinner.

Karier, Clarence J. *Scientists of the Mind: Intellectual Founders of Modern Psychology*. Urbana, Ill.: University of Illinois Press, 1986. Critical essays on major psychologists, including William James, Edward Thorndike, and G. Stanley Hall.

Kliebard, Herbert M. *The Struggle for the American Curriculum 1893–1958*. Boston: Routledge & Kegan Paul, 1986. Kliebard's history of curriculum in the twentieth century stresses the conflict between social-efficiency advocates, humanists, social meliorists, and developmentalists.

Rousseau, Jean-Jacques. *Emile*. New York: Dutton, 1911. Rousseau's plan for the ideal natural education based on stages of development.

4

The Social Structure and American Education

Equality of Opportunity

From the nineteenth century to the present America's democratic ideology has sought a means of providing equal opportunity for everyone. "Equality of opportunity" means that all members of a society are given equal chances to enter any occupation or social class. This does not mean that everyone can choose any social position; rather, all have an equal chance to compete for any place in society. Ideally, equality of opportunity should result in a social system in which all members occupy their particular positions as a result of merit and not as a result of family wealth, heredity, or special cultural advantages.

Within the ideology of equality of opportunity an individual's life is viewed as a social race in which all members of society begin at the same starting line but finish the race in a different order. The most important thing is to assure that all have equal opportunity to run the social race. This means making sure that all begin at the same starting line and that the race is fair.

The role of the school in the provision of equality of opportunity has changed from the nineteenth century to the twentieth century. In the nineteenth century, the school was to provide everyone with an equal education or the same education and the social race was to be run after leaving the schoolhouse. In other words, equality of opportunity was to be a function of competition outside of the schoolhouse, with the social starting line at the point of exit from the school. In the late nineteenth and early part of the twentieth centuries it was argued that competition outside of school was not fair because of the possible influence of family wealth and other social factors. To make equality of opportunity fair, it was argued, the school had to play a greater role in determining equality of opportunity.

As the school played a larger role in attempting to provide equality of opportunity, the social starting line shifted from the point of completing school to the beginning of school. Students began to be separated according to their abilities, interests, and future occupations. The result was that students began to receive unequal and different educations. For instance, some students might graduate with vocational training and others with preparation for going to college. What this meant was that the school no longer provided an equal education with competition occurring outside of school. It provided instead an unequal education with competition for social positions taking place in the schoolhouse. It was argued that standardized tests, teacher judgments, and counselors could make a fairer decision about where a person could go in the social structure than could be achieved through competition outside of school.

A brief history illustrates the changes in the role of the school in the provision of equality of opportunity. In the common school of the nineteenth century, differences of social class and special advantages were supposed to disappear, as everyone was given an equal chance to get an equal education. This was one of the reasons for the support of common schools in the nineteenth century. During the 1830s, workingmen's parties advocated the establishment of publicly supported common schools and the end of the pauper schools that had been the only free schools up to that time. It was asserted that with public schools for the poor and private schools for the middle class and the rich, education reinforced social differences and doomed the children of the poor to a perpetual lower-class status. Only common schools could provide for equality of opportunity.

The most extreme statements came from one faction of the New York Workingman's party. This group argued that sending students to a common school would not in itself eliminate differences in social background, because the well-to-do child would return from school to a home richly furnished and full of books, whereas the poor one would return to a shanty barren of books and opportunities to learn. School, in the opinion of these workingmen, could never eliminate these differences. Their solution was that all children in New York should be removed from their families and placed in state boarding schools where they would all live in the same types of rooms, wear the same types of clothes, and eat the same food. In this milieu education would truly allow all members of society to begin the race on equal terms. This extreme solution to the problem did not receive wide support, and debates about it eventually led to the collapse of the New York Workingman's party.

In the late nineteenth and early part of the twentieth centuries, the development of intelligence tests was considered a means by which equality of opportunity could be made fairer. Some people argued that intelligence tests could be an objective measure that could be used to determine one's best place in society. The first intelligence test was developed in the early 1900s by the French psychologist Alfred Binet, who wanted to find a method of separating children with extremely low levels of intelligence from those with normal intelligence levels. The assumption of the test was that an inherited level of intelligence existed and could be measured independent of environmental factors such as social class, housing conditions, and cultural advantages.

In the United States the movement to measure native intelligence spread rapidly because of its link to the ideology of equality of opportunity. The doctrine of native intelligence provided the premise that the role of the school was to eliminate all hindrances to the full development in individual intelligence. In other words, individuals would be given an equal chance to develop their particular level of intelligence. Identifying a particular characteristic such as intelligence and recognizing that all members of society would achieve different positions in the race because of differences in native intelligence seemed to give scientific validation to the arguments for equality of opportunity. The movement to measure intelligence allowed for equality of opportunity and at the same time justified a hierarchical social structure, based on intelligence, in which all people were not equal. Within this framework democracy was viewed as a social system in which all people were given an equal chance to reach a level in society that corresponded to their individual level of intelligence.

The major problem in the link between attempts to measure native intelligence and to provide equality of opportunity has been that levels of measured intelligence tend to be related to social class and race. That is, the poor and minority groups in the United States tend to get lower scores on intelligence tests than middle- and upper-class majority groups. This situation has resulted in the claim by some people that the measurement of intelligence discriminates against certain social classes and minority groups.

Discussions about the relationship between the measurement of intelligence and discrimination have centered on whether an inherited native intelligence exists and, if it does exist, whether it can be measured. For instance, those who believe that an inherited level of intelligence exists and is measurable by tests state that the differences in measured levels of intelligence accurately reflect the conditions of society. Alfred Binet contended that the reason the lower social class did poorly on intelligence tests was because they did in fact have lower levels of intelligence and, moreover, that was why they were in the lower social class. More recently, psychologist Arthur Jensen has argued that existing tests accurately measure inherited intelligence and that differences in performance by certain racial and social groups are accurate. On the other hand, there have been those who believe in the existence of inherited intelligence but feel that the questions asked on existing tests reflect the cultural and social bias of the dominant middle class in the United States. The poor, and certain racial groups, perform poorly on existing tests because many of the test questions deal with things that are not familiar to those groups.

Within this framework, the solution to the problem is the creation of an intelligence test that is free of any cultural bias.

Another approach to the problem is the complete rejection of the idea of inherited intelligence and the acceptance of the view that intelligence and abilities are primarily a result of environment. This is the famous "nurture-nature" debate. Those who see nurture as being more important argue that differences in measured intelligence between social and racial groups primarily reflect differences in social conditions. The poor grow up in surroundings that are limited in terms of intellectual training: an absence of books and magazines in the home; poor housing, diet, and medical care; and lack of peer-group interest in learning all might account for the poor performance on intelligence tests. This approach suggests that the school can act positively to overcome differences caused by social and cultural conditions.

Most recently, schools have tended to act from the premise that differences in backgrounds can be overcome in the schools. The argument for equality of opportunity has been placed in the context of the culture-of-poverty argument described in Chapter 1. Through compensatory education and Head Start programs the schools have attempted to end poverty and provide equality of opportunity by trying to compensate for social conditions. Head Start and early-childhood education programs are designed to counteract the supposedly poor learning opportunities of the children of the poor, and compensatory education is designed to provide special instruction in reading and other skills in order to offset cultural and economic disadvantages.

Of fundamental concern in current discussions is whether the school can make any contribution to equality of opportunity. One issue has been whether the school reproduces and reinforces the social-class structure of the United States. The other important issue concerns the degree of contribution the school makes to social mobility.

Social-Class Differences in Education

One of the major criticisms of public schools has been the apparent internal duplication of the social-class structure of society. This has been particularly true in the tracking and ability-grouping practices of the school. *Tracking,* primarily a practice of the high school, separates students into different curriculums such as college preparatory, vocational, and general. Ability grouping involves placing students in different classes on the basis of their abilities. These abilities are usually determined by a combination of teacher assessment of the student and standardized tests.

The pattern within American schools is for the social class of the students to parallel the levels of ability grouping and tracking. That is, the higher the social-class background of the students, the more likely it is that they will be in the higher ability groups and/or a college-preparatory curriculum. Conversely

Table 4.1 Social Class in Elmtown

Social Class
1   Upper class, wealth primarily a result of inheritance
2   Income from profession, family business, or a salaried executive
3   Income from small businesses, farms, and wages from white-collar jobs in mines, mills and public service
4   Income from blue-collar occupations in mills and mines
5   Income from unskilled, part-time labor and welfare

SOURCE: Summarized from Chapter 5 of A. B. Hollingshead, *Elmtown's Youth* (New York: John Wiley & Sons, Inc., 1949).

the lower the social-class status of the students, the more likely it is that they will be in the lower ability groups and/or the vocational curriculum.

Studies have shown the existence of this condition in the American public schools from the 1920s to the present. One of the first major studies of social-class differences in relationship to adolescent culture and the high school was conducted in a small town in Indiana by a team of sociologists headed by A. B. Hollingshead. Their findings, which they titled *Elmtown's Youth,* can still be found duplicated in a majority of high schools throughout the country.

The Hollingshead study divided the population of Elmtown into five social classes as shown in Table 4.1. The tracks, or courses of study, at Elmtown's high school were college preparatory, general, and commercial. When the social-class origins in each track were determined, it was found that children from social classes 1 and 2 concentrated on college-preparatory courses (64 percent) and ignored the commercial course. Class 3s were found mainly in the general course (51 percent), with 27 percent in college preparatory and 21 percent in commercial. Class 4s slipped down the hierarchical scale of curriculums; only 9 percent were in college preparatory, 58 percent were in general, and 33 percent were in commercial. Only 4 percent of Class 5s were in the college-preparatory curriculum, whereas 38 percent were in commercial and 58 percent in general curricula.

That the distribution of students in the various curriculums of a school reflects social class does not in itself indicate a problem or that the school is responsible. Hollingshead found that social pressures from family and peer group contributed to the decision to enter a particular course of study. Upper-class parents tended to be more oriented to college, while lower-class parents thought in terms of training for jobs within their own particular social class.

Pressures outside the school existed to support the differences in social classes, but Hollingshead also found that the school, through a variety of methods, gave support to the differences in social class. Differences of response to a given educational situation tended to vary with the social class of the student. For instance, the parents of students were counseled differently according to social class. Although children from social classes 2 and 3 received better grades than lower-class children, parents of social classes 2 and 3 were more often called to school to discuss the work of their children. The parents of lower-class children, however, were more often called to school to discuss the behavior of their children. This situation was paradoxical because not only did lower-class children tend to receive lower grades but they also tended to fail courses more often than children from the upper classes. Objectively, one would assume that if the school were acting free of social-class bias, parents of lower-class children would have received more counseling about school work than about behavior.

In the situation described by Hollingshead, problems related to children of the lower social class tend to be considered behavior problems in school, whereas those related to the upper classes tend to be considered learning problems. Nothing so dramatically tells the story of institutional response to social class than the tale about the enforcement of the school lateness rule. Elmtown High School had adopted a new tardy rule, which the principal and superintendent intended to enforce with vigor. The first violator of the tardy rule was the son of a Class 1 family, who arrived late to school in his father's Cadillac. The student was told by the principal to report for detention after school. When the student did not appear for detention after school, the principal phoned the father, who brought the student back to school. The superintendent, nervous about offending the father, greeted the boy at the school door and had him sit for 10 to 15 minutes in his outer office before sending him home. The superintendent later stated that he did not want the boy to have to sit with the other students in the detention room.

The opposite response occurred that next day when a son of a Class 4 family arrived late to school. The principal and superintendent made joking comments about the student's dress and statements about his father being a laborer at the local fertilizer plant. When school ended, the superintendent and principal roamed the halls, and when they saw the Class 4 student trying to leave the building, the principal grabbed him and began to shout at him. The student broke from the grasp of the principal and ran through the halls, where he was eventually caught by the superintendent, who shook and slapped him three or four times. Eventually the principal and superintendent physically pushed the student out of the school.

In the cases described above the school officials were able to identify the social-class origins of their students through their personal contact within the local community. In larger educational systems social-class identification is often made through the dress of the student, the ethnic or racial background, the location of the home within the community, and informal discussions. For instance, a student might be referred to as coming from a particular section of town, which when mentioned is understood to be an area inhabited, say, by blue-collar workers in a local factory or by executives in major industries. Ethnic names in large metropolitan areas can also cause a response related to the social-class nature of the family or attitudes toward learning.

A more recent example of the relationship between social class and track-ing in schools has been given by Jeanne Ballantine in her book, *The Sociology of Education*. Ballantine's example, taken from a study of two Midwestern school systems, compares the number of students from differing social-class back-grounds who were in the top academic track with the actual number of students qualified for admission to that track. For students from upper-class backgrounds it was found that 80 percent of those qualified to be in the top academic track were in that track. On the other hand, it was found that only 47 percent of those students from lower-class backgrounds who qualified for the top academic track were actually in that track. In other words, 53 percent of the lower-class students who were qualified for the top academic track were not being given the full benefits of an academic education. For middle-class students, 65 per-cent of those qualified for the top academic track were in that track.

Jeanne Ballantine also provides evidence that race is a factor in the separation of students into academic tracks, with the differences in tracking between whites and blacks increasing over time. In the evidence presented, 44 percent of the white student body of a seventh-grade class was in the academic track, whereas 33 percent of the black student body of the same seventh-grade class was in that track. The percentages changed dramatically as the same group of students moved through the eighth and ninth grades. In the eighth grade the percentage of the white student population in the academic track increased to 47 percent, whereas the percentage of the black population in that track decreased to 20 percent. In the ninth grade the percentage for whites decreased to 30 percent whereas the percentage for blacks decreased to 10 percent.

One of the contributing factors to social-class and racial bias in schools is level of expectations. Teachers and other school officials begin to expect certain students to act in certain ways. In its simplest form, this stereotyping results in the expectation that students from middle- and upper-class families will do well in school, whereas children from lower-class backgrounds are expected to do poorly. Research findings suggest that one problem with such stereotyping is that students live up to expectations about them. If students are expected to do poorly, they do poorly; if expected to do well, they do well. This is referred to as the *self-fulfilling prophecy*.

The most famous study of the tendency to live up to expectations is Robert Rosenthal and Lenore Jacobson's *Pygmalion in the Classroom*. In the first part of the study, a group of experimenters was given a random selection of rats and told that certain rats came from highly intelligent stock. The rats labeled as coming from highly intelligent stock tended to perform better than the other rats, even though they had been randomly grouped. The two psychol-ogists tested their results in a school to see if teacher expectations would affect student performance. After giving students a standardized intelligence test, they gave teachers the names of students whom they called "late bloomers" and told teachers to expect a sudden spurt of learning from them. In fact, the names of these students had been selected at random from the class. A year later the intelligence tests were administered again. The scores of the supposed "late bloomers" were compared with those of other children who had received scores on the original test similar to the supposed "late bloomers'." It was found that those students who had been identified to teachers as "late bloomers" made considerable gains in their intelligence-test scores when compared with students not designated as "late bloomers."

The principal inference of this study is that teacher expectations can play an important role in determining the educational achievement of the child. This might be a serious problem in the education of children of poor and minority groups, where teachers develop expectations that these children will either fail or have a difficult time learning. Some educators, such as teacher and educational writer Miriam Wasserman, argue that teacher expectations are one of the major barriers to educational success for the poor and for certain minority groups.

Wasserman, in her case study of the New York school system, *The School Fix: NYC, USA,* relates the issue of teacher expectations to what she calls the "guidance approach to teaching." The guidance approach means that when planning instructional units, the teacher tried to take into account the student's family background, social life, and problems outside school. On the surface this sounds like good educational practice in relating teaching methods and materials to the background and needs of the student. In practice, Wasserman discovered the tendency to label all students from poverty areas as having learning problems, as not being interested in school, and as probably not succeeding in school. Teachers tended to provide not-very-challenging material to students so labeled or explained their own failure to teach the student in terms of the student's background.

In further investigation of this problem, Wasserman interviewed students from poverty backgrounds who had been successful in school. She found that these students believed the major element in their successful educational career was having a teacher who was primarily interested in the student's learning and who emphasized and demanded high-quality work. These teachers had high expectations for their students, expectations that were not influenced by the social-class backgrounds of the students.

The combination of the classification of students according to abilities and curriculum plus the expectations of teachers and other school officials all seem to contribute to the social-class divisions of the surrounding society being reflected in the placement and treatment of students in the school. In addition, it has been found that in terms of educational achievement the differences between children from different social classes become progressively greater from the first grade through high school.

Progressive differences between social-class groups were noted by Patricia Sexton in her major study of a large urban center, which she called Big City. Her study, *Education and Income,* divided the parents in Big City into income levels and compared these divisions with ability grouping, achievement scores, and tracking. She found a direct correlation between the income level of the parents and the child's performance on achievement tests and placement in ability groups and curriculum tracks. Children from lower-income levels tended to be placed in lower-ability groups and non-college-preparatory tracks. In addition, she found lower-income groups receiving lower scores on standardized tests than children from parents in the upper-income levels. This began occurring in the elementary grades, with the differences between the scores of the children of upper- and lower-income groups increasing as the children went from elementary to secondary schools. Sexton's explanation of this result was that if a child did not achieve well in reading in the lower grades, this increasingly affected school work as the student moved through grades requiring increasing amounts of reading.

In addition to inequalities between groups within a school, Sexton found inequalities between schools within a large district. These inequalities were also related to the income level of the parents. She found that the money spent on schools and the quality of education offered varied in direct proportion to the income of families in the school's neighborhood. The differences were reflected in the quality and adequacy of school buildings, school and class overcrowding, quality of teaching staff, methods of testing and estimating pupil performance, quality of secondary curriculum, use of school buildings by the community, and other facilities and services.

The inequalities Sexton found between schools has become a major issue in the courts of the United States. Court cases have centered on the differences in school expenditures between school districts. School districts with a low-income population tend to spend less or have less to spend on schools than school districts with a high-income population. The legal issues involved are discussed in greater detail in Chapter 10, which focuses on the courts and education. For present purposes, it is important to understand the extent of these differences in terms of social class.

Christopher Jencks, in his assessment of national data in the early 1970s, found that different individuals and groups received unequal shares of national education resources. Jenck's conclusion in *Inequality* was that in terms of use of educational resources, working-class children spent 13 percent less time in school than white-collar children. But, Jencks argued, the differences in time people spend in school tend to be less than other social-class differences in society.

In terms of inequalities in school expenditures, Jencks found that the children of the richest fifth of all families in the United States are in schools that spend about 20 percent more than do the schools serving the poorest fifth. These differences in expenditures do not necessarily mean that the schools are guilty of promoting gross inequalities. For instance, Jencks contends that the inequalities in school expenditures are less than the inequalities in income in the United States. The top fifth of all families receive 800 to 1,000 percent more income than the bottom fifth. When this difference is compared to the difference of only 20 percent in school expenditures, Jencks feels, the schools appear as a triumph of egalitarianism.

The differences found in treatment, place in the school curriculum, and access to educational resources among social classes do indicate unequal treatment between social groups but do not necessarily mean that education reinforces the existing social-class structure, according to Jencks. That is, because these differences in schooling exist does not mean that the children of lower-income families will tend to enter low-income careers or that children of high-income families will have the opposite experience.

In terms of the argument for equality of opportunity, the most important questions that must be asked are whether education is a major factor in determining future careers and social class, and whether unequal treatment in school of children from different social classes affects their future position in the social structure.

Social Mobility and Education

The key to understanding whether inequalities in education reinforce the social-class structure and whether education can contribute to equality of opportunity lies in the investigation of the relationship between schooling and social mobility. To understand this relationship one must consider some of the problems inherent in describing social mobility as an entity. Mobility can cover a wide range of definitions including income, occupation, status, and political or social power. The son of the owner of the local construction company who becomes a university professor might be upwardly mobile in terms of status or prestige but not in terms of income. In a similar manner the son of a minister who becomes a small-store owner might be upwardly mobile in terms of income but not in terms of status. Mobility also depends on the perspective of the person making the judgment. The son of a leading manufacturer who becomes a talented musician might be considered downwardly mobile in terms of status by his father and upwardly mobile by friends of the art.

In a society that prizes education, schooling will always provide a means for individuals to achieve upward social mobility. Some immigrant groups that came to the United States viewed the well-schooled person as having great status in society. They viewed the school as a means of mobility because having an education provided them with prestige in the community. The increased status given by schooling might exist independently of other indicators of mobility. The son of an immigrant store owner who completes college and becomes a high school teacher is upwardly mobile in terms of the prestige his father gives to his son's diplomas and occupation, but not necessarily in terms of income.

One of the problems in discussing the link between education and social mobility is the widespread acceptance of the idea that schooling contributes to social mobility. One of the reasons for the acceptance of this idea is that educational diplomas by themselves have become status indicators. More schooling, of course, actually can mean more status if the individual and society genuinely place great value in academic achievement, but the fact is, in our society, one can have many degrees and still be poor and socially ineffective.

Another problem in talking about schooling and social mobility is that of distinguishing between mobility that results from structural changes in society and mobility related to educational achievement. For instance, occupational mobility is the form of mobility most often discussed. In most cases it is considered in terms of intergenerational mobility. That is, mobility is assessed by comparing individuals' current occupations with jobs held by parents. Social mobility is measured in terms of the differences in occupations of parents and their sons and daughters.

In the United States, the link between schooling and occupational mobility has been conditioned directly by certain structural changes in American society. One might describe occupational mobility in a static society as two people exchanging occupational roles; that is, there exists only a set number of occupations, thus the upward mobility of one person is dependent upon the downward mobility of another person. Ideally, the school as a selective mechanism would assure that this type of mobility takes place in terms of merit and competency. But the United States has not been a static society in which mobility has been achieved on the basis just described. Significant structural changes have increased the number of jobs in certain occupational areas and at the same time decreased the number in other occupations. The social mobility resulting from these changes in the social structure has often been credited to the school. Nevertheless, while the school has facilitated the flow of the population from one occupational area to another, it has not directly caused these changes.

The most significant structural changes in American society affecting social mobility have been the rapid rise in the number of white-collar (business government, and professional) occupations, and the rapid decline in the number of agricultural occupations. In 1900 farm workers, including owners and laborers, composed 37.5 percent of the labor force; by 1965 this number had declined to 5.8 percent. White-collar workers, on the other hand, represented 17.6 percent of the labor force in 1900 and 43.8 percent in 1965. White-collar workers include managers, sales personnel, professionals, and clerical help.

Schools, of course, provided the necessary education for those filling the expanded white-collar positions. Public belief in the relationship between mobility and schooling was reinforced by those who were able to move from the farm or factory into white-collar positions. They tended to see their new opportunities not in terms of the structural changes in American society but in terms of their own effort through education to attain these new positions. Schooling did facilitate the structural changes, but the direct causes were outside the province of the school.

Seymour Lipset and Reinhard Bendix, in their study of *Social Mobility in Industrial Society,* found that changes in the occupational structure had an important impact on mobility rates. Their study involved a comparison of mobility rates in different industrial societies. The authors found little variation in mobility rates in industrialized countries, as measured by shifts from manual to nonmanual occupations. This conclusion contradicted the widely held belief that there is greater opportunity for occupational mobility in the United States than in other countries.

Lipset and Bendix did find that in occupations where there were significant differences in mobility rates between industrial countries, these were related to differences in educational opportunity. High-ranking civil service jobs and professional occupations fall within this category. In both cases variation in mobility rates could be attributed to different educational opportunities. These variations are logical when one considers what the school is best able to do. In most countries, one can attain professional status only through the school. In the United States the high rate of mobility into professional ranks is a result of the expanded opportunities for higher education. It should be noted that, for many, upward mobility into professional ranks has been a result of changes in the occupational structure caused by the expansion of schooling, which, in turn, has created a large professional class of professors, administrators, and other school officials. Access to these positions is only through the school.

One of the major conclusions of the Lipset and Bendix study was that schooling is a direct factor in mobility only for those occupations that can be reached exclusively through the school. In other areas, such as manual and white-collar jobs, the determining factor is changes in the occupational structure. In terms of mobility into political elites, Lipset and Bendix found that opportunity to enter the political elite through the electoral path was greater in Europe than in America. The reason, they asserted, is that in Europe labor and working-class political parties provide a means by which members of lower social classes can be elected to government positions.

Peter Blau and Otis Duncan arrived at similar conclusions in their study of *The American Occupational Structure.* They argued that mobility rates in the United States have been affected primarily by technological progress, immigration, and differential fertility rates. The substitution of machines for manual workers made it possible for large numbers of workers to be engaged in white-collar work, thus fostering upward mobility. The millions of disadvantaged immigrants who moved into the lower ranks of the occupational hierarchy made it possible for the sons and daughters of workers in these lower strata to move up to higher occupational levels. In addition, they contended, the relatively low birthrates of the white-collar class opened up other opportunities for upward mobility.

Like Lipset and Bendix, these authors found that structural changes in society are the primary causes of mobility. Their major disagreement with

Lipset and Bendix is in comparing mobility rates between the United States and other industrial countries. Both studies found little difference among countries in mobility rates between manual and nonmanual occupations. But Blau and Duncan did find greater opportunity in the United States to move from the working class to the top occupational stratum of society. They asserted that this greater mobility between the extremes in American society has helped foster Americans' continued belief in equality of opportunity and in America as the land of opportunity.

While most studies agree that the rate of mobility is more dependent on technological changes and changes in the occupational structure than on education, there have been proposals to increase the rate of social mobility by changing the methods of measuring educational attainment. The most famous of these proposals was made by Christopher Jencks in his previously cited work, *Inequality*. Jencks found, as have others, that the most important detriment to educational achievement is family background. This means that a person who comes from a family with a high income and high educational attainment, whose father has an occupation high on the occupational hierarchy (such as professional or corporate executive), is more likely to receive more education and a more advanced educational diploma than a person from a low-income family whose father has a low-status occupation. In addition, Jencks concluded that occupational status is strongly related to educational attainment.

These conclusions suggest that a certain rigidity is built into the social structure; family background determines education, which determines occupational status. Jencks has suggested that one way of breaking through this apparently self-perpetuating system is to measure educational attainment in terms of grades and test scores and not in terms of diplomas. In other words, educational attainment would be determined by a score on a standardized test or by grades, and not by diplomas earned at the end of four years of high school or college. Jencks found that family background is not as strongly related to test scores as it is to educational attainment. A child from a lower social class has a greater chance of achieving equal or better scores on a standardized test, compared to a child from an upper-class background, than he or she has the chance of reaching the same level of educational attainment. Jencks found even less of a relationship between family background and grades received in school.

Based on these findings, Jencks argues that the rate of social mobility would increase if occupations were open to people on the basis of test scores or grades and not on the basis of educational credentials. For instance, if high-status occupations were open exclusively to people with high test scores and if all people with high test scores wanted to enter the highest-status occupations, then there would be greater social mobility. That is, there would be a greater chance of children ending up in social classes different from those of their parents. Children of high-status parents would have a greater chance of entering lower-status jobs, and children of lower-status parents would have a greater chance of entering higher-status occupations. The rate of mobility, according to Jencks would be even higher if high-status occupations went exclusively to those students with high grades.

Education and Income

An individual can value education for the intellectual stimulation it provides and for the increased status and higher income it offers. Certainly one of the promises of American education has been an increase in personal income through higher educational attainments. While a relationship exists between greater amounts of education and higher personal income, there are some major problems in this relationship.

First, one must realize that the relationship between education and income conforms to certain laws of supply and demand. If there is a high demand for high school graduates, and only a few members of the population have graduated from high school, then the high demand and low supply will result in relatively high incomes being offered to high school graduates. The incomes in this case are high relative to the situation in which there is a large number of high school graduates and a small demand.

What this means is that an inherent conflict exists between the goals of equality of educational opportunity and quality of economic opportunity. If everyone has an opportunity to receive a maximum amount of education, the value of that education in terms of personal income will decrease as the supply of educated people increases. For instance, if everyone were to have a college degree, then the value of that degree in terms of personal income would be lower than if only a few had college degrees.

Another way of expressing this is in terms of educational inflation. Educational inflation appeared on the American scene in the late 1960s and early 1970s when the job market was flooded with college graduates who were often forced to take jobs considered lower in income and status than had been traditionally accepted by college graduates. People with bachelors and masters degrees, and even doctorates, had to find employment as cab drivers, store clerks, and a host of other occupations previously filled by persons having no more than high school diplomas.

In this situation, educational inflation means the declining value, in terms of personal income, of each year of education or each educational diploma. Educational inflation is related to increased educational requirements for occupations, without any basic change in the nature of the occupation. For example, consider the following situation: An employer has five applicants for a job as a general clerk in a business office. Four of the applicants have high school diplomas, while the other applicant has a high school diploma and also attended college for two years. The employer hires the applicant with two years of college on the assumption that the additional two years of education reflect more intelligence and a better ability to learn the job.

If we assume a flow of information in the labor market, the essential message given to the applicants who were not hired is that they need more years of schooling to compete successfully for jobs. The four rejected applicants decide to attend their local community college for two years to get Associate of Arts degrees. Two years later each of the four job seekers applies for another clerk job. This time, however, the fifth job applicant is a graduate of a four-year college.

The situation just described occurs when the labor-market demand for a particular level of education is smaller than the supply. This sometimes happens in a cycle of supply and demand. For instance, in the late 1960s the demand for lawyers increased, causing large numbers of college graduates to enter law schools. In fact, the demand was so great that it led to an increase in the number of law schools. By the late 1970s the supply of law school graduates had begun to be higher than the demand; people began to talk about the market for lawyers being saturated.

Another way of discussing educational inflation, and the more general relationship between education and income, is in terms of rates of return on an investment. For instance, let us consider a college education as an economic investment. The cost of this investment is the sum of the costs of tuition and supplies plus the amount of money that could have been earned if the individual had elected not to go to college. If education is pursued for increased income, then one must compare one's lifetime income without a college degree to one's lifetime income with a college degree. The difference between the two lifetime incomes will be the return on one's investment in a college education. One's rate of return will be the difference in the percentage of annual return on investment in education as a result of the differences in income that result from having or not having a college education.

For instance, the economist Richard Freeman in his book *The Overeducated American,* estimated that during the educational inflation of the late 1960s and early 1970s, the rate of return on a college education declined from 11.0 percent to 7.5 percent. Economists recognize the difficulty in estimating rates of return on an investment in education due to the difficulty in knowing how long a person will be active in the work force and the future incomes for different occupations. Even with these difficulties, however, economists agree that education conforms to the laws of supply and demand and that rates of return on investment in an education will be determined by conditions in the marketplace.

Returns on investment in education vary among racial groups and between sexes because of prejudice and social conditions. For example, the U.S. Bureau of the Census reported that in 1977 white men with high school diplomas earned an average of $14,786 a year; black men with the same number of years of education earned $10,821. The difference is even greater between white and black college graduates: White men averaged $19,329 a year, and black men averaged $13,334 a year in 1977.

The difference in income between men and women is even greater than the racial difference. In 1977 a white woman with a high school diploma earned $8,493 a year (a white male earned $14,786 and black male $10,821). Black females with high school diplomas earned even less: $8,185 a year. The same differences occur between male and female college graduates. White women averaged $11,040 a year in 1977 (white men averaged $19,329); black women averaged $12,049 a year (black males averaged $13,334). It is interesting to note that in 1977 a black female college graduate earned on the average more than a white female with an equivalent education.

These figures demonstrate that the value of an education depends on social conditions. To establish a meaningful link between education and equality of opportunity, changes will have to be made in the society to overcome the disparities shown in the preceding comparisons of yearly income.

Inequality of Educational Opportunity and Equality of Opportunity

Do inequalities in educational opportunities directly affect equality of opportunity? It was shown in the first part of this chapter that sociologists and educators are in agreement about the existence of unequal educational opportunity. Although they debate the extent of inequality, they agree that different social classes and racial groups receive unequal treatment in the public schools (as will be discussed in Chapter 5). There is also agreement that education is not a primary determiner of rates of mobility. That is, the amount of education provided in a society does not determine the amount of mobility. On the other hand, the level of educational achievement in the United States *is* related to occupational status, and the primary determiner of educational achievement is family background. Given these sets of findings, what is the effect of inequalities in education on equality of opportunity?

A major national study that looked at this question was a survey conducted at the request of the U.S. Congress as part of the 1964 Civil Rights Act. The survey was organized and planned by sociologist James Coleman and published as *Equality of Educational Opportunity*. This survey, known as the Coleman Report, has become one of the most famous and controversial studies of American education.

Coleman and his group began the survey by outlining five approaches that could be taken in measuring inequality in educational opportunity. The first approach defined the problem in terms of the degree of racial segregation that existed in school systems. The second approach was in terms of inequality of resource inputs, items such as books, school facilities, and student-teacher ratios. The third approach was in terms of inequality of intangible resources, such as teacher morale. The final two approaches to the problem of inequality asked broader questions of the meaning of inequality. The fourth approach measured the inequality of inputs in terms of their effectiveness for educational achievement. In other words, did differences in resources such as books, buildings, student-teacher ratios, and other school items have any effect on how well a student achieved? The fifth approach involved determination of whether inequality of output was evidence of inequality of opportunity.

Within the framework of these five approaches, the Coleman Report asked some basic questions about the relationship between the school and the social structure. Of primary importance for school people was the question of what factors in schooling have the greatest effect upon educational achievement. This question was to be answered in the fourth approach, which related inequality of inputs to educational achievement. The major overall task of the report, of course, was to measure the extent of racial segregation and inequalities of resources as related to race and not social class. This aspect of the study is discussed in more detail in the next chapter.

The Coleman Report found that in terms of school resources, white children as compared to minority children attended schools with smaller class sizes, more science and language laboratories, more books in the library, and more opportunities for participating in college-preparatory and accelerated academic curricula. The Coleman study then compared these differences in resources with student achievement as determined by achievement tests. The report assumed about achievement tests that "what they measure are the skills which are among the most important in our society for getting a good job and moving up to a better one, and for full participation in an increasingly technical world." The Coleman Report found that, except for Asian Americans, all other minority groups attained significantly lower achievement scores than whites, and that the differences increased from the first through the twelfth grades.

When these differences in achievement-test scores were compared to school resources, it was found that "differences between schools account for only a small fraction of differences in achievement." The evidence for this finding included differences in the effect of school resources for white and for minority students. The achievement of white students seemed to be affected less by the strengths or weaknesses of curricula and school facilities, whereas these did seem to have some effect on the achievement of minority students. Student achievement, however, was strongly related to the educational backgrounds and aspirations of the other students in school.

The conclusions of the Coleman Report led to a complex set of questions. It should be noted that the report did give strong support to the policy of school integration. Because the most important factor affecting achievement was pupil backgrounds, the report could conclude that "the analysis of school factors described...suggest that in the long run, integration should be expected to have a positive effect on Negro achievement." In general, the conclusions of the report seemed to suggest that the quality of school curricula and facilities bore little relationship to the question of equality of educational opportunity.

The conclusions of the Coleman Report startled those people who believed that schools would be the answer to the problems of poverty and would provide equality of opportunity. The study seemed to say that the school could do little in terms of teaching, curriculum development, and facilities to improve educational achievement and equalize opportunities for advancement in American society. The most important factors were peers and family background. This meant that the school could not play an important role in providing equality of opportunity. Schools could equalize educational opportunities by providing equal facilities and curricula, and quality teachers, but this would only solve the problem of the injustice of unequal treatment of different social classes and groups and not the problem of unequal opportunity.

This was also the major conclusion of Jencks's study, *Inequality*. Jencks's study combined the data of the Coleman work with other major national studies. He concluded that equalizing the amount and quality of schooling would have only a minor effect on cognitive skills as measured by standardized tests. The major determiners of cognitive skills, he found, are a person's total environment and heredity. It should be mentioned that the tests used to measure cognitive skills have been criticized for cultural and social-class bias.

The study found that qualitative differences between high schools explain only a minor part of the variation in students' educational attainment. Jencks also concluded that school resources do not have any influence on students' educational attainments, and that attending high school with bright, highly motivated classmates had both positive and negative effects on a student's chances of attending college. The one measurable factor that obviously influenced educational attainment was the curriculum track to which a student is assigned.

Both the Jencks study and the Coleman Report suggest that inequalities in educational opportunity have very little effect on educational attainment and, consequently, on intergenerational occupational mobility. This would mean that no matter how much a society equalized educational opportunities for all groups or provided superior educational opportunities for the poor and minority groups, there would be little or no change in the rate of upward occupational mobility. In other words, the schools cannot provide equality of opportunity.

It is possible to argue this particular problem from an entirely different perspective. Rather than ask what factors contribute to increased rates of social mobility, one can ask about the factors that contribute to intergenerational immobility. In other words, why isn't there more upward occupational mobility from parents to children in Western industrialized countries?

Economist Samuel Bowles contends that the school is one of the causes for occupational immobility. This argument completely reverses the idea that the school creates occupational mobility to the idea that the school has the opposite effect. Bowles, in constructing his thesis, accepts the findings that mobility rates are consistent throughout Western industrialized countries and that family background is one of the major factors in determining economic and social advancement. What Bowles argues is that the school is a medium through which family background is translated into occupational and income opportunities.

This translation occurs with regard to personality traits relevant to the work task; modes of self-presentation such as manner of speech and dress; ascriptive characteristics such as race, sex, and age; and the level and prestige of the individual's education. Bowles considers these four factors integral to the process of intergenerational immobility. It is these traits that emerge from the family background and are reinforced in the schools before entrance into the workforce. Cognitive skills seem to have little significance in this process. Bowles asserts, and Christopher Jencks in *Inequality* agrees, that adult cognitive abilities have a minor influence on occupational success when considered independent of family background and level of schooling.

Bowles insists that the four factors—personality traits, self-presentation, ascriptive characteristics, and level of educational attainment—are all significantly related to occupational success. They also are all related to the social class of the family. For instance, family background is directly related to level of educational attainment and the prestige of that attainment. In this particular case the economic level of the family is translated by the school into educational attainment. Children from low-income families do not attain as high a level of education as children from rich families. From this standpoint the school reinforces social stratification and contributes to intergenerational immobility. In terms of ascriptive characteristics such as race, the social advantages or disadvantages of a particular racial group are again translated by the school into levels of educational attainment.

Personality traits and self-presentation are, according to Bowles, important ingredients in occupational success. These characteristics are a direct product of child-rearing practices and reflect the social class of the family. Also, Bowles asserts, child-rearing patterns are directly related to the occupation of the head of the family. This argument is based on the work of Melvin Kohn, whose study of *Class and Conformity: A Study of Values,* found that middle-class parents are more likely to emphasize children's self-direction and working-class parents to emphasize conformity to external authority. By self-direction, Kohn meant internal standards of direction for behavior, whereas conformity meant externally imposed rules. Within this framework, working-class parents value obedience, neatness, and honesty; higher-status parents emphasize curiosity, self-control, and happiness. Even when racial and religious divisions are considered, Kohn found that social class still stands out as the more important determinant in child-rearing values.

There is, says Kohn, a direct relationship between the degree of occupational self-direction experienced by the head of the family and child-rearing values. In fact, he argues that this is the most important factor in determining child-rearing practices. The more self-direction experienced on the job by the head of the family, the more likely it is that child-rearing patterns will emphasize self-direction. Self-direction on the job is directly related to the social class of the family. Higher-status and higher-income jobs usually involve self-direction; lower-status and lower-income jobs tend to be more routine and require more conformity to imposed rules.

Bowles, in his book entitled *Schooling in Capitalist America,* supports Kohn's conclusions. Child rearing, Bowles declares, is important in developing personality traits related to entrance into the workforce. Personalities evidencing a great deal of self-direction tend to have greater success in high-status occupations. The differences in child-rearing patterns, Bowles states, are reflected in the schools attended by different social classes. Schools with populations from lower-income families tend to be more authoritarian and to require more conformity than schools attended by children from higher-income families. This is often reflected in the differences between educationally innovative schools in high-income suburbs and the more traditional schools in low-income, inner-city neighborhoods. In some cases, parents place pressure on local schools either to be more authoritarian or to allow more self-direction. The nature of this pressure tends to be related to the social class of the parents. The same pattern emerges in higher education, according to Bowles, when one compares the social relations of a community college with those of an elite four-year college. In this manner, Bowles argues, the child-rearing patterns of the family are translated through the medium of the school into the occupational structure. The school thus contributes to intergenerational immobility and limits equality of opportunity.

Effective Schools and the Mediation of Family Background

The studies discussed in the previous section paint a dim picture of what schools can do to overcome problems caused by differences in the social-class backgrounds of students. Schools are portrayed as being unable to improve the achievement of students, and as inevitably reproducing the family background of students. Other studies have suggested a more complex and hopeful picture of the role of the school. The more-effective-schools movement is premised on the idea that certain improvements in schools will lead to improvements in the academic achievement of children from lower socioeconomic backgrounds. Other studies have argued that the school does not simply reproduce social-class background, but that a mediation occurs between the culture of the school and the culture of the student's family. This mediation has its own consequences for the academic and social development of students.

The book that provided the first insights into how schools might be reformed to improve the academic achievement of students from lower-class backgrounds is Michael Rutter's *Fifteen Thousand Hours.* The title refers to the number of hours a child spends in British schools from the age of five to the age of leaving school. The study focused on 12 schools in the inner city of London.

The general purpose of the study was to find the relationship between educational inputs and outcomes—in other words, to find the things a school can do that will make a difference in the education of children. The study was conducted at a time when a great deal of research was saying that the school makes very little difference and that the primary determiner of educational outcomes is family background. Previous research had found that the amount of money spent, the types of buildings and libraries, and other educational inputs were not as important as family background.

Fifteen Thousand Hours concluded that certain variations that exist between schools in the social and academic outcomes of students could *not* be explained by family background, size of school, age of buildings, space available, or administrative organization. The study found that some schools had better attendance, better student behavior, less delinquency, and better examination scores because of the characteristics of the school as a social institution. The characteristics found to be related to better behavior, less delinquency, and better examination scores were degree of academic emphasis, how teachers acted during lessons, system of rewards and punishments, degree of responsibility assumed by students, and social conditions of the pupils in school.

More specifically, the study found better behavior in the classroom when the teacher prepared a lesson in advance, arrived on time, and taught the class as a whole. It found classroom conditions to be better when the teacher provided ample praise; frequent disciplinary actions by the teacher were linked to disruptive behavior. Like other experts, the researchers for *Fifteen Thousand Hours* found better student behavior and performance linked to expectations and standards. Students had higher academic success when there was a frequent assignment of homework and when teachers expressed high academic expectations to the students. In more commonsense terms, when teachers prepare their lessons and expect their students to learn, there is a greater chance for academic success.

The study also found that if teachers act as if they care about their students, and if good care is taken of school buildings, then students receive the message that schooling and student activities are valued. In addition, attendance was better and delinquency less frequent in schools where the entire staff planned the curriculum and the methods for handling discipline. Positive results were also found when there were shared activities between students and staff, and when students were given positions of responsibility in the school.

Fifteen Thousand Hours found a relationship between all the above factors and educational outcomes. No single factor could be identified in isolation from other factors as causing better behavior, higher attendance, and higher examination scores. All the factors combined to create a social ethos that affected educational outcomes. They also found a relationship between behavior, exam success, and attendance. Schools with high rates of exam success had good attendance and few behavior problems. The social ethos of a school creates a general pattern of social behavior among students.

The findings of *Fifteen Thousand Hours* suggest that it is meaningful to talk about equality of educational opportunity in terms of educational outcomes. In the context of the study it would mean that some schools are better than others for children from the same family background. Children from lower-class backgrounds *can* attend schools that will make a difference and that difference is primarily determined by the factors making up the social ethos of the school. Equal educational opportunity can be improved if teachers prepare lessons and have high expectations of their students, if there is an ample system of reward, if the staff and administration work cooperatively, and if students assume responsibility. The major limitation of *Fifteen Thousand Hours* is that it focused on schools attended by a particular social group.

The findings reported in *Fifteen Thousand Hours* had a strong impact on what has been referred to as the "more-effective-schools" movement in the United States. It reinforced many of the findings of researchers working in the early 1980s in elementary schools located in low-income areas of inner cities. These researchers were finding that schools with characteristics similar to those found by Rutter in successful schools in England were having a positive effect on achievement-test scores. These characteristics have been identified as the following:

1. A principal with strong leadership in instruction
2. Teachers with high levels of expectations for student learning
3. School climate
4. Increased time on instructional tasks
5. Regular and systematic student evaluations
6. Community support and adequate resources

The reader should understand that the effective-schools movement has a very distinct definition of a successful school. It is a definition that makes the results of achievement-test scores the major criteria of educational success. The most common definition of educational success in the more-effective-schools movement is bringing an equal percentage of a school's upper and lower social classes to minimum mastery of basic skills. By describing success in these terms it has been hoped that an equal emphasis will be given to the learning of students from both upper and lower social-class backgrounds.

As effective-school projects have been instituted in many cities, there has been some variation in what are considered the characteristics of a successful school. For instance, Daniel U. Levine and Robert J. Havighurst report in their book, *Society and Education,* that the Connecticut School Effectiveness Project defined the characteristics of effective schools as follows:

1. A safe environment that is conducive to learning
2. Clear school goals
3. Instructional leadership from the principal
4. A climate of high expectations
5. A high percentage of time on task
6. Frequent evaluation of student performance
7. Community support

Levine and Havighurst also report the findings of a survey conducted by Phi Delta Kappa on the characteristics of effective inner-city elementary schools, in which the only additions to the above lists would be low adult-child ratios in the schools and greater parental involvement.

In some cities, the characteristics of effective schools have been given as basic assumptions in school-improvement projects. In their book, *Schools in Central Cities,* Kathryn Borman and Joel Spring report that in Milwaukee the effective-schools project named RISE (Rising to Individual Scholastic Excellence) adopted as three assumptions: (1) virtually all students, regardless of their family background, can acquire basic skills; (2) inappropriate school expectations and practices are the major cause of low achievement by low-income and minority students; and (3) the literature on effective schools has identified expectations, norms, practices, and policies associated with high achievement.

Many of the characteristics identified with effective schools appear on the surface to be common sense. Certainly, a school should have a leader who is interested in instruction. The problem is that many school principals have been overwhelmed with the noninstructional aspects of their jobs. Many principals spend endless hours worrying about paperwork, maintenance of school buildings, the school cafeteria, community relations, and discipline problems. Very often principals have not been adequately trained to be instructional leaders. Placed in this context, the expectation that principals should be instructional leaders represents a major revolution in the activities of many school leaders.

In a similar manner, one would expect teachers to have expectations that their students will learn. But, as was described earlier in this chapter, teachers have tended to have low levels of expectations for children from minority backgrounds and lower social classes. Many teachers in inner-city schools have come to view their jobs as primarily baby-sitting and have reduced their levels of instructional expectations. This is why the effective-schools movement has placed a great deal of emphasis upon teachers expecting and demanding high-quality academic work from all children.

One would also assume that the majority of time in a school and in a class-room would be spent on instructional tasks. In many cases this has not been so, because of all the noninstructional tasks that have been given to schools and the amount of time spent in the classroom by teachers on noninstructional activities. For instance, a great deal of school time can be devoted to assemblies, playground activities, collecting money for various activities, the filing of reports, attendance monitoring, and other noninstructional activities. Placing emphasis upon time on task in instruction is simply stating that the primary goal of the school should be instruction in subject matter.

School climate and community resources are two related aspects of the effective-schools movement. School climate refers to the general atmosphere of the school. In many ways it cannot be clearly defined to a person who has not visited a variety of inner-city schools. Some schools look dirty, are poorly maintained, and have students drifting through the halls, and the noise from the classrooms suggest more chaos than engagement in instructional activities. Other inner-city schools project just the opposite impression, with chaos giving way to reasonably happy students interested in school activities. Obviously, school climate depends to a great extent on the leadership of the principal. But it also depends on community resources and support. Without that support it is difficult to maintain the physical plant of the school, provide teachers with adequate instructional materials, and maintain reasonable class sizes. Under poor conditions teacher and student morale begins to decline and the general atmosphere of the school is no longer conducive to learning.

The emphasis in the effective-schools movement on constant monitoring of student progress has two important aspects. On the one hand, it is reasonable to assume that good teaching requires knowing how your students are progressing. This could mean testing them at regular intervals to determine how well they are advancing through their lessons. On the other hand, testing does take time away from instructional tasks and does increase the work of the teacher. This is particularly true if the school system requires that the teacher report test scores to some central office.

Also, testing has become increasingly political as teachers, principals, and superintendents are evaluated on the basis of students' test scores. For instance, merit pay for teachers could be based on the test scores of their students; principals in many school districts are being evaluated on this basis. In the same manner, superintendents are often evaluated on the basis of the test scores for the entire district. For these reasons, test scores have become important for job security and advancement in school systems. As a result there is an increasing tendency to teach to the test. In other words, the primary objective of school administrators and teachers under these circumstances can become teaching for improvement on specific test items. In these cases, the test determines the content of instruction.

Although some criticism can be directed at the more-effective-school movements' overreliance on testing, a very positive aspect of the movement is the emphasis it places on the ability of lower-income students to learn. This emphasis is a major change from the despair of the 1960s and 1970s when many people began to abandon any hope of improving schools. Rather than seeing educational outcomes as inevitably linked to family background, the effective-schools movement holds out some hope that schools can make a difference.

Another major change in thinking about the relationship between family background and educational outcomes has been a realization that this relationship is not a simple one-to-one correspondence. The school not only reacts to the family background of the student, but the student also reacts to the school. The pioneer study of this phenomenon is Paul Willis's *Learning to Labour*. Willis studied a group of students from working-class backgrounds who attend an all-male comprehensive high school in an industrial area of England. These students learned to manipulate the environment of the school in order to make sure that they would have a good time. They created a peer culture that was antischool. Their culture differed sharply from what they called the "ear-'oles." The "ear-'oles"—students who appeared to do nothing but sit and listen in school—represent the student who conforms to the authority and the expectations of the school.

The working-class students resented both the "ear-'oles" and the authority of the school. They felt that the school was out of touch with real life and had little relationship with the male working-class world that they came from and expected to enter as adults. They took every opportunity to play pranks on school officials, teachers, and "ear-'oles." Their culture was a rejection of hopes for upward mobility through schooling and the values of schooling and learning.

Ironically, Willis portrays this antischool culture as preparation for the generalized labor force the students will be entering. The pranks they play in school are similar to the pranks they will later play on the shop floor. The peer culture they develop is similar to the culture of their fathers at work and the culture they will experience when they enter the workforce. This interpretation provides a more complex picture of the interaction between family background and the school. In this case, the students create an antischool culture, which plays a determining role in assuring the perpetuation of their working-class status.

In Willis's account, the school is not the villain that takes account of family background to reproduce existing social classes. Rather, the culture of the school comes into conflict with the culture of the students. The result is the creation of a student culture that rejects the values of the school and is preparation for continued working-class status. One leaves the reading of Willis's book with the feeling that the only resolution to the situation is for the school to change its culture to accommodate that of other cultures, so that students do not find it necessary to create a peer culture that is antilearning.

If the above reasoning is correct, then it suggests that another ingredient must be considered if the schools are to be effective in educating children from all social classes. Added to the list of characteristics of the more-effective-schools movement should be the requirement that the school consider placing students in a situation where they do not find it necessary to develop an anti-school culture. What this would mean is not clear at this time. It does provide the hope that the link between family background and educational outcomes is not immutable.

Exercises

1. A major issue discussed in this chapter is the relationship between social class and inequality of educational opportunity. Was this a factor in your education? Can you remember if social class was related to ability grouping or different curriculum tracks?
2. Select a high school in your community and determine whether social class is related to the curriculum in which the students are placed. Are students at this school from particular social groups the major participants in extracurricular activities?
3. Make a chart tracing the major occupational changes in the last several generations of your family. Try to determine the major factors that caused social mobility in your family.
4. In a group discussion or essay discuss whether you think the school should be used as an institution to foster equality of opportunity.

Suggested Readings and Works Cited in Chapter

Ballantine, Jeanne. *The Sociology of Education*. Englewood Cliffs, N.J.: Prentice-Hall, 1983. Chapter 3 of this study of the sociology of education contains information on the relationship between education and social stratification.

Blau, Peter and Duncan Otis. *The American Occupational Structure*. New York: John Wiley, 1967. The classic study of mobility patterns in the United States and the effect on mobility of different social factors including education.

Borman, Kathryn and Joel Spring. *Schools in Central Cities*. New York: Longman, 1984. Chapter 7 of this study of central-city schools provides an analysis of the more-effective-schools movement.

Bowles, Samuel, and Herbert Ginitis. *Schooling in Capitalist America*. New York: Basic Books, 1976. This book by two neo-Marxist economists argues that schooling in the United States maintains the existing social-class structure for the benefit of an economic elite.

Coleman, James. *Equality of Educational Opportunity*. Washington, D.C.: Government Printing Office, 1966. The famous Coleman Report that deals with the relationship between inequality of educational opportunity and student achievement.

Freeman, Richard B. *The Overeducated American*. New York: Academic Press, 1976. Freeman provides a summary of research on education and income and a study of the effects of supply and demand on that relationship.

Hollingshead, A. B. *Elmtown's Youth*. New York: John Wiley, 1949. The classic study of the effect of social class on adolescent life in a small town.

Jencks, Christopher. *Inequality*. New York: Harper & Row, 1972. A major study of the effects of family and schooling on inequality.

Kohn, Melvin. *Class and Conformity: A Study of Values*. Homewood, Ill.: Dorsey, 1969. A study of the relationship between child-rearing practices and social class.

Levine, Daniel, and Robert Havighurst. *Society and Education: Sixth Edition*. Boston: Allyn and Bacon, 1984. Chapters 3, 4, and 5 of this study of the sociology of education are devoted to the issue of education and opportunity.

Lipset, Seymour, and Reinhard Bendix. *Social Mobility in Industrial Society*. Berkeley: University of California Press, 1959. The first major comparative study of social mobility in industrial countries.

Persell, Caroline. *Education and Inequality*. New York: Free Press, 1979. The best available summary of research on the causes and consequences of inequality of educational opportunity.

Rosenthal, Robert, and Lenore Jacobson. *Pygmalion in the Classroom*. The classic study of the effects of teacher expectations.

Rutter, Michael et al. *Fifteen Thousand Hours*. Cambridge, Mass.: Harvard University Press, 1979. A study of the differences between 12 inner-city schools in London and how those differences are related to behavior and academic achievement.

Sexton, Patricia. *Education and Income*. New York: Viking, 1961. A study of the relationship between family income and ability grouping, tracking, and achievement in a large city.

Wasserman, Miriam. *The School Fix: NYC, USA*. New York: Outerbridge & Dienstfrey, 1970. First section of the book has case studies of students who did or did not make it successfully through the New York schools.

Willis, Paul. *Learning to Labour*. Lexington, Mass.: D.C. Heath, 1979. A study of the development of an antischool peer culture among working-class students in England.

5

Equality of Educational Opportunity

There is an important distinction between equality of opportunity and equality of educational opportunity. As defined previously, equality of opportunity means giving everyone the same chance to compete for positions in society. On the other hand, equality of educational opportunity means giving everyone the same chance to receive an education. It can be argued that equality of educational opportunity is essential for equality of opportunity in a society. But this argument can be maintained only if there is proof that education does provide equality of opportunity. And, as shown in Chapter 4, the ability of education to provide equality of opportunity is still debatable.

The debate about the precise relationship between education and equality of opportunity should not detract from the importance of arguments in favor of equality of educational opportunity. The provision of equality of educational opportunity can be defended solely on the grounds of justice. If government provides a service like education, then all citizens should have equal access to that service. One of the great political revolutions in the nineteenth century was the introduction of equality before the law. Prior to that time, in many Western nations the law was applied differently to different classes of the population. For instance, the aristocracy was usually given preferential treatment under the law.

Equality before the law can simply mean that if a government has a law that provides free public education, then all classes of citizens should have equal access to that public education. Therefore, providing equality of educational opportunity can be defended apart from any claims that it results in social benefits. Stated simply, everyone should have the right to an education, if that education is provided by the government.

The problem that has existed in the United States is that all groups have not had equal access to public schooling. In some cases this has occurred by law. For instance, prior to 1954 southern states had laws requiring segregation by race in the public schools. As I will discuss in more detail later in the chapter, it was the opinion of the U.S. Supreme Court that such laws prevented equal access to education because segregation is inherently unequal. On the other hand, in northern states the practices of school officials, and not the law, were responsible for school segregation. In both cases, courts have ruled that segregated education is a denial of equality or equal treatment by the law.

Denial of equal access to an education can also be the result of a variety of other factors. For instance, for many years handicapped people were denied equal access to an education because of the lack of provisions to accommodate their special needs. Entry into buildings was difficult for many handicapped people because they could not negotiate stairs and ramps for wheelchairs were not provided. Movement between floors in buildings was difficult for similar reasons. Providing equality of educational opportunity for handicapped people has meant making physical changes in buildings.

Equality of educational opportunity has also been denied to children from homes where English is not the spoken language, when no special provision for this language problem has been made by the schools. Courts have argued that children who do not fully comprehend the language of the school are being denied equal access to instruction. Equality of educational opportunity in this situation means that the schools must provide special help for children with non-English-speaking backgrounds.

Equality of educational opportunity also refers to how children are treated once they are in the educational system. For instance, as discussed in Chapter 4, when the result of tracking in high schools is the placement, in most cases, of different racial groups in separate tracks, there is good evidence that some form of internal segregation is occurring within the school. In this situation, tracking might result in a denial of equal educational opportunity.

Inequality of educational opportunity in schools has been an important issue in relation to the rights of women. The most dramatic example of this has been the question of equal access and equal treatment in different educational programs. For many years, male athletic programs in schools received more financial support and attention than female athletic programs. This has been a clear violation of equality of educational opportunity. Also, many curriculums, particularly in vocational education, were serving males primarily and not females, with the result that women have been denied the benefit of equal treatment by the law.

Although it is clear that equality of educational opportunity is distinct from equality of opportunity, there is still a tendency to link the two together, because both concepts promise an improvement in social and economic benefits. Historically, both concepts have been linked in struggles for increased civil rights.

The Struggle for Civil Rights

American history is the story of the steady struggle for increased civil participation in society. Usually the term *civil rights* means the right to an equal opportunity to gain economic and social advantages, and equal treatment by the law. Since the founding of the Republic, groups have struggled to remove barriers that deny equal access to economic opportunities, institutions, and political power. It is important to understand that an increase in civil rights has occurred only because of active participation and struggle by citizens. The reason people have had to struggle to gain civil rights is that equalization of civil rights has usually meant reducing the advantages held by one class of citizens over another class of citizens.

The two most important struggles for equal civil rights have been by women and by racial minority groups. For both groups the struggle has been for equal political power, equal access to economic opportunities, equal treatment and access to social institutions, and equality of educational opportunity. The most important struggle for women in the United States was for the right to vote. Although the suffrage movement was international, in the United States its final resolution was the adoption in 1920 of the Nineteenth Amendment to the Constitution.

The other important struggle for women has been to gain equal access to economic opportunities. Historically, women have been relegated to certain sectors of the labor market. In the nineteenth century, the primary sources of employment for women outside the home were as domestic help, teachers, factory workers, and in other service occupations. These employment opportunities were usually occasions for economic exploitation. For instance, women and children comprised a large sector of industrial employment in the nineteenth century because they were a cheap form of labor. As pointed out in Chapter 2, women were allowed to enter the ranks of teaching primarily because they were viewed as a cheap and steady workforce. In the latter part of the nineteenth and early part of the twentieth centuries, women came to dominate the professions of nursing and social work, which are often referred to as the helping professions. Again, the wage scales of these professions were considerably below those in professions dominated by men.

With the growth of white-collar occupations in the twentieth century, women became the major source of workers for office positions such as secretaries, typists, and clerks. In the twentieth century, schools have played an important role in assuring the perpetuation of women in these occupations. One of the most successful vocational education programs has been in business and secretarial skills. These programs have tended to enroll women primarily.

This has meant that a sex-segregated curriculum has contributed to the maintenance of a sex-segregated sector of the labor market.

Educational institutions have been central to the struggle by women for equal access to occupations. First, although women have predominated in the role of teacher in public schools since the nineteenth century, they have not held an equivalent number of administrative positions in public schools nor have they held an equivalent number of positions on university faculties. Second, educational training is the primary means of entering many professions, such as law and medicine. Gaining equal access to these educational programs has been an important part of women's struggle for equality of opportunity.

One of the important gains for women was the passage by the federal government of the Higher Education Act of 1972. Title IX of this legislation provided both for sex equality in employment in educational institutions and for sex equality in educational programs. The legislation applied to all educational institutions, including preschools, elementary and secondary schools, vocational and professonal schools, and public and private undergraduate and graduate institutions. A 1983 U.S. Supreme Court decision, *Grove City College* v. *Bell,* restricted Title IX in its application to specific educational programs within institutions. This decision will be discussed in more detail in Chapter 8.

Minority groups have had struggles similar to those of women in their quest for equal civil rights. For blacks, the major problem has been struggling against the legacy of slavery. After the Civil War, two amendments to the Constitution promised to give blacks equal political status. The Fourteenth Amendment to the Constitution, ratified in 1868, guaranteed equality before the law. This amendment has proven to be extremely important in arguments for equality of educational opportunity. It will be discussed and mentioned throughout this chapter and other chapters in the book. The Fifteenth Amendment to the Constitution, ratified in 1870, guaranteed that the right to vote would not be denied on account of race, color, or previous condition of servitude.

The promise of equality before the law was denied to blacks in southern states in the latter part of the nineteenth century with the passage of "Jim Crow" laws. These laws made it extremely difficult for blacks to vote, and mandated segregation in public schools and other public institutions. The abolition of these restrictive laws was a major focus of the black community's civil rights struggle, beginning in the late-nineteenth century and continuing through the 1960s, when Congress passed legislation protecting civil rights and the right to vote for blacks.

Like women, minority groups have also found themselves relegated to low-wage sectors of the labor force. In fact, there is a direct relationship between segregation in education and economic exploitation. One clear example is found in the state of California, which at different periods in history has segregated Chinese, Japanese, Chicanos, Indians, and blacks. Segregation of these groups coincided with their exploitation as workers. For instance, Chinese were segregated in California during the period when they were brought into the country as inexpensive labor to work on the railroads; Japanese were segregated at the time they were being brought in as agricultural workers. In the South, blacks were segregated during a period when their labor was considered necessary for the building of the new industrial South.

Segregation carries with it the stigma of racial inferiority. The belief in the racial inferiority of one group allows other groups to rationalize its place at the bottom of the labor market. In other words, one can justify placing racial groups in positions of economic exploitation by claiming that they are inferior and unsuitable for other positions. Historically, segregated education in the United States and other countries has been a means of perpetuating myths of racial superiority and inferiority.

The black community in the United States saw the ending of racial segregation in the schools as a means of improving equality of opportunity, because desegregation would help to remove the stigma of racial inferiority and would provide greater opportunities for upward occupational mobility. This is why educational aspirations have been so high in the black community. Historically, much of the hope of the black community has centered on gaining equality of educational opportunity.

After the Civil War, the major debate between black leaders such as W. E. B. DuBois and Booker T. Washington did not focus on whether education should play the major role in the advancement of black people, but on what kind of education would be best. In the twentieth century, the major area of concern of the National Association for the Advancement of Colored People (NAACP) has been desegregating American schools and achieving equal educational opportunity for black children. Current sociological research has found that black educational aspirations are higher than the educational aspirations of whites within the same social class.

The high educational aspirations of the black community in the United States have contributed to one of the great tragedies of American life, because they have not resulted in equal economic gains. One of the great burdens of being black or of Spanish-American origin is that the economic value of each stage of educational attainment is less than it is for the majority white population. In their study of *The American Occupational Structure* (discussed in Chapter 4), Peter Blau and Otis Duncan found that education did not produce the same benefits for blacks as for whites in terms of occupational achievement or mobility. The difference between mean occupational status of whites and nonwhites increased with higher educational levels; Blau and Duncan's data showed that approximately the same amount of educational investment yielded considerably less, in the form of superior occupational status or upward mobility, to nonwhites than to whites. For nonwhites in the United States, the burden of discrimination is that equal educational effort does not result in equal economic and social gains.

The other tragedy of the high educational aspirations of the black community has been that the quality of education provided tends to reflect institutional discrimination in terms of the quality of teaching, types of books and resources available in the schools, and the tracking of black students into vocational and nonacademic curricula.

Institutional racial discrimination occurs in the same form in which social-class discrimination occurs. There is a tendency for white schoolteachers and principals to have lower expectations for black students than for white students. This is not necessarily an example of overt racism but is primarily a result of the cultural isolation of the white community from the black community and the lack of awareness by the white community of the high educational aspirations of black parents and students. In addition to the problem of teachers' low expectations, there is a tendency in large school systems for younger and less experienced teachers to be placed in schools that are predominantly nonwhite.

The greatest impact of civil rights struggles on the schools has been the process of desegregation. Desegregation has not only helped to fulfill the promise of equal educational opportunity, but has also changed the organizational structure of education by fostering the development of magnet schools. This chapter will next explore the process of desegregation, the problems of institutional segregation and racism, and the effects of the struggle of women for equal rights.

Desegregation of American Schools

The historic 1954 Supreme Court school desegregation case, *Brown* v. *Board of Education of Topeka,* gave legal meaning to the idea that segregated education means unequal education. Until 1954, segregated schools in the United States operated under a ruling given by the Supreme Court in 1895, *Plessy* v. *Ferguson,* that segregation did not create a badge of inferiority if segregated facilities were equal and the law was reasonable. The decision in both cases centered around the meaning of the Fourteenth Amendment to the Constitution. This amendment was ratified in 1868, shortly after the close of the Civil War. One of its purposes was to extend the basic guarantees of the Bill of Rights into the areas of state and local government. The most important and controversial section of the Fourteenth Amendment states: "No State shall make or enforce any law which shall abridge the privileges or immunities of citizens...nor ...deprive any person of life, liberty, or property, without due process of law; nor deny to any person within its jurisdiction the equal protection of the laws."

The 1895 decision, *Plessy* v. *Ferguson,* involved Homer Plessy, who was one-eighth black and seven-eighths white. He was arrested for refusing to ride in the colored coach of a train, as required by Louisiana state law. The

Supreme Court's decision in this case, that segregated facilities could exist if they were equal, became known as the "separate but equal" doctrine.

The 1954 desegregation decision, *Brown* v. *Board of Education of Topeka,* overturned the "separate but equal" doctrine by arguing, on the basis of the findings of social science, that segregated education was inherently unequal. This meant that even if school facilities, teachers, equipment, and all other physical conditions were equal between two racially segregated schools, the two schools would still be unequal because of the fact of racial segregation.

In 1955 the Supreme Court issued its Enforcement Decree for the desegregation of schools. One problem facing the Court was the lack of machinery for supervising and assuring the desegregation of schools. The Court resolved this problem by relying on federal district courts as the determiners of equitable principles for desegregation. The Court argued that each local school district had its own set of problems with regard to how desegregation would affect the use of buildings, school transportation systems, and the determination of boundaries of school districts. These problems, it was felt, could best be handled on a local basis through the district courts.

The Enforcement Decree began the long and hard process of attempting to end inequality in American education caused by racial segregation. It was and is an attempt to use the federal courts as a means of extending equality of educational opportunity to all Americans. One problem in enforcing the Supreme Court decision was the statement in the Enforcement Decree that the district courts should issue orders and decrees "as are necessary and proper to admit to public schools on a racially nondiscriminatory basis with all deliberate speed the parties to these cases." Many Americans in the 1950s and early 1960s felt that "all deliberate speed" had been interpreted by the district courts as meaning a snail's pace, and were upset at the slow progress of school desegregation in the South.

In 1964 Congress took a significant step toward speeding up school desegregation by passing the important Civil Rights Act. In terms of school desegregation, Title VI of the 1964 Civil Rights Act was most important because it provided a means for the federal government to force school desegregation. In its final form, Title VI required the mandatory withholding of federal funds from institutions that practiced racial discrimination. Title VI stated that no person, because of race, color, or national origin, could be excluded from or denied the benefits of any program receiving federal financial assistance. It required all federal agencies to establish guidelines to implement this policy. Refusal by institutions or projects to follow these guidelines was to result in the "termination of or refusal to grant or to continue assistance under such program or activity."

Title VI of the 1964 Civil Rights Act was important for two reasons. First, it established a major precedent for federal control of American public schools, by making explicit that the control of money would be one method used by the federal government to shape local school policies. (This aspect of the law is discussed in more detail in Chapter 8.) Second, it turned the federal Office of Education into a policing agency with the responsibility of determining whether or not school systems were segregated, and if they were, of doing something about the segregated conditions.

One result of Title VI was to speed up the process of school desegregation in the South, particularly after the passage of federal legislation in 1965 that increased the amount of money available to local schools from the federal government. In the late 1960s southern school districts rapidly began to submit school desegregation plans to the Office of Education.

With the passage of the 1964 Civil Rights Act it was possible to attack segregated school conditions either through the courts or through the threat of withholding federal education funds. A pattern of enforcement emerged in the 1960s in which the Office of Education was relied upon in southern segregation situations and the courts were relied upon in segregation cases in the North. One reason for this was that in the South, it was more difficult to prosecute desegregation cases in district courts because the judges tended to share the prejudices of the local community. The enforcement of Title VI was effective in the South because local southern school districts needed the money. In the North the courts were more often used because of the nature of national politics. The first attempt to withhold money from a northern city ended in dismal failure. In 1965 the Office of Education announced that $32 million was being withheld from the Chicago public school system pending investigation. After the announcement by the Office of Education, Mayor Richard J. Daley, one of the major political powers in the Democratic party, and congressional leaders from Illinois placed pressure on Democratic President Lyndon Johnson. After Johnson quickly let it be known that he wanted the funds to begin flowing to Chicago, the major thrust of Title VI was directed primarily at the South.

In the North prosecution of inequality in educational opportunity as it related to school segregation required a different approach from that used in the South. In the South, school segregation had existed by legislative acts that required separation of the races. In the North there were no specific laws requiring separation of the races. But even without specific laws, racial segregation existed. In fact, the U.S. Commission on Civil Rights reported in 1967 that the level of racial separation in northern city schools was increasing; 75 percent of the black elementary students in cities attended schools whose populations were almost entirely black, whereas 83 percent of the white students attended all-white schools. The trend in northern cities was toward increasing racial segregation.

Since actual laws requiring racial segregation did not exist in the North, it was necessary for individuals bringing complaints against northern school districts to prove that the existing patterns of racial segregation were the result of purposeful action on the part of the school district. In other words, it had to be proved that school officials intended racial segregation to be a result of their educational policies.

The conditions required to prove segregation were explicitly outlined in 1974, in the Sixth Circuit Court of Appeals case, *Oliver* v. *Michigan State Board of Education*. The court stated, "A presumption of segregative purpose arises when plaintiffs establish that the natural, probable and foreseeable result of public officials' action or inaction was an increase or perpetuation of public school segregation." This did not mean that individual motives or prejudices were to be investigated but that the overall pattern of school actions had to be shown to increase racial segregation. In the language of the court this meant that "the question whether a purposeful pattern of segregation has manifested itself over time, despite the fact that individual official actions, considered alone, may not have been taken for segregative purposes...."

If a school district was found guilty of segregation, in either the North or the South, it was required to submit a plan, or have a plan developed by an outside expert, for the desegregation of the school district. This was true for both court actions and actions taken by the Office of Education under Title VI of the 1964 Civil Rights Act. The usual procedure in court cases where the school district is found guilty of segregation is for the judge to request the development of a desegregation plan within a specified time period. The Office of Education, on the other hand, usually requires proof from educational institutions receiving federal money of some affirmative action to end segregation. During the 1960s the Office of Education required southern school districts to submit specific desegregation plans.

The most politically explosive and controversial aspect of both court actions and actions under Title VI have been desegregation plans. Some of these plans have required forced busing, which in some northern communities has resulted in riots, demonstrations, and the closing of schools. Desegregation plans quickly became an issue in local and national political campaigns, where candidates were forced to define their positions, particularly about forced busing. Communities going through the process of desegregation without violence or major strife still had to use a large number of community-relations experts to prepare the local population.

The earliest desegregation plans were developed in the South. One of the major responses of southern school districts to the enforcement of Title VI was the development of freedom-of-choice plans. These plans allowed students in any school system using the plan to attend any school of their choice within the system. In the South this proved to be another method of maintaining segregation, because the tradition of white control was entrenched and also because the harassment of black parents forced them to choose all-black schools for their children. To counter this situation, the Office of Education began to establish racial quotas for desegregation plans. This meant that local school districts had to keep records of the degree of racial balance within their schools.

The issue of busing as a means of desegregation hit the national scene with full force in 1971, when the Supreme Court in *Swann* v. *Charlotte-Mecklenburg Board of Education* supported busing as a legitimate tool for bringing about the desegregation of school districts. The Court warned that "schools all or predominantly of one race in a district of mixed population will require close scrutiny to determine that school assignments are not part of state-enforced segregation." The implications of this decision were that segregation in northern urban school districts would come under close scrutiny of the courts and that busing would be considered a legitimate tool for implementing desegregation plans. Traditional arguments about the value of neighborhood schools could no longer be used to avoid integration. Also, school districts would be viewed as unitary systems within which racial integration had to be achieved wherever possible.

By 1972, presidential politics entered the picture directly when President Richard Nixon sent a special message to Congress requesting a moratorium on student busing. Nixon's actions reflected the growing reaction of white parents in northern cities to the issue of forced busing. Some communities were able to accomplish desegregation with a minimum of problems; others, such as Boston, suffered a great deal of strife. During 1975 and 1976 the Boston public schools faced problems of demonstrating parents, interracial fights between students, and clashes between community members and police.

What has often been lost in the rhetoric of politicans and the controversy surrounding busing is the essential issue that desegregation is an attempt to provide equal educational opportunity to all Americans. Not only in terms of the Supreme Court decision are segregated educational facilities inherently unequal, but also in terms of what has actually occurred in northern schools. As court cases have been prosecuted against northern school districts, it has become quite clear that past segregative practices resulted in unequal educational opportunity for minority groups.

The following case study of Cleveland, Ohio, demonstrates how past segregative practices resulted in inferior educational opportunity for blacks, and how school officials are now attempting to end segregation. The material for the case study is taken directly from the decision issued by the U.S. District Court in 1976, which found the Cleveland Board of Education guilty of school segregation. Other documents include the appeals by the Cleveland Board of Education after the decision and the response of the NAACP to that appeal.

CLEVELAND, OHIO

The findings of the U.S. District Court against the Cleveland school district are examples of how segregated school practices are directly related to unequal educational opportunity.

Racial segregation had increased in Cleveland between 1940 and 1975. Table 5.1 gives the percentage of black students attending schools that were one-race schools, for various years during that period. The chart shows the

Table 5.1 Percentage of Black Students in One-Race Schools

Year	Percent
1940	51.03
1950	58.08
1955	57.72
1960	76.03
1970	90.00
1975	91.75

steady trend toward the concentration of black students in segregated schools in Cleveland, a trend that is not in itself proof of intentional segregation. What needs to be proved is that this pattern is a result of actions by school officials.

The most important issues are pupil assignment and school capacity. "Pupil assignment" refers to the method used by the school system to assign students to different schools, either by drawing lines for school districts or through special placement. Obviously pupil assignment is a key issue because it results in either segregated or integrated conditions. What must be shown is whether or not the methods used by school officials in pupil assignment were affected by the race of the students.

The evidence used to prove that segregative intentions influenced pupil assignments by Cleveland school officials was school capacity. "School capacity" refers to the number of students a school building was designed to serve. It is assumed that a school district would attempt to assign students in a way that would leave no building either overcrowded or underutilized.

In the Cleveland decision, the district court found that black pupils tended to be assigned to overcrowded schools despite the fact that some schools with a majority of white students had unused classrooms. This situation occurred in areas where district lines could easily have been redrawn to correct the problem. One example given in the court decision involved 13 elementary schools where the proportion of black students ranged from 95.4 to 100.0 percent. Only one of these schools had unused classrooms, and most schools were overcrowded. For instance, one school, designed to hold 980 pupils, had an enrollment of 1,350; another school, built to hold 945 students, had 1,446 enrolled pupils.

The court found that these 13 schools were surrounded by 12 other schools, all but 3 of which had proportional black enrollments substantially below the percentage of black students in the Cleveland public schools. Eight of the 12 surrounding-area schools had enrollments that were at least 200 students below their basic capacity; in all, these 12 schools had a total of 51 unused classrooms. The court reasoned that if school assignments had been made without consideration of race, then students would have been more evenly divided between schools. Situations such as this one resulted in the court's decision that school-district lines had been drawn to maintain racial segregation.

In addition, the court found that pupil-assignment policy concerning special transfers was influenced by racial considerations. "Special transfers" could be granted to students when school officials determined some need for a student to change from one school to another. The court found that some school-board employees placed a handwritten "W" on applications believed to be from white students. Thus special transfers were used to allow white students to attend predominantly white schools rather than their "neighborhood" schools, which happened to be predominantly black.

The court also found intentional racial segregation in terms of faculty assignment. The pattern it found was that as a school's black student enrollment increased, so too did the number of black faculty assigned to that school. One school employee, who had worked for the system for 37 years, told the court, "Well, I don't know whether you want to call it policy or custom or understanding or whatever it is, but if you were black, you went to a school with a predominantly black enrollment."

The most important fact about the above patterns of intentional segregation is that it resulted in inferior education for black people in Cleveland. Overcrowding in black schools resulted in the establishment of "relay" between 1955 and 1961—an effort to get twice the mileage out of a school day by teaching one group of students in the morning and another in the afternoon. The court stated in its decision that "the instruction thus received was abbreviated, and therefore inferior, to that received by pupils not on relay classes and, in fact, fell far short of the minimal education standards set out by law." The court reported that the vast majority of the schools that employed relay classes had majority or predominantly black student enrollments.

The fact that inferior education was provided in overcrowded black schools —whereas classrooms in surrounding white schools remained empty—was one basis on which Ohio was found guilty of supporting racial segregation in the schools. The court ruled that in predominantly black schools, state officials had failed to fulfill their statutory obligation to enforce the statewide minimum standards established for public schools. During the periods when such minimum standards were not enforced, it was argued, "many of the schools in Cleveland which were identifiably black were demonstrably inferior to other schools in the Cleveland system and, therefore, unequal."

Specifically, the court found that in certain schools the state board and the state superintendent had expressly exempted Cleveland school officials from the requirement of providing at least five hours of classroom instruction per day; the overwhelming majority of the exempted schools had populations that were almost totally black. The court stated, "The result was that in these schools, students were put on relay classes, that is, they attended school for only three-and-a-half hours per day, rather than five."

As school desegregation proceeded across the country it caused a fundamental change in the organization of school curricula, with the introduction of magnet or alternative schools. Magnet or alternative schools are designed to provide an attractive program that will have wide appeal throughout a school district. Theoretically, magnet schools will attract enough students from all racial backgrounds to achieve integrated schools. For instance, a school district might establish a school for creative and performing arts that would attract students of all races from all areas of the district. If one critiera in selecting students is the maintenance of racial balance, then that school becomes a means of achieving integration.

The great attraction of magnet schools, and a major reason why they have been widely supported, is that they provide a means of voluntary desegregation. They have received support also because of a belief that they will reduce the flight of middle-class and white families from school districts undergoing desegregation. In other words, it is hoped that by providing unique and attractive programs, school districts will retain their populations as voluntary desegregation takes place.

The concept of magnet schools also received support from the federal government, which aided in their rapid adoption by school districts. The 1976 amendments to the Emergency School Aid Act (ESAA) provided financial support specifically for magnet school programs. In addition, President Ronald Reagan's administration in 1984 used magnet-school plans as its method of achieving out-of-court settlements of desegregation cases. This will be discussed in more detail in Chapter 8.

Some school districts have developed elaborate plans for magnet schools. In Houston, Texas, magnet schools have been established ranging from Petro-Chemical Careers Institute to a High School for Law Enforcement and Criminal Justice. In most school districts, magnet schools have been introduced by first offering a program in creative and performing arts. For example, both Philadelphia and Cincinnati established a School of Creative and Performing Arts as their early magnet-school offering. In Philadelphia, school-desegregation plans have led to schools offering programs that range from the study of foreign affairs to community-based education. In many cases, special programs already in existence, particularly for academic excellence and vocational training, were classified as magnet schools.

In evaluating the desegregation aspect of magnet schools, a distinction must be made between mandatory and voluntary desegregation plans. According to Mark Smylie in a 1983 article for *Urban Education*, "Districts implementing mandatory plans achieved over three times the racial balance among schools achieved by districts implementing voluntary plans." In some situations, magnet-school programs established as a part of involuntary desegregation plans are viewed as a means of reducing the potential hostility of parents. In these situations, the choice is not between a segregated neighborhood school and a desegregated magnet school, but a choice between (1) forced reassignment to a desegregated school, (2) leaving the school system, or (3) selecting a desegregated magnet school. Christine Rossell in a 1979 article in *Urban Education* reported that in Boston, where magnet schools were part of a court-ordered desegregation plan, they "reportedly have long waiting lists...and were perhaps the only 'successful' aspect of the plan despite greater busing distance and numbers bused."

Segregation within Schools

While most of the efforts of courts and the federal government have focused on the desegregation of school districts, a continuing problem of segregation within schools has prevailed. In fact, the integration of some school districts has resulted in the segregation of students within a school by academic programs and school activities. It often happens that racial differences are translated into socioeconomic differences, which results (as noted in the previous chapter) in tracking and in segregation by ability group.

A number of studies of the process of segregation have examined what takes place within schools after a school district has undergone desegregation. One of the most interesting studies was compiled by Ray Rist in the late 1970s and published in 1979 as *Desegregated Schools: Appraisals of an American Experiment*. The research describes the subtle forms of segregation that began to occur as white and black students were placed in integrated schools for the first time. For instance, in one recently integrated school, black students were suspended for committing the same offenses for which white students received only a reprimand. A teacher in the school complained that, unlike black students, when white students were sent to the principal's office, they were immediately sent back to class. In this school, equal opportunity to attend the school did not result in equal treatment within the school.

Unequal treatment of different races within the same school is one problem in integrated schools; the establishment of racial boundaries among students creates another. One study in the Rist book describes how racial boundaries were established in a high school in Memphis, Tennessee, after the students of an all-black school were integrated with the students of an all-white school. Here, white students maintained control over most student activities. Activities in which black students began to participate after integration were athletics and cheerleading. When this occurred, the status of these activities was denigrated by white students. On the other hand, whites were able to maintain control of the student government, ROTC, school clubs, and the staff of the yearbook.

This division of control among student activities reflected the rigid social boundaries that existed in the high school between the two groups. Individuals who crossed these social boundaries had to adapt to the social customs of those on the other side. For instance, black students had to change their style of dress and social conduct in order to be accepted by white students. Black students who crossed racial lines by making such changes found themselves accused by other black students of "acting white" and were subsequently rejected by "unchanged" black students. The same was true of white students who crossed racial boundaries.

The racial boundaries that continued to exist in the high school after integration reflected the racial barriers that continued in the larger society. The social life of a school often reflects the social world outside the school. Integration of a school system can help assure equality of educational opportunity but it cannot break down society's racial barriers. Although schools attempt to deal with this problem, its solution requires a general transformation of racial relationships in the larger society.

There are steps that school administrators and teachers can take to lower racial barriers. Attention can be paid to the racial composition of school activities so that no racial group dominates an activity. It is important to see that no single school event (e.g., a school dance) becomes identified with a particular racial group. Attention to the racial composition of activities can extend into the classroom, with the teacher making sure that seating patterns and work groups do not reflect racial barriers.

Also, school people must remain sensitive to the possibility of racial differences being translated into socioeconomic differences. By the end of the 1970s debate had begun over whether to direct concern toward racial differences or socioeconomic differences. Sparking this debate was a book by the sociologist William J. Wilson, *The Declining Significance of Race: Blacks and Changing American Institutions*. Wilson argued that as a result of the civil rights movement, racial differences had become less important in explaining social differences between blacks and whites; socioeconomic differences were now more important than differences of race.

To support his argument, Wilson cited statistics on the changing pattern of the occupational structure in the black community and the increasing gap in social conditions between middle- and lower-class blacks. Wilson noted a dramatic change in black social mobility during the 1950s and 1960s. In 1950, 16.4 percent of black males were employed in middle-class occupations. In 1960, this percentage reached 24 percent; and in 1970, it rose to 35.3 percent. These changes reflect the dramatic increase in civil rights for minority groups during these two decades.

But during the 1970s, Wilson argued, the gap between middle-class and poor blacks began to increase, thus making it more difficult for blacks born into a state of poverty to experience social mobility. He noted the steady decrease in the number of blacks below the poverty line, from 48.1 percent in 1959 to 29.4 percent in 1968; in the 1970s, however, this percentage underwent *no* significant change, with the percentage of blacks below the poverty line persisting at 27 to 28 percent.

Not only has the percentage of blacks below the poverty line remained about the same since the 1960s but the gap in income between middle-class and lower-class blacks has been increasing. The unemployment rate for young blacks from poor families also has been increasing, and many have given up looking for work. In addition, there has been a steady increase in single-parent families among poor blacks, which has a direct effect on family income. What all this adds up to, according to Wilson, is deteriorating social and economic conditions for poor blacks.

In other words, advances in civil rights have benefited middle-class minority members to a greater extent than lower-class minority members. What this could lead to is the creation of a permanent underclass of minority groups locked into poverty while middle-class minority members become successfully integrated into the social and economic structures.

Thus, teachers and administrators must be aware of not only racial barriers but also socioeconomic barriers. It would be relatively easy for school people to integrate student activities and classrooms with middle-class blacks, without giving consideration to social-class differences within the black community. Integration of middle-class students only could give teachers or administrators a false sense of having solved racial problems when, in fact, they might be contributing to the development of a permanent underclass.

A major problem that could result from the accomplishment of equal educational opportunity between races is increased inequality in educational opportunity between social classes. For instance, magnet schools might bring about racial balance but also might result in a social-class stratification in particular schools. It is not beyond the realm of possibility that white and black children of working-class parents both might receive counseling that sends them to vocational schools, while upper- and middle-class children are counseled to select academic programs. Although the high aspirations of middle-class black parents might be satisfied, there would be a danger of increased segregation between social classes.

This is particularly important when we consider the relationship between education and social mobility, as discussed in the previous chapter. The high educational aspirations held by the black community are related to a belief that schooling is a means of social mobility. It is also true that segregated education has been a means of maintaining a stratified society by keeping black people separated from the career routes available to the majority population. Integrated education will be a means of moving the black population into the mainstream of occupational mobility in the United States. This could be one of the important consequences of integration.

On the other hand, as discussed in Chapter 4, receiving equal education does not guarantee social mobility, which is not directly related to the school but to the job market. In addition, there is some evidence that the school's role includes a combination of facilitating the movement of people into new occupations as they occur and maintaining stratification between social classes. It is certainly good that poor black people receive equal education, but the frustrations now felt by poor whites in using the school as a means of social mobility might well be shared by poor blacks as the middle-class black population reaps the rewards of integration.

One important consequence of school integration might be the stabilization of urban housing patterns and integrated neighborhoods. The quality of the schools often determines where people choose to live. White parents, in particular, will choose one neighborhood over another because one area's school is all-white while another's is all-black. This has been the pattern in northern urban areas. With school integration, this factor is no longer important in selecting housing. Quality and price will become more important determiners of housing patterns than the quality and racial composition of the neighborhood school. School integration might contribute to the growth of more racially integrated neighborhoods as blacks achieve their dream of equal educational opportunity.

Black Suburbia

One particular suburban community of about 40,000 people is on the border of a major midwestern industrial city. Prior to the 1960s, the majority of the population was white; family incomes were primarily in the lower-middle and middle range. During the mid-1960s, the population of the community began to shift rapidly from a majority of white residents to a majority of black residents. This was dramatically reflected in the school enrollments. In 1965, the percentage of black students enrolled in the school system was 10 percent. By 1970, the percentage of black students was 87 percent, and in 1974 it was 97 percent. By the middle of the 1970s the few remaining white children were in one elementary school in the more affluent section of the suburb.

The black population that moved into Black Suburbia was primarily in the middle-income range and very concerned about the quality of the educational system. When income figures from the 1960 and 1970 censuses for this suburban area are compared and 1960 dollars are adjusted to 1970 dollars, it is revealed that the black population moving into Black Suburbia in the 1960s had slightly higher incomes than the whites moving out of the community. The bulk of the black population moving into the area during this period was in the middle-income range and could be viewed as a group interested in upward mobility.

A study of the community in the late 1960s showed the mobility concerns and educational aspirations of the new black population. The study provided profiles of nine different social groups, including old and new white residents at different income and age levels and new black residents at different income and age levels. The study found that both middle-aged and young middle-class black residents had high expectations of upward mobility and believed that quality schools were a major element in a quality community. The population group labeled "new, middle-aged, black middle-class residents" were earning more than $10,000 a year and were employed as managers, proprietors, and professionals. This group was found to have an "extraordinarily high degree" of expectations for continuing upward mobility and a concern about the quality of schools. The same expectations and concerns were held by the "new, young, black middle class," who were earning between $6,000 and $9,000 per year and also were employed as managers, proprietors, and professionals. (It should be remembered that the incomes quoted are in 1960 dollars, which were worth considerably more than current dollar.)

The middle-aged and young black working class described in the study evidenced varying degrees of concern about the quality of schooling. For the middle-aged black working-class family, schools were not an important reason for moving to Black Suburbia. This group comprised unskilled workers earning between $6,000 and $7,000 per year. On the other hand, the quality of schools was important to the young black working-class residents, who were earning between $5,000 and $9,000 per year and were employed primarily in skilled and semiskilled jobs.

During the early 1970s the high mobility and the educational aspirations of black residents who arrived in Black Suburbia in the 1960s were threatened by the rapid influx of a poor black population. The introduction of a large group of low-income black families was reflected in the percentage of children from welfare families in the school system. Between 1965 and 1970 the percentage of children from welfare families in Black Suburbia increased from 6 to 16 percent as the racial composition of the population changed. Between 1970 and 1973 the percentage of children from welfare families increased dramatically, from 16 to 51 percent. In other words, the migration of upwardly mobile middle-class blacks was followed by the rapid migration of black welfare families.

The educational aspirations of those in the early black migration were frustrated both by the response of the local school system to these new residents, and by the later migration of poor blacks. One of the first things to happen was that the educational expectations of the mainly white teachers and administrators in the school system began to fall. This seemed to be caused by the assumption of the white school staff that the blacks moving into the community were not interested in education and would create major problems in the school system. This assumption is most clearly shown when the educational expectations of elementary school principals are compared with the educational expectations of the black community.

In the early 1970s, a local government survey of Black Suburbia included a question dealing with the level of educational aspirations. The survey asked parents how far they would like their sons or daughters to progress in school. Seventy-three percent of the parents wanted their sons to complete college, and 71 percent had that goal for their daughters. More important, when asked how far they believed their sons or daughters would actually go in school, 60 percent believed their sons would complete college, and 62 percent believed their daughters would do the same.

The contrast between the educational aspirations of the parents and the expectations of the elementary school principals illustrates the problems and frustrations encountered by black residents. When I asked elementary school principals what percentage of the students in their schools they felt would go to college, the responses from three of the principals were 3 percent, 12 percent, and 10 percent. Two elementary school principals evaded the question and claimed it had nothing to do with their work in the elementary school, and one elementary school principal gave a figure of 50 percent.

One of the important things about these responses is that the 50-percent figure was given by a new black elementary principal, who clearly was closer to understanding the values of the local community. All the other principals were white, and had been principals in the school system before the racial change occurred. The educational expectation levels of these principals not only were considerably below those of the community but were also below those of the teachers. A survey of elementary school teachers found that they thought that 29 percent of their students would graduate from college. Although this figure was still lower than the figure for the community, it was at least closer to community expectations than were the principals' estimates. One of the reasons for this might be that the teaching staff had changed more than the elementary administrative staff, and there had been a recent effort by the school district to recruit black teachers.

Several examples can be used to show how the lower expectations of school staff translated into practice. When I interviewed the head of the local community library, he informed me that in the years prior to the racial change, scholarly and professional journals were heavily used by high school students. This was not because the students read these journals for pleasure, but because teachers gave homework assignments in the journals. After the racial change, teachers stopped giving homework assignments in these advanced journals. In other words, the blacks who moved to the community because of its relatively high educational standards suddenly found those standards being lowered as their children entered the system.

The director of the local YMCA stated that a person who really wanted to know what was going on in the local school system should park his car outside the high school at closing time and count the number of students carrying books home from school. The director claimed that only a few students carried books, and this was another indication that teachers were no longer giving homework assignments and had given up trying to teach.

Complaints about teachers not teaching were echoed by students in the tenth and twelfth grades of the high school. A random sample of the tenth grade was interviewed and asked about their future plans and about any complaints about the school system. Fifty-eight percent of the tenth-grade students who were interviewed had expectations of attending and graduating from college. The major complaint of the students was the quality of the teaching staff.

Twelfth-grade students were chosen to be interviewed from a list of those students designated by the school administration as the "best." Sixty percent of these students expressed concern and even bitterness about the teaching staff. Their major complaint was that certain teachers made no effort to teach and wasted most class periods. One student stated that he had teachers who probably accomplished one day's worth of teaching out of every five days in the classroom. Another student stated that many teachers did not seem to care whether or not students did the work or learned. No attempt was made to make students want to come to class. One student argued that the reason teachers did not care was because they were so upset at trying to control "rowdy" students.

The issue of "rowdy" students entered almost every discussion about the quality of education in the local high school. There seemed to be an underlying assumption in any conversation with a community member that the "rowdy" students came from low-income black families. This reflected a tension between the middle-class blacks who moved into the community in the 1960s and the low-income blacks who moved into the community in the 1970s. Low-income families represented a threat to the aspirations and status of the middle-class residents of Black Suburbia.

One example of this was a black member of the local school board who pounded the table and exclaimed that all he wanted was to live a middle-class existence and provide a home and future for his family. This, he stated, was why he had moved to the community. Now he felt his dreams were not being realized, as crime increased in the community, and he feared that his children were not receiving an adequate education at the local school. He complained that every time his children left the house, he worried that they would get involved with the "rowdy" youths of the community. Currently he was sending his daughter to a private school, but his son went to the local high school. He worried constantly that his son would get in with the "wrong" group in the school.

This particular school board member led a group in the community that demanded a strict dress code. The reason for this was that those students identified as "rowdy" very often wore large hats and high-heeled shoes. The community members demanding the dress code saw it as a means of controlling and disciplining "rowdy" students. One result of this campaign was signs throughout the high school restricting the wearing of hats.

That the community related "rowdiness" with low-income background was evident from discussions with other community members. One leader of a community welfare organization claimed that "rowdy" juveniles were organized into natural street groupings, with one street in rivalry with another street. These street groupings, he argued, were primarily based on economic differences; kids from better streets put down kids from poorer streets. The community social welfare worker saw "rowdy" juveniles as a product of poverty, and characterized by their lack of a sense of direction, which led to an easy drifting into a life of stealing, drugs, and gambling. Another social welfare worker, who dealt directly with cases of juvenile delinquency, described middle-class youth in the community as walking a thin line where, at any time, pressures from this delinquent subculture could persuade the student to join the "rowdy" culture. This was very much the fear expressed by the school board member.

Students at the high school tended to see the issue of "rowdy" students as one of the problems with the teaching staff. Teachers generalized from the misbehavior of a few students to all students. One of the common complaints of tenth graders was the way teachers handled discipline problems. The majority of students felt that teachers were unable to control students in a just and fair manner. The problem was compounded, students believed, because teachers did not know how to control "rowdy" students and, consequently, acted "mean" toward all students.

The process of generalizing from a few students to all students might have been one of the factors contributing to the failure of teachers in the school system to understand or attempt to respond to the educational aspirations of the middle-class black community. Perhaps the delinquent subculture reinforced existing stereotypes held by white teachers and administrators about the way black students acted and learned. This would have influenced the levels of teacher expectations, reflected in specifics such as not assigning homework or not expecting students to use the community library.

For middle-class blacks who entered the community in the 1960s with high aspirations for upward mobility and quality education for their children, the school system became a source of frustration and disillusionment. Teachers did not provide the instruction parents had hoped for and, in addition, they came to fear that their children might enter a delinquent subculture. For the more-affluent black residents, the solution was a rejection of the public school and the transfer of their children into private schools.

Black families and students who were not interested in college but hoped that the school could provide some form of immediate job training also were frustrated in attaining their goals, as a direct result of racial discrimination. In the early 1970s the school system in Black Suburbia had built a new vocational high school directly connected to the traditional high school. The vocational school was the product of a state master plan for vocational education, which mandated the establishment of joint vocational school districts or individual vocational schools within each district. The problems of the vocational school in Black Suburbia were directly related to the discriminatory policies of the surrounding white suburban communities.

The story of Black Suburbia's vocational school came from the local superintendent and his staff, as well as a superintendent in the district next to Black Suburbia. After the resolution of the vocational-school issue, these superintendents were no longer on speaking terms. The problem began when a meeting of all the superintendents in one suburban area of this metropolitan area was called to discuss the formation of a joint vocational school district as a method of complying with state requirements. The suburbs in this area were mostly white, except for three integrated suburban communities and Black Suburbia. Before the actual meeting, the superintendents of the predominantly white suburbs agreed by telephone to form their own vocational district, which would exclude the three integrated school districts and Black Suburbia. When the four school superintendents representing the suburbs having sizable black populations arrived at the meeting, they found that all decisions had been made and that they would be forced to work together in establishing a separate vocational district.

There is no agreement on what happened after this meeting. The superintendent of Black Suburbia claimed that the three integrated suburbs were hesitant about working with his school district, because those three communities had a higher-income population. Consequently, the superintendent of Black Suburbia was forced to build a vocational high school next to the one regular high school in the community. The superintendent of the adjoining integrated community claims the whole situation was a misunderstanding and that his community was willing to work on a joint vocational-school district.

The establishment of a separate vocational school in Black Suburbia had the effect of increasing the degree of segregation between white and black suburban schools. A joint vocational school covering the entire eastern area would have made a major contribution to school integration. The segregation of Black Suburbia's vocational school assured that its training programs would be inferior to the joint vocational school's programs, because an all-black school faces major problems in establishing links with unions, which have traditionally excluded blacks, and with white businesses. Because it is difficult for an all-black school to establish these contacts, it is very hard to place students graduating from the vocational program.

This problem was highlighted in conversation with the head of the vocational high school. In his vocational training programs he could claim the placement of only three welders in the last three years. The superintendent admitted conducting his own telephone survey to determine the problems in placement of the graduates in cosmetology. He found that only a few black graduates were able to get jobs in beauty parlors, and those jobs were at very low wages. Even those who got jobs found they lasted only a short time, because beauty parlors depend on a high turnover of personnel.

Another problem faced by the Black Suburbia school system is that it now has a vocational building that must be filled and a teaching staff that needs to protect its own jobs by attracting students. The size of the vocational school requires that almost half the students in the eleventh and twelfth grades enroll in its programs. In the tenth grade the students are shown through the school and given a choice between entering the vocational program the following year or continuing in an academic program. From the perspective of the staff of the vocational school, it is important to persuade students to enter their programs.

When the guidance counselor in the vocational school was asked what methods were used to persuade students to enter programs that could not promise jobs, his response was that they lied to the students. He justified this in terms of needing students to build good programs in the future, and said that even though jobs would be difficult to find for the students, the training they would be receiving in the vocational program would be more useful than that received in the traditional academic program. From his perspective, very few of the students in the secondary school were capable of going on to college.

A different interpretation was given by the black director of the local YWCA. She felt that the vocational school was keeping students from going to college. When she was asked what percentage of local high school students she felt would go on to college, she stated that before the vocational high school had been established, about 70 percent of the girls attending the YWCA planned on attending college. After the establishment of the vocational school, the number dropped to 30 or 40 percent. She argued quite strongly that if the community had been all-white, the vocational school never would have been built. It was, she felt, a racist institution designed primarily to give black students an inferior education. Another observer referred to the vocational program as "education for welfare."

The story of Black Suburbia highlights some fundamental problems encountered by minority groups in the United States. The fact that the expectations of teachers and school administrative staffs can be far below the aspirations of the minority group can cause a major decrease in the quality of education. In addition, the school staff can generalize from the behavioral problems of children from low-income families to all members of the minority group. In this case study, students directly felt this process of generalization.

The problems caused by the segregation of minority students are illustrated by the vocational-education program in Black Suburbia. But even if a joint vocational district that included students from Black Suburbia had been established, there would have been no guarantee that other forms of discrimination, such as the school staff having lower expectations for blacks as opposed to whites, might not have occurred. Indeed, one would expect that, given the previous history of relationships between these school districts, there probably would have been discriminatory actions in a joint vocational district.

What the story of Black Suburbia represents is the struggle in the United States of minority groups to attain a quality education when faced with problems of segregation between schools and discriminatory actions within schools. The history of the black struggle for equal education has focused on the ending of segregation, because segregated education can mean unequal education and a denial to minorities of access to all resources in a community.

The difficulty of job placement for students from an all-black vocational school is only one example of the inherent inequality in segregated education.

Sexism and Equality of Educational Opportunity

The historic struggle of women for equal civil rights was discussed in an earlier section of this chapter. Education has played a role in this struggle for several reasons. First, equality of educational opportunity has promised equal access to occupations. Historically, women have tended to dominate certain professions, whereas they have found it difficult to enter other professions. For instance, Daniel Levine and Robert Havighurst report in their book, *Society and Education,* that in 1980 the nursing profession was 96 percent female, and the teaching profession was 71 percent female. On the other hand, only 4 percent of engineers, and only 13 percent of lawyers and judges were females. One should immediately note in these examples that the professions in which women are the majority are the lower-paying occupations. Probably the most revealing contrast is between nurses and physicians. In 1980, 14 percent of physicians and osteopaths were women. In this case men, as physicians, are in authority over women, as nurses.

Second, women have sought equality of opportunity in order to gain access to occupations within the field of education. For instance, Patricia O'Reilly and Kathryn Borman report in their essay, "Sexism in Education: Documented Biases, Destructive Practices and Some Hope for the Future," that in 1980, "99 percent of school superintendents and 97 percent of high school principals [were] male." When contrasted with the fact that 71 percent of teachers are female, the disparity becomes obvious. O'Reilly and Borman describe this situation as "men rule women and women rule children."

To solve the problems represented by the preceding occupational statistics, equal treatment is required for women as students and as employees of educational institutions. This means that sexual discrimination needs to be eliminated in curricula in which men are the majority. Second, women need to be encouraged to enter curricula such as engineering and law. In order to accomplish this, socialization patterns need to be changed in families and in schools. Within educational institutions, affirmative action needs to be taken to assure equal access to administrative positions.

An important issue related to encouraging women to enter occupations where men are presently in a majority is sex-role stereotyping. During childhood certain activities become associated with one sex as opposed to the other. For instance, active and aggressive behavior is associated with boys, whereas passive and nurturing behavior is associated with girls. This type of socialization can contribute to boys and girls selecting occupations that reflect learned patterns of behavior. An obvious example is that of boys selecting work as policepersons or firepersons, and girls selecting work as nurses and teachers.

Avoiding sex-role stereotyping in educational institutions is very important in assuring equal opportunity for women and men. It is important to remember that sex-role stereotyping also places limits on male actions. Of course, sex-role stereotyping provides economic benefits primarily to men. One issue in sex-role stereotyping is the content of materials used in the classroom. For instance, elementary-school readers might picture only women working in the kitchen while men work outdoors. History textbooks might contain very little about the role of women in history. Of particular importance is the history of women's struggle for civil rights. Jeanne Ballantine reports in *The Sociology of Education* that recent studies still find girls and women being placed in stereotypic roles. She writes, "For instance, math problems involving girls often show them jumping rope, buying clothes, sewing, cooking, or calculating the grocery bill. This can limit what girls see as viable options and uses for their studies." In other words, girls learning arithmetic from these types of texts are not being prepared to see themselves using mathematics in engineering or science. Many of these discriminatory features of textbooks have been corrected, but it is important that all educational material be closely checked to assure that it does not contain any sex-role bias.

Sex-role bias also exists in the way many teachers treat students. O'Reilly and Borman report in their previously cited study that "from nursery school on most teachers talk more to boys than they do to girls and interact more with boys, whether 'asking questions, criticizing, accepting or rejecting ideas, giving approval and disapproval.'" It has been found that teacher tend to do tasks for girls, whereas they give boys instructions on how to accomplish tasks by themselves. Obviously, this provides boys with more training for independent action than is received by girls. In addition, teachers tend to react to boys no matter where they are in the classroom, whereas they respond mainly to girls who are physically near. This supports independent activity by boys and clinging, dependent behavior by girls.

These differences in treatment have been found to be related to occupational choice. Ballantine finds this most obvious in the fact that women enter college less inclined than men to select majors in math, science, and engineering. The avoidance of these majors is related to the tendency for women to underrate their abilities in these areas. Using the research of Donna Kaminski, Ballantine writes that the social, cultural, psychological, and educational factors influencing women not to enter math-related areas are "perceived incompatibility with raising children; sterotypes of appropriate gender behavior; few role models for women; less preparation from high school courses; early socialization experiences; and parental values and attitudes which are unsupportive." Ballantine argues that the middle-school years are the most crucial years for determining the choices women will make about their future areas of study.

Sex-role bias also appears in other areas of the curriculum. It is often difficult to determine if this is the result of socialization, or pressures from the educational institution on women to select particular areas of the curriculum.

In either case sexual discrimination is involved. As in math and science, there are clear patterns of sexual discrimination in vocational-education programs. Levine and Havighurst report that according to enrollment figures for vocational-education programs in 1979, men are in the majority in fields of study such as agriculture, technical, and trade and industrial. In agriculture, the enrollments are 83 percent male and 17 percent female; technical education is 80 percent male and 20 percent female; trade and industrial education is 82 percent male and 18 percent female. On the other hand, office education is 72 percent female and 28 percent male, and health education is 75 percent female and 25 percent male.

Correcting the sex bias of the curriculum involves not only changes in patterns of socialization and in the content of textbooks, but also legal action. The most important legislation to deal with these problems is Title IX of the Higher Education Act of 1972. As mentioned earlier in the chapter, Title IX guarantees equal educational opportunity for women, as employees in educational institutions and as students. This means that educational institutions must take positive action to assure that women have equal access to all curricula.

Levine and Havighurst report that the National Advisory Council on Women's Educational Programs reviewed changes since the passage of Title IX and concluded that there has been significant progress in extending equality of educational opportunity to women. The council found improvements: student services such as counseling, health, and financial aid were being operated on a more equal basis between men and women, and more equal support was being given to extracurricular activities, particularly athletics. But the council also expressed disappointment that women were not gaining significant improvements in employment by educational institutions as principals, school superintendents, and full professors.

There is a certain tragedy in the fact that women are not more equally represented in the administration of American schools. Studies tend to show that women make superior educational administrators. The previously mentioned study by O'Reilly and Borman argues that women principals are likely to be more interested than are their male counterparts in instructional supervision, democratic leadership styles, and involvement with students and with the community. These are generally considered to be the traits most associated with the principals of effective schools. The tragedy is in the previously cited figure that 97 percent of high-school principals are male. In fact, according to O'Reilly and Borman, in recent years the total percentage of women holding positions as both assistant principals and principals fell from 15.2 percent in 1970–71 to 12.9 percent in 1976.

During the period of decline in the percentage of women in educational administration, there was an actual increase in the number of women receiving master's and doctorate degrees in educational administration. Most states require a certain number of courses in educational administration before they will grant a certificate to hold a position as assistant principal, principal, or superintendent. According to O'Reilly and Borman, in 1970 women earned only 2 percent of the master's degrees and 6 percent of the doctorate degrees in educational administration. By 1976, these percentages had increased: 29 percent of the master's degrees and 20 percent of the doctoral degrees in educational administration were earned by women.

The decline in the percentage of women in school administrative roles during the same period in which there was an increase in the number of women earning degrees in educational administration suggests that the core of the problem is discriminatory hiring practices in the schools. This is also suggested by statistics dealing with regional patterns of employment of women. O'Reilly and Borman report, in one survey, that 35 percent of all female principals were employed in the highly urbanized mid-Atlantic states, and only 14 percent of female high school principals held positions in cities with a population of less than 149,999.

What these figures suggest is that there is more discrimination against women in rural and suburban school districts than in urban school districts. O'Reilly and Borman quote one researcher who stated, "Those in rural regions and those with less education express more prejudiced attitudes even when respondent age and acquaintance with a female administrator are taken into account." One way of interpreting this finding is to say that the attitudes held by current school administrators and school boards are primarily responsible for the denial to women of equal access to jobs in educational administration.

Although many improvements have been made in the elimination of sexual bias from the curricula of educational institutions, there remains the important issue of allowing women to have equal employment opportunities. This primarily is an issue of power. Positions in educational administration are positions of power within the educational system. Providing equal employment opportunities for women also challenges the prevailing concept of leadership in educational institutions. Traditionally, as O'Reilly and Borman argue, "prevailing school organization mythology is based upon a 'masculine ethic' emphasizing the leadership strength of a (white, male) rational planner." In other words, the struggle for civil rights for women has not been completed. The legislation exists to protect those rights but the struggle must be continued to put those rights into practice.

The struggle for the continuing expansion of civil rights is one of the most positive aspects of the history of the American people. That struggle will continue to direct its efforts at educational institutions, because the promise of education to provide equality of opportunity has not yet been fulfilled. Equality of educational opportunity is a prerequisite for equality of opportunity. The discussion of equal educational opportunity will continue in Chapter 10, which deals with the role of the courts in education. A major part of the struggle for equal educational opportunity has occurred in relation to court decisions dealing with a range of school practices from tracking to the language used in the schools.

The New Immigrants

Time magazine calls them the "new whiz kids." In the fall of 1987 *Time* reported that Asian-Americans comprised 25 percent of the entering class at the University of California at Berkeley, 21 percent at the California Institute of Technology, 20 percent at the Massachusetts Institute of Technology, and 14 percent at Harvard. In Los Angeles, New York City, and towns scattered across the country, neighborhoods identified with immigrants from particular South American, Caribbean, Asian, and Central American countries sprang up in the 1970s. In New York City, a traditional home for new immigrants, a Spanish Yellow Pages telephone directory was issued in the 1980s, and most advertising on the subway system is now in Spanish. Throughout New York, immigrants from South Korea took over greengrocer businesses and opened manicure salons, while other immigrant groups took over newspaper stands and restaurants. In the Brighton Beach section of Brooklyn, the presence of Jewish immigrants from the Soviet Union can be seen in the ethnic goods in stores and the foreign titles in bookstores.

The new wave of immigration into the United States in the 1970s and 1980s was made possible by the Immigration Act of 1965. Prior to 1965, immigration was determined by the ethnic quota section of the 1924 Immigration Act. Under the 1924 act, passed during a period of extreme racism, the annual quota of a national group allowed to immigrate to the United States was determined by the percentage that national group comprised of the total U.S. population in 1920. The openly stated purpose of the 1924 immigration legislation was to limit immigration of nonwhite populations.

As a consequence of the 1924 Immigration Act, the depression of the 1930s, and World War II, immigration to the United States declined from the late 1920s through the early 1950s. Immigration began to increase again in the 1950s and underwent a dramatic change after passage of the 1965 Immigration Act. Before 1965, the proportion of immigrants from Europe had remained approximately constant relative to those from Asia and the rest of the Americas. But after 1965, the proportion of immigrants from Europe dramatically declined and the proportion from Asia and the Americas dramatically increased.

Between the late 1960s and the early 1980s, the largest number of immigrants each year came from Mexico. In recent years, more and more immigrants have arrived from Asian sources, although Mexico continues to provide more than any other single country. In 1969, the order of immigrant sources to the United States was Mexico, Italy, the Philippines, Canada, and Greece. By 1973, Canada and Greece had dropped off the list, which read Mexico, the Philippines, Cuba, Korea, and Italy. Two years later Italy was replaced by China-Taiwan. Through the rest of the 1970s, the proportion of immigrants from Asia and the Pacific steadily increased. In 1980, the top five sources of immigrants were Mexico, Vietnam, the Philippines, Korea, and China-Taiwan.

The primary reasons for immigration during this period were economic, political, and familial. The 1965 Immigration Act established a preference system that favored family ties. In the distribution of immigration visas preference is given to spouses, children, and siblings of U.S. citizens. Also, preference is given to professionals and persons of exceptional ability who will benefit the U.S. economy and to skilled workers who are needed in the economy. Finally, preference is given to political refugees from communist or communist-dominated countries.

This preference system has resulted in immigrants with differing economic and educational backgrounds. For instance, large numbers of Mexicans have been able legally to enter the United States because of family ties with Mexican-Americans. Many of these Mexicans, along with those entering the country illegally, were poorly educated and were escaping the harsh economic conditions in Mexico.

On the other hand, the large Cuban and Vietnamese immigration of the 1970s fell under the political refugee preference category of the 1965 legislation. Many of these refugees were from the professional and business classes of their countries.

The preference given to professionals provided the means for large numbers of medical doctors and other educated workers to immigrate. Most often, the foreign professional immigrates because of higher salaries in the United States. For instance, by the mid-1970s more than half of the interns in municipal hospitals in New York City were Asian immigrant doctors. By 1976, about 40 percent of all Filipino doctors practiced in the United States. The most dramatic case was in 1972 when almost the entire graduating class of a new medical school in Thailand chartered a plane and flew to the United States.

In *Still the Golden Door: The Third World Comes to America,* David Reimers describes a typical pattern for Asian immigration, which begins with an Asian student coming as a nonimmigrant to complete his or her education. Near the end of the student's studies, the student finds a job and is given immigrant status. After a few years, the immigrant becomes a citizen and is able to sponsor, under the preference system, brothers and sisters as immigrants. In turn, the brothers and sisters can use the preference system to sponsor their spouses and children. This is why, according to Reimers, the 1965 legislation is often called the "brothers and sisters act."

The educational response to the new immigration is quite different and more complicated than the response in the early twentieth century. In an essay in a book he edited titled *Clamor at the Gates: The New American Immigration,* sociologist Nathan Glazer points out that immigrant education programs of the 1920s emphasized the teaching of English and the American way of life. Often, these Americanization programs included saluting and pledging allegiance to the flag, teaching an American diet, and convincing the student of the decadence of most foreign governments when compared to the United States.

The educational response to the new immigration, however, is complicated by court decisions and political divisions. The most important U.S. Supreme Court decision affecting new immigrants is *Lau et al.* v. *Nichols* (discussed in detail in Chapter 10). This 1974 decision required schools to provide special aid to students from families in which English was not the spoken language. Government and school officials assumed in the 1970s that the requirement for special help meant bilingual education. The use of bilingual education in the schools resulted in bitter political disputes in the 1980s.

Bilingual education is the product of efforts by leaders of the Mexican-American community to have the schools respond to the educational needs of their community's children. Essentially, they want their children to learn to function in the majority culture and at the same time maintain the traditions of the Mexican-American culture. This means using Spanish to teach English and teaching Mexican-American heritage. Bilingual education is important to political leaders dependent on the continuation of a cohesive Mexican-American bloc vote. Traditional Americanization programs threaten ethnic bloc votes because of the potential disintegration of ethnic ties as immigrants are integrated into the majority culture.

The political dispute over bilingual education erupted in the 1980s when the Reagan administration attacked bilingual education and supported English immersion methods. Immersion methods surround the child with English and do not use the language of the immigrant family for instruction. One reason for this attack was that most Mexican-American leaders were in the Democratic party, and from the Republican standpoint breaking up ethnic bloc votes was a means of reducing Democratic power. In fact, some members of the Republican party joined a movement opposing bilingual education and supporting the adoption of English as the official language of the Unites States. The movement for making English the official language is led by an organization called U.S. English, founded in 1983 by former Republican Senator S. I. Hayakawa.

In 1986, in reaction to the Reagan administration stand on bilingual education, the National Association of Bilingual Education announced increased political activities and intensified public relations efforts for bilingual education. Gene T. Chavez, the president of the association, warned, in reference to former Senator S. I. Hayakawa and U.S. English that "those who think this country can only tolerate one language" were more motivated by politics than educational concerns. At the same meeting the incoming president of the organization, Chicago school administrator Jose Gonzalez, attacked the Reagan administration and the Department of Education for entering an "unholy alliance" with right-wing groups opposing bilingual education, such as U.S. English, Save Our Schools, and the Heritage Foundation.

Within the Reagan administration, Secretary of Education William

Bennett attempted to reduce support for bilingual education by appointing opponents to the government's National Advisory and Coordinating Council on Bilingual Education. The new appointees expressed preference for immersing non-English-speaking children in the English language, rather than teaching them in a bilingual context. In addition, the new appointees favored giving more power to local officials to determine programs.

The current dispute over bilingual education reflects the traditional problem for the public schools in educating immigrants. Should the public schools strive to protect the culture of immigrant groups or should they focus on integration into the dominant culture? Certainly, the Americanization programs of the 1920s worked for cultural integration. Creating a homogeneous culture is one of the historic goals of American public schools. However, current arguments stress the contributions diverse ethnic groups can make in shaping American culture. Also, there is less certainty in the 1980s about who will define the dominant culture for Americanization programs.

Besides the problem of the language and culture of the public schools, there is the continuing problem of educational discrimination against immigrant groups. Current discrimination against Asian-Americans can be compared to the plight of the Jews in the 1920s who were discriminated against in higher education by a quota system on enrollments. *Time* magazine reported in 1987 that as a result of quota systems many qualified Asian-Americans were being refused admission to major universities. The largest number of complaints centered on the admission policies of the University of California at Berkeley. *Time* quotes the cochairperson of the Asian American Task Force on University Admissions, Alameda County Superior Court Judge Ken Kawaichi, that university administrators envision a campus that "is mostly white, mostly upper class with limited numbers of blacks, Hispanics and Asians. One day they looked around and said, 'My goodness, look at this campus. What are all these Asian people doing here?' Then they started tinkering with the system."

The issues of discrimination and Americanization probably will be resolved for most immigrant groups through the use of political power in the educational system. Those groups that are able to organize sufficient political power will have the schools serve their needs. Those who are unable to exercise political power will have to accept whatever programs are developed within the schools. In this context, achieving equality of educational opportunity is primarily a political issue.

Exercises

1. To understand educational aspirations and debates over education in the black community, read and compare Booker T. Washington's *Up From Slavery* and W. E. B. DuBois's *The Souls of Black Folk*.

2. Check with a local school district to find out how it has complied with Title VI of the 1964 Civil Rights Act.
3. Investigate a local school to determine the distribution of minority students in the curriculum and in ability groups.
4. Contact a local school system to find out the degree of faculty integration and student integration.
5. Conduct a small survey of students in a local school system to determine levels of educational aspirations.

Suggested Readings and Works Cited in Chapter

Ballantine, Jeanne. *The Sociology of Education.* Englewood Cliffs, N.J.: Prentice-Hall, 1983. Chapter 4 is devoted to a discussion of sexism in education.

Borman, Kathryn M. and Joel Spring. *Schools in Central Cities.* New York: Longman, 1984. Chapter 6 analyzes the impact of desegregation on the curriculum.

Brand, David. "The New Whiz Kids." *Time* 130, no. 1 (August 31, 1987). A report of the educational aspirations and problems of Asian-American students.

Crawford, James. "Bilingual Educators Seeking Strategies to Counter Attacks." *Education Week* 5, no. 28 (April 9, 1986): 1, 9. A report of recent political battles over bilingual education.

Glazer, Nathan. "Immigrants and Education." *Clamor at the Gates*: The New American Immigration, edited by Nathan Glazer. San Francisco: Institute for Contemporary Affairs, 1985, pp. 213–241. Analysis of education policies regarding the new immigrants.

Kluger, Richard. *Simple Justice.* New York: Random House, 1975. A good history of *Brown* v. *Board of Education* and the struggle for equality.

Levine, Daniel, and Robert Havighurst. *Society and Education: Sixth Edition.* Boston: Allyn and Bacon, 1984. Chapter 18 is devoted to women and education.

O'Reilly, Patricia, and Kathryn Borman. "Sexism in Education: Documented Biases, Destructive Practices and Some Hope for the Future." *Theory into Practice* 23, no. 2 (Spring 1984). A good summary of information on institutional sexism in education.

Orfield, Gary. *The Reconstruction of Southern Education: The Schools and the 1964 Civil Rights Act.* New York: Wiley-Interscience, 1969. A study of the desegregation of southern schools following the passage of the 1964 Civil Rights Act.

Reimers, David. *Still the Golden Door: The Third World Comes to America.* New York: Columbia University Press, 1985. A history and portrait of recent immigrants to the United States.

Rist, Ray. *Desegregated Schools: Appraisals of an American Experiment.* New York: Academic Press, 1979. This book contains a collection of six studies of the process of desegregation within both northern and southern schools.

Rossell, Christine. "Magnet Schools as a Desegregation Tool." *Urban Education* 14, no. 3 (October 1979). A study of the role of magnet schools in desegregation plans.

Smylie, Mark. "Reducing Racial Isolation in Large School Districts: The Comparative Effectiveness of Mandatory and Voluntary Strategies." *Urban Education* 17, no. 4

(January 1983). A good analysis of the different types of school desegregation plans.

Spring, Joel. *The Sorting Machine: National Educational Policy Since 1945.* New York: Longman, 1976. Chapters 4, 5, and 6 provide a history of the civil rights movement and school desegregation.

Wilson, William J. *The Declining Significance of Race: Blacks and Changing American Institutions.* Chicago: University of Chicago Press, 1979. A study of the history and recent social and economic conditions of the black population in the United States.

II

POWER AND CONTROL IN AMERICAN EDUCATION

6

Power and Control in the Local School District

Two of the major issues related to the control of American education in local school districts have been the extent to which members of the local boards of education represent the population of the schools, and the actual amount of power wielded by boards of education in relation to the professional staffs of schools. The issue of representation concerns whether the membership on boards of education should reflect the social composition of the local population. The question of the power relationship between boards of education and professional staffs of schools considers what educational matters should be controlled by boards of education and what educational matters should be controlled by school administrators and teachers.

To understand the importance of these issues, one must first consider the organization of education at the local level in the United States. In most American communities some form of appointed or elected board of education has the responsibility of representing public opinion in school matters. Whether or not the board is appointed or elected and how it is appointed or elected varies from community to community. In general, boards of education formulate educational policy, which is then administered by the school staff. In the local school district the superintendent of schools has the responsibility for administering educational policy and advising the board on the needs of the local school system.

The central office staff is usually composed of an administrative staff, which deals with the overall organization of the school system's curriculum, financial matters, personnel policies, and any programs that affect all schools within a district. In terms of the control of local education, the central office staff is very important because it often controls the lines of communication between the building principals and teachers and the superintendent. Building principals have the responsibility of administering school policy within their particular elementary or secondary school.

The reader should be cautioned that this description of organization in the local district is a gross oversimplification of the actual lines of power and communication that exist within each district. For instance, teachers often deal directly with the board of education when they are organized into a local association for the purpose of collective bargaining for wages and work conditions. One of the purposes of this chapter is to help the reader understand the complicated nature of these relationships.

The first two sections of this chapter deal with the social composition of boards of education, the political world in which they function, and the extent of their governing power over schools. The third section deals with the internal relationships between members of the school staff. The fourth and final sections deal with the relationship between the board of education and the professional staff with regard to control of educational policy.

The Social Composition and Political World of Boards of Education

A traditional criticism of boards of education in the twentieth century has been that their membership constitutes an elite. What is meant by "elite" is that the membership primarily is drawn from the professional and business groups in the local community. This is not as true in rural communities, where there is often heavy representation from the farm community. Most boards of education in the United States tend to be composed of white male professional or business persons. The representation from this group on boards of education tends to be out of proportion to their actual numbers, in comparison with the rest of the population. In other words, the membership of boards of education in the United States tends not to reflect the social composition of the local community.

This general picture of the composition of boards of education in local school districts is reflected in national statistics. Nationally, a disproportionate number of board members are male, have college educations, are in upper-income groups, and have high-status occupations. There are regional variations in the social composition of school boards. These variations are reflected in the annual survey of school board members published each January in the *American School Board Journal*. In their survey published in January 1984 they found that, nationally, 64.9 percent of school board members had four or more years of college, 55 percent held professional or managerial positions, 93.1 percent were white, 62.9 percent were men, and 53.2 percent had total family incomes over $40,000.

The preceding national figures reflect neither recent important changes nor regional differences. For instance, the percentage of women on school boards has increased dramatically in recent years. Between 1982 and 1983 the percentage of women on school boards increased from 28.3 percent to 37.1 percent. During the same period the number of school board members holding professional and managerial positions declined from 66.6 percent to 55 percent. It is impossible to determine from the *American School Board Journal* survey how much of this change in the occupations of school board members is a reflection of increased participation by women. It is also difficult from these figures to identify the general social and economic status of women board members because many are identified as homemakers. The actual status of homemakers varies with the income and occupation of the head of the household.

If these figures are broken down by region, the southern states located south of a line running from Texas to Virginia appear to have the most elite school boards. In these southern states 66.4 percent of school board members (as opposed to 53.2 percent nationally) have total family incomes over $40,000. Indeed, the southern states have the highest number of board members with family incomes over $100,000. For the southern states, the figure for incomes over $100,000 was 14.4 percent, whereas it was 6.8 percent for the nation as a whole. On the other hand, there was a larger minority population on southern school boards, with membership being 79.7 percent white.

The western region bounded by Montana, North Dakota, New Mexico, and Oklahoma has the lowest average income for school board members. In this region 42.9 percent have family incomes over $40,000, with 3.7 percent over $100,000. In this region 41.9 percent of the school board members are women. The other region of the country tend to be similar to each other. The Pacific region bounded by Alaska, Utah, California, and Hawaii reported 53 percent of family incomes of board members over $40,000, with a female membership of 44.8 percent and a white membership of 94.8 percent. In the central region bounded by Minnesota, Ohio, Kentucky, and Missouri, 53 percent of board members have family incomes over $40,000; female membership is 34.9 percent and white membership is 95.4 percent. In the northeast region bounded by Maine, Pennsylvania, and Maryland, 50.5 percent of board members have family incomes over $40,000, with a female membership of 35.2 percent and a white membership of 96.6 percent.

Some educators view the elite nature of the social composition of school boards as a positive asset to the local school district. Joseph M. Cronin in his history, *The Control of Urban Schools,* found that educators during the early part of the twentieth century believed it was important to have successful and well-educated men on the school board because this social group was more knowledgeable and more interested in education than the rest of the popu-lation. In fact, the whole trend in the early part of the twentieth century toward centralization and reduction in size of urban school boards was premised on the idea of limiting public participation in school affairs to the social leaders of the community. Opposition to this trend came from organized labor, which felt that board membership drawn from only one sector of the community would result in the domination of school policy by certain political and economic views.

One way to approach this issue is to compare the educational priorities of school board members with those of the general public. The major problem in these comparisons is that the nature of the school board member's job might create different priorities than those held by the general public. For instance, according to the survey published in the January 1982 issue of the *American School Board Journal,* the two top concerns of school board members were decreasing enrollments and the declining tax base. Of course, these concerns reflected the reality of problems facing local school districts. On the other hand, the general public rated discipline and drug abuse as their two top concerns.

The differences between the public and board members on these two different sets of concerns can be explained by the nature of the board members' tasks. This is the case with curriculum reform. The general public ranks curriculum reform as its third highest concern. School board members rank curriculum reform as sixth, after decreasing enrollment, declining tax base, cutting staff, collective bargaining, and evaluating teachers. In general, when one compares the concerns of board members with those of the public, one can conclude that board members are more concerned with the financial and business aspects of schooling while the public, which votes them into office, is more concerned with interpersonal actions of students, learning, and teaching. One could argue that the business and financial orientation of school board members is a reflection of their own business backgrounds. One could also argue that school board members tend to rely upon the school staff to deal with problems of curriculum and instruction, whereas they focus on general management issues.

Whatever the explanation, there is a recognized difference between public and board member concerns about the educational system. This raises the issue of elite representation on boards of education. Whether or not school boards should be composed of elite members of the community depends on one's concept of representation. There are two types of representation—trustee or delegate. A trustee form of representation acts to achieve a general common good or public interest. For instance, a school board member acting as a trustee would make decisions based on what she or he believes is good for the general public. These types of decisions might often be contrary to what the public actually wants. In other words, the public interest or general good as defined by the board member might not represent the true wishes of the public. Support of trustee forms of representation is premised on the idea that decisions, particularly about social institutions such as schools, should be removed from the immediate control of the general population. The reason one wants an elite board membership that is well educated and successful is to assure that decision making conforms to what the elite believes is the public good.

Delegate form of representation attempts to conform to the desires of the population. Decision making is based on what the representative believes is wanted by the public. This form of representation is preferred by those who believe that social institutions should function according to what people want and not on the basis of some individual's personal interpretation of the public good. It is argued that those who try to make decisions based on a set of beliefs about what constitutes the public good cannot separate their own beliefs from the decision-making process. The issue of trustee versus delegate representation has become an important issue in the controversy over representation of minority groups on boards of education. To understand this issue one must consider the relationship between what type of representation is used and the particular organization of school board elections that results from it.

Most school board elections in the United States have been organized around the concept of trustee representation, in order to limit public participation in direct control of school board affairs. This has been accomplished through at-large and nonpartisan elections. In at-large elections a person running for the school board must be elected by the entire voting population of a school district. This means a person must have enough money and organizational support to campaign throughout the entire school system. In contrast, during the nineteenth century the voting districts for many school board elections were confined to limited geographical areas within a school district. In such situations a person did not need a great deal of financial backing to campaign within a small area and could win elections based on neighborhood contacts. This method of election made it easier for the average person to win elections to the school board. It can be argued that at-large elections tend to favor trustee forms of representation, while the other type of election favors delegate forms of representation because there is more direct contact between the elector and the elected.

Nonpartisan elections also tend to favor the election of elites to school boards. In one of the most complete studies of the issue, *Nonpartisan Elections and the Case for Party Politics,* Willis Hawley argues that nonpartisan elections create a partisan bias in favor of Republicans. In this argument he is associating "Republican" with community elites. Nonpartisan means that regular political parties cannot nominate and campaign for a particular candidate. When this is the case, Hawley argues, informal networks begin to operate to select and provide support for candidates. These informal networks are generally composed of civic-business clubs such as the Chamber of Commerce, Kiwanis Club, Rotary, and other luncheon-service clubs.

As mentioned previously, at-large and nonpartisan elections have created a problem for those seeking representation of minority groups on boards of education. Members of minority groups do not often have access to the informal networks described in the previous paragraph. In addition, it is often difficult for a member of a minority group to win election in an at-large campaign because of lack of support from white voters. On the other hand, it would be much easier for minority groups to win representation on school boards if board members were elected from a small geographical area that primarily included members of that minority group.

An example of this is the change that took place in the Dallas, Texas, school district that ended in 1974 its method of electing a nine-member board of education by at-large elections. The new method of election, which was mandated by the Texas legislature in 1973, divided the school system into nine districts of approximately 89,500 each. The change to election by district did have a significant effect on the social composition of the board of education, because it allowed representation of minority members. Before 1974 the board of education was composed primarily of whites. After 1974 the board has been composed of six Anglos, two blacks, and one Mexican-American.

In most cases, local school board membership still tends to be closely related to the informal power structure of the local community. This is reflected in the importance of civic business clubs and educational organizations as routes to board membership. It is also reflected in board members' statements about the kinds of encouragement they received. Although in most elections to government positions the support of a political party is very important, this is not the case in elections of school board members. L. Harmon Zeigler and M. Kent Jennings report in their study, *Governing American Schools: Political Interaction in Local School Districts,* that nearly a quarter of their national sample of school board members claimed that no individual or group requested them to run for the board. On the other hand, 29 percent of board members claimed they received encouragement from other board members to run for the board, 21 percent received requests from formal citizen groups, 13 percent claimed they received requests from governmental and political figures to become members of the board, and the remainder of board members stated they were requested to run for the board by friends and professional school personnel.

What all this means is that understanding the informal power structure of a local community is extremely important for understanding the politics and policies of local boards of education. This has been highlighted in recent years in struggles over school desegregation. David Kirby et al. in their study of *Political Strategies in Northern School Desegregation* found that school desegregation has been a political decision made by elites and not by the masses. Their study surveyed 91 cities ranging in size from 50,000 to large cities over 250,000. The primary goal of the study was to look at the major political actors in relationship to the characteristics of the cities and the political structure of their educational systems. The study looked specifically at the civil rights movement, the school board, the superintendent, civic leaders, and white protest against desegregation plans. To support their conclusion that elites made the most important decisions regarding school desegregation, they provided a statistical overview of elite membership on school boards. In their sample drawn from 91 cities, over 50 percent of the membership of civic elites were bankers, industrialists, and heads of local businesses. The others included lawyers, heads of local utilities, newspaper people, civic association executives, clergy, university administrators, and professionals. Only 5 percent of this civic leadership were identified as liberals representing labor and civil rights organizations.

The nature of the informal power structure varies from community to community. In their study entitled *Politics, Power, Polls, and School Elections,* Michael Y. Nunnery and Ralph B. Kimbrough have defined several different power structures that can exist within local schools. They argue that understanding the nature of the local power structure is important for understanding both the politics of the board of education and the community support structure and the methods used to gain support for educational policies.

Nunnery and Kimbrough argue that there are four basic types of local power structures, ranging from monopolistic systems to those characterized by democratic pluralism. A community with a monopolistic power structure is controlled by a single group of businessmen, professionals, and politicians. Sometimes this occurs in one-industry towns or in rural areas governed by groups of large landowners. Within a monopolistic system, a few top influentials make the major decisions for the community. In these systems there is characteristically very little conflict and confrontation.

A second, somewhat-closed system is the multigroup and noncompetitive power structure. In this power structure, although rival groups exist within the structure seeking their own economic advantage, there is still general agreement about the basic policies to be followed within the local community. For instance, leaders of the different groups within this power structure might compete for such things as contracts for building schools and who will provide the schools with insurance, but still agree upon general educational policy.

The third type of power structure that affects board of education politics is one characterized by competition between elite groups. This very often occurs when a community is undergoing social change, such as a rural community rapidly changing into a suburban community. In this case, major competition is seen between the established and the newer elite groups over questions such as zoning, planning, industrialism, and education. There are frequent differences of opinion between competing elite groups about basic school policy. For instance, a traditional rural-community elite might place less emphasis on preparation for college than a new elite associated with suburban development. Although strong conflict exists in this structure between competing elite groups, there is still little general citizen participation in the power structure.

The fourth type of power structure is characterized by democratic pluralism, where the system is continually open to new persons and groups gaining positions of power. Very often, the people who are influential in the community decision-making process change, depending upon the issue being considered. For instance, people who are influential in the educational decision-making process might be different from those involved in other community affairs. Within this structure there is a great deal of citizen participation.

Nunnery and Kimbrough believe that for a school administrator to work effectively, it is eessential that he or she understand the power structure within the local community. It is equally true that in order to understand the politics of the local school board and its policies, one must understand the power structure that is responsible for election or appointment to the board. One of the difficulties in doing this is being able to generalize from one community to another. No two communities are necessarily alike in terms of their power structures and the informal networks that lead to board membership. Each community must be studied to determine its particular power structure.

Nunnery and Kimbrough have suggested some methods that school administrators can use to determine the nature of the local power structure. These methods are also valuable to the student and local citizen in coming to understand the political and social forces behind the school board. Nunnery and Kimbrough recommend the following procedure. First, a person should become acquainted with the variety of literature on community power structures as a basis for interpreting any data gathered. Second, a person should become acquainted with the leaders in different areas of the community. Nunnery and Kimbrough recommend beginning with the heads of the local chamber of commerce, women's clubs, unions, churches, political parties, newspapers, and radio and television stations. In addition, prominent attorneys, physicians, and bankers should be contacted.

In discussions with these persons questions should be asked about important issues, problems, and decisions; notes should be taken with regard to the names most frequently mentioned. Also, discussion should be encouraged about whom the community leaders think are the most influential people in the community. From these conversations a person can begin piecing together an outline of the relationships between those people considered the most influential in the community. Next, one should check the membership lists of local boards of directors of financial institutions, community groups, and the chamber of commerce. With this information a person should be able to outline the informal power structure of the community. After this is done, the results can be tested through participation in community activites, in order to observe the degree of citizen participation and the importance of the power structure in the decision-making process.

The same methods recommended by Nunnery and Kimbrough can be directly applied to a study of the membership of the local board of education. Interviews with current and former board members can reveal why they got involved in board activities and their relationship to the general community power structure. Of extreme importance in this regard are informal contacts. One can determine through both membership lists of organizations and direct questions whether or not a great deal of informal contact takes place among board members or between themselves and other members of the local power structure. Very often decisions about school issues and school board participation are made at informal social gatherings and parties in homes and in social clubs. This is true both for economic elite groups such as businessmen and professionals, and for social-interest groups such as racial and ethnic organizations.

Although the linkage between the school board and the community power structure is important for understanding the actions of board members, it is also important for understanding the linkages between the board and the school administration. It is essential in terms of being effective and for job protection for the superintendent of schools to have a cooperative and friendly board of education. For this reason, school administrators tend to favor school board members who have successful business or professional backgrounds.

In *The School Managers: Power and Conflict in American Public Education,* Donald McCarty and Charles Ramsey provide a classification of the relationships between community power structures, school boards, and administrative styles. They assume that the type of community power structure determines the nature of the school board and the administrative style of the superintendent. They divide community power structures into the following:

1. dominated
2. factional
3. pluralistic
4. inert

In dominated communities majority power is exercised by a few persons or one person. In most cases, these people are part of the community's economic elite, though in some cases they could be leaders of ethnic, religious, or political groups. Factional communities are characterized usually by two factions competing for power. Very often these factions differ in values, particularly religious values. Pluralistic communities have a great deal of competition between a variety of community-interest groups with no single group dominating school policies. And in inert communities, there is no visible power structure and there is little display of public interest in the schools.

McCarty and Ramsey argue that the following relations exist between these power structures and types of school boards and superintendent styles:

Community *Power Structures*	*Types of* *School Boards*	*Superintendent* *Styles*
1. Dominated	1. Dominated	1. Functionary
2. Factional	2. Factional	2. Political
3. Pluralistic	3. Pluralistic	3. Adviser
4. Inert	4. Sanctioning	4. Decision making

In a *dominated* community, the local elite control access to membership on the school board and, consequently, control school board policies. In order to retain his or her position, the superintendent must follow the wishes of the community elite. McCarty and Ramsey studied one dominated community where a superintendent protested his firing by a school board acting against the wishes of the local power elite. In response to the situation, the community elite met in the offices of a local bank and decided, in order to avoid community conflict, to let the superintendent be fired. At the same time, they decided the school board had gotten out of control. The most respected member of the elite group was made chairman of the school board's nomination committee and its membership was selected to assure elite control. Traditionally, those recommended by the nomination committee were elected to the school board without opposition. And finally, the leading members of the community kept a close watch on the nominating committee for several years to assure the selection of candidates they approved.

In a *factional* community, the survival of a superintendent depends on his or her ability to function as a political strategist balancing the concerns of each community faction. In a factional community studied by McCarty and Ramsey, the major competing groups were a permissive Jewish and a conservative Catholic population. The two groups represented almost equal populations in the school district, and the control of the school board shifted from group to group in each highly contested election. The campaigns were very emotional, with each group accusing the other of undermining the quality of education. When McCarty and Ramsey arrived in the community, liberals on the school board had lost their majority to conservatives who immediately fired the superintendent. The fired superintendent, according to McCarty and Ramsey, failed as a political strategist because he appeared to favor the previous liberal majority.

The competition among a variety of groups in a *pluralistic* community results in constantly shifting coalitions on the school board. In the community studied by McCarty and Ramsey, a dispute over a bond issue created a coalition of Catholics, the Chamber of Commerce, and a labor union in opposition, and Protestant churches and the PTA in support. The superintendent in this community played the role of the professional adviser. On the bond issue, his support was given in professional statements about the need for additional classrooms and more teachers. In performing the role of professional adviser to a pluralistic board, the superintendent should move cautiously to avoid adverse community reaction to proposals for change.

And finally, *inert* communities give the majority of power over school issues to the superintendent. McCarty and Ramsey describe inert communities as being ideologically homogeneous and without a sense of purpose. In most situations, the composition of the board is indirectly controlled by the superintendent. Board members turn to the superintendent for leadership and decision making. In some cases, McCarty and Ramsey report, the superintendent claimed that board members accepted 99 percent of his or her proposals. Very seldom in inert communities does the board turn to leaders outside of the school system for advice on educational matters.

In all four of these categories, superintendents prefer school board members who have successful business or professional backgrounds. In *Governing American Schools,* Zeigler and Jennings found that board members from lower socioeconomic groups tend to be more involved in administrative detail than those from higher social and economic groups. From the standpoint of the superintendent, board-member involvement in administrative details can restrict the actions of the administrative staff. In most cases, superintendents prefer board members to restrict their activities to general educational policies.

This finding supports the argument given in the early part of the twentieth century that board membership should be restricted to the successful and educated because of their greater interest in educational policy. But this does not mean that lower-status board members are not interested in educational policy. What it does mean is that they have a greater interest in the actual control of the educational system. In fact, higher-status board members gave more importance than did lower-status board members to the opinion of the superintendent; consequently, there was less conflict between higher-status board members and the superintendent than between lower-status board members and the superintendent. This might be because the superintendent and the higher-status board members tend to share the same social world. They often attend the same social gatherings and belong to the same civic-service clubs and other social organizations. This situation may result in the superintendent and the board members sharing the same point of view about the components of a good educational program and other social and economic policies.

The major objection to the elitist composition of American school boards is that they do not reflect the interests and opinions of all members of the community. Basic disagreements can occur between social groups in our society over educational policy. For instance, higher-status groups in a community may give strong support to a vocational program for lower-status children, whereas lower-status groups may disapprove of this type of program because they want a college-preparatory program for their children as a means of providing upward mobility. Which group is right in this case is not important in terms of this discussion. What is important is that fundamental differences between social groups can exist over educational policy. Because of the social composition of school boards and their linkage to the informal power structures of local communities, however, these differences are not reflected in debates between school board members.

The Governing Power of Boards of Education

The discussion of elite membership of boards of education may seem meaningless when one begins to consider the actual authority of school boards. Although boards of education are supposed to be important mechanisms for achieving local control of the schools, most board members today feel that they have very little real power over the schools and that what little power they have is being rapidly eroded by other areas of government and other organizations.

During the 1970s a flood of articles began to appear in education magazines about the lost authority of boards of education in the United States. Lee K. Davis, a member and former chairperson of the Orange County School Board in Florida, summarized this point of view in an article in the November 1976 issue of *Educational Leadership* titled "The School Board's Struggle to Survive." Among the factors listed by Davis as causing the erosion of school board authority are increased state and federal involvement in education policy, increased regulation from court decisions, and the unionization of teachers. For instance, Davis cited the example of his own school district, the thirty-second largest in the United States, where the majority of time-consuming education-related issues were initiated outside the local system.

Court decisions dealing with desegregation, student rights, teacher rights, and corporal punishment have forced school boards to devote a great deal of attention to complying with these court orders. State legislatures and the federal government increasingly have become involved in matters concerning school curricula and, consequently, they have limited the degree of control exercised by school boards over these issues. State legislatures are mandating specific programs such as vocational education, sex education, and social studies courses, as well as programs in other areas of the curriculum. In addition, financial pressures have forced local school districts to seek more and more federal money. Most money from the federal government is "categorical," which means that it is designated for use in particular programs and in compliance with federal guidelines. Like state-mandated curricula, all federal guidelines have restricted the power of the local board of education to control the local school curriculum.

Teacher unionization has restricted the power of boards to control personnel matters. In the past, boards of education had the final voice about the hiring of teachers in the local district. Boards also had greater control over issues of salary and hiring and firing. Today, in many districts around the country this power is shared with teacher organizations, which function as collective bargaining units. Highly detailed contracts are negotiated between teacher organizations and school boards. In addition, many teacher organizations are demanding greater control of educational policy and the curriculum.

All these conditions have led to a general attitude of despair among board members around the country who feel that the authority of boards of education has been eroded. To put this situation in perspective, one must consider how school boards have traditionally functioned in the twentieth century.

Most literature on the history of education seems to agree that school boards have been most active and involved when there is some crisis within the schools and the community. In most such cases, board members tend to rely heavily upon the actions and opinions of the local school administrative staff. The situation that is most likely to make school boards the center of political activity is when major changes occur in the social composition of the local population or some particular school controversy arises dealing with sex or religion.

Examples of major school board activity resulting from population shifts can be found in a number of community studies. Herbert Gans's study of Levittown provides one example of a new population coming into conflict with the local power structure and school administration. Levittown was a planned community built in what had been a rural area. As the new residents moved into the community from nearby urban areas they began to demand improved college-preparatory programs and the introduction of what were considered more educationally advanced programs. When new residents began to participate in elections to the school board, their candidates placed direct pressure for change upon the rather traditional rural school administration that had previously existed in the area.

The community of "Robertsdale" described in Lawrence Iannaccone and Frank W. Lutz's *Politics, Power and Policy: The Governing of Local School Districts* is another example of studies of heightened school board involvement and activity. This study of "Robertsdale" is about a school controversy in a growing suburban community, where a new power structure begins to come into conflict with an already existing structure. In this case the school superintendent had direct connections to the existing informal power structure and was forced to resign after the incumbents on the board lost in the election.

Along with changes in the social composition of the local population, controversies over sex, religion, and politics can spark increased school board activity and involvement in the schools. Such controversies are very difficult to predict. Sometimes a controversy begins when only a few people in a community object to books that are being used in classes or made available to students in the libraries. During the 1950s, members of so-called patriotic organizations stood watch in many communities to ensure that books considered "communistic" did not enter the school system. Many communities and school systems were torn apart during this period by attacks from such vigilante-type groups. Sex education and books with sexual content can create similar conflicts. In the early 1970s, the novels of the well-known writer Kurt Vonnegut were removed from the shelves of school libraries and the reading lists for English classes in some communities because of pressure from local groups. One school system in North Dakota burned Vonnegut's books in the school furnace.

The most famous school controversy of the early 1970s took place in Kanawha County, West Virginia, in September 1974, when protestors appeared at the schools demanding their closure because in their opinion teachers were using allegedly dirty, anti-God, anti-American textbooks. Local coal miners struck in sympathy with the protest. The miners' strike and spreading school boycott resulted in a $2 million loss, the shooting of two men, firings on school buses, and the bombing of elementary schools. State troopers and the FBI were required to restore order to the school system.

In some ways these examples illustrate the lack of involvement in and control of most school matters by local boards of education. Textbook and library selections are usually determined by the school administrative staff or a teacher committee and become major concerns of the community and school board only when a local person or group protests their contents. Schoolbook controversies are not common to all school systems; in fact, when one considers the number of school systems in the United States, they are rare. The content of books is certainly an important part of education, and in most communities control over the choice of textbooks is largely in the hands of the professional staff. The increased involvement and activity of school boards during periods of population change also highlights their lack of activity when these conditions are not present.

The important point about these examples is that the erosion of school board authority is not simply a product of the 1970s, but has been a problem for some time. In the 1960s James Koerner wrote a book called *Who Controls American Education?* in which he argued that the control of American education had been taken over by the professional educator. At the local level this meant that the majority of control was held by the school staff, with the board of education just rubber-stamping the decisions made by the administrative staff. Only situations like those described above sparked board involvement in the actual control of the schools.

If the real control of local education is in the hands of the administrative staff, then the discussion of the elite membership of boards of education is largely academic. The combination of local administrative power, state and federal regulation, and court decisions may have destroyed any pretense of local control of education, as supposedly exercised by boards of education. To understand the interrelationships between board and administrative control of local education issues, we must next look at the political world of the local superintendent and administrative staff.

The Political World of the School Administrative Staff

In the November 1975 issue of *Educational Leadership*, Lee Hansen, an associate superintendent for the Ann Arbor Public Schools, Michigan, predicted the imminent rise of what he called the "political superintendent." Hansen argued that such an individual would be a politican first and an educator second. The important qualities of the political superintendent would be communication skills, ability to manage public opinion, ability to use the informal power structure, and ability to create an atmosphere of openness and trust.

Hansen based his prediction of the rise of the political superintendent upon what he viewed as the collapse of the traditional political world of the superintendent. He argued that superintendents in the 1960s could feel fairly confident of their ability to collect, control, and use power. During this period, community power structures were relatively dominant over the community and stable; coalitions of support were easy to assemble and maintain; and a basic faith in education and educators still existed. Since the 1960s there has been a steady collapse of the power base of most superintendents. Like boards of education, superintendents are finding more and more areas of decision making being assumed by state and federal governments. State-aid formulas, mandated programs, and educational standards have taken away many decisions that traditionally would have been made by the administrative staff. In addition, federal programs have turned superintendents into administrators of programs that they did not initiate and in whose basic design they did not participate.

On the local level, the modern superintendent has had to contend with community power structures that are more competitive than those in the past. In many communities, monopolistic power structures have changed and are being replaced by ones based on democratic pluralism, in which there are ideological splits between liberals and conservatives, as well as pressures from organized minority groups and community groups lobbying for special programs. In addition, teacher unionization and organized student-rights groups have made it difficult for superintendents to deal in areas they have traditionally controlled.

The growth in democratic pluralism in local community power structures is an extremely important factor in changing superintendents' actions within local communities. As mentioned, the traditional political world of the superintendent was most often centered around a fairly stable and clearly defined informal power structure. To both attain and remain in the position of superintendent, an individual had to be accepted by the local power structure. Most superintendents joined the local chamber of commerce or other civic-service organizations and mixed informally with members of the community's elite. Once established within a community, a superintendent often participated informally in the selection of local candidates for school board elections. An astute superintendent would build a power base by creating a loyal community following through organizations like the PTA, and by winning the loyalty of the community elite through formal and informal contacts.

In both the traditional and emerging political worlds of superintendents, their actions in relationship to the power structure are conditioned by their aspirations. Ernest House, in *The Politics of Educational Innovation*, has described two aspirations that are characteristic of superintendents. One superintendent aspires to remain within the community as long as possible and eventually plans to retire from the position. House calls this type of superintendent "place bound." The other superintendent views his current position as one step to another, better superintendent's position. House calls this type of superintendent "career bound" and characterizes his actions as primarily directed toward gaining recognition outside the local community, as a means of attracting other job offers.

These two types of superintendents have different types of relationships with the local power structure. Both depend on its support for initial appointment to the position. But after acquiring the job, the "place bound" superintendent is concerned about acquiring a loyal following among members of the community and establishing support from the local power structure, whereas the "career bound" superintendent is more interested in winning recognition at either the state or national level. The "career bound" superintendent tends to show less loyalty to desires of the local power structure and spends less energy on building a following within the local community.

The relationship between the superintendent and the local power structure is important in determining the relationship between the school board and the superintendent. In situations where the school board is directly linked to a monopolistic power structure and a "place bound" superintendent has close ties and support from the local structure, there will probably be little conflict between the board and the superintendent; the board will probably give more and more of its prerogatives and authority to the superintendent. On the surface, it would thus appear that the superintendent and administrative staff really run the schools, and that the board has a diminished role. In reality, the superintendent is given increased authority as long as his actions and decisions are congruent with the desires and educational goals of the monopolistic power structure.

The opposite situation prevails when there is a "career bound" superintendent and a power structure characterized by democratic pluralism. This is very often the situation today in large and medium-sized cities. In these cases there tends to be more conflict between the board and the superintendent and more school board involvement in school affairs. Superintendents might find themselves dealing with both the traditional community power structure and new pressure groups representing the demands of racial and ethnic minorities, women's groups, and other groups representing specific demands on the schools. It is for these situations that Hansen has called for the training of political superintendents who are able to build a power base on the demands of these often conflicting groups.

Relationship with the community is only one aspect of the political world of the superintendent. The other is relationship with the central office staff of the local school system, which includes the assistant superintendents, a financial officer, recordkeepers for the school system, and the directors of special programs. This group is supposed to help the superintendent run the school system. This group also can exercise a great deal of control over the superintendent and school policy.

A study by Joseph McGivney and James Haught titled "The Politics of Education: A View from the Perspective of the Central Office Staff" argues that one of the inherent goals of the administrative staff is to maintain control over the educational system. Techniques used by the staff to maintain its power include controlling communication between groups attempting to place pressure on the school system. In addition, the members of the central office staff play a key role as gatekeepers of information flow between a school's building principal and school staff, and the superintendent and the board of education. Members of the central office staff hold meetings with principals, teachers, and students. They also hold meetings with the superintendent and school board committees, in which they convey information and concerns from the rest of the school system. This gatekeeping function can be very important in influencing educational policy.

McGivney and Haught found that through the control of information the central office staff has a major effect on the decision-making process of the board of education. Boards of education seldom reject proposals that come from the central office. Proposals from outside groups that are contrary to the desires of the central office staff are often intercepted by the staff before they reach the board. One technique the central office staff can use against outside groups is to question their information base and their sincerity.

House has argued in *The Politics of Educational Innovation* that the gatekeeping functions of the central office staff are pivotal to any attempts to change or introduce new programs into a local school system. The staff controls the flow of information to teachers about the program and the flow of information from the system to outside sources. House found in one case that the central office staff tended to manipulate information. In a special-education program for gifted children, the central staff of a local district did not tell one-third of the teachers that they had been listed in a proposal to the state as teachers of the gifted. Teachers also received this information from the state office only when the central office staff had informally approved the information.

House has described the central office staff as a type of elite governing group that can be found within any organization. There is some debate about whether the superintendent or the central office staff is more influential. In terms of introducing change into the educational system, it was found that the values of the inner-circle elite were more important in predicting innovation than those of the director and staff. In other words, the attitudes of the central office staff tend to be more important than the attitudes of the superintendent or teachers in influencing educational policy within a school system.

The central office staff cannot, of course, function independently of the superintendent. A new superintendent will attempt to organize a staff that will reflect his or her policies. But total staff change when a new superintendent begins usually is not possible, and there are usually many members of the central office staff who maintain their positions through a successive number of superintendents. These long-term staff members very often exercise a great deal of power within a school district.

The combined power of the central office staff and the superintendent has led writers (such as James Koerner in *Who Controls American Education?*) to argue that the real control of the school is in the hands of the professional educators who occupy those positions. Most decisions in a school district are turned over to the expertise of these professional groups. The role of the school board in most cases is to place its stamp of approval on decisions recommended by the superintendent and the central office staff. When this is the case, it can be argued that local public control of education has been replaced by local professional control of education.

On the other hand, the position can be taken that the real power in a local school district is actually in the hands of the informal power structure, which remains silent as long as the professional staff pursues policies that it approves. The approval of the informal power structure can be indicated through silence or through informal communication with the administrative staff. Informal communication can take place at social gatherings or at functions of civic-service organizations such as the chamber of commerce. It also can be the case that the informal power structure will choose a superintendent who will reflect its values and goals for the educational system. In turn, the superintendent will select and organize the school staff to reflect those values. In this situation, indirect control of the educational system by the local power structure is achieved by turning control of the school over to a "friendly" professional staff.

An argument can also be made that the expertise of the school staff can influence the board members and the informal power structure. That is, the superintendent and central office staff can attempt to control the opinions about education of the local power structure. One way of understanding this is to look at the relationships between superintendents and boards of education.

The Superintendent and the Board of Education

Zeigler and Jennings in their study, *Governing American Schools*, tried in their national survey to measure the methods a superintendent might use to control and influence the local board. They argued that there are specific ways in which this can be done. One way is through gatekeeping, or control of information received by the board. According to this argument, the superintendent is ideally situated to select the information that he or she wants the board to hear. In addition, superintendents can convince boards that most issues require technical expertise and should be decided on the basis of advice from the school staff.

Zeigler and Jennings attempted to measure the degree of gatekeeping in superintendent and board relationships, in the United States, by determining the degree of control exercised by superintendents over agenda setting at board meetings. Agenda setting is a very important political function at board of education meetings because it determines what will be discussed and in what order. In some situations a member of the board or a board committee may have responsibility for determining the agenda. In other cases it may be the superintendent, or the superintendent and a board member. If the superintendent determines the agenda, it means that he or she has a great deal of power as a gatekeeper to decide what issues will appear before the board.

Zeigler and Jennings found in their national survey that in 70 percent of the school districts in the United States the superintendent had the primary responsibility for setting the agenda, and in two-thirds of the districts superintendents were solely responsible for agenda setting. Zeigler and Jennings felt these findings indicated that superintendents did occupy powerful gatekeeping positions and had the potential power to strongly influence board members.

The other measurement made by Zeigler and Jennings was to ask board members to name their four most important sources of educational information of a technical or professional nature. The purpose was to determine how much control superintendents had over the information received by the board. The study found that in over half the districts, the proportion of information received from the superintendent was over 30 percent. Even though this indicated that a sizable amount of information passed through the hands of the superintendent to board members, it was not enough to support the argument for the gatekeeping function of superintendents with regard to educational information. Determination of the agenda was a more important function.

Another attempt made by the same team to measure the influence of superintendents over board members was to look at the number of hours per week a superintendent was in contact with board members. They found that the median number of hours was fewer than four per week, and that one-third of districts had superintendents who spent more than five hours per week with board members. Zeigler and Jennings compared these findings with the level of board opposition to the superintendent. They found that there tends to be more interaction between board members and superintendents when there is greater conflict between them. This finding supports the argument that boards become more active and involved in school affairs during periods of conflict.

Zeigler and Jennings's national study highlighted important differences between urban, suburban, and small-town school boards and superintendents. For instance, Zeigler and Jennings were interested in the role played by indoctrination of new board members in the gaining and maintaining of power by superintendents. They found that superintendents in small towns who socialize with their new board members have a reasonable chance of winning future battles with the board. On the other hand, early socialization with and indoctrination of board members by the superintendent has little effect in suburban and urban areas, and in fact it is more associated with board victories in these areas.

In terms of building community political support, 31 percent of city superintendents, 29 percent of suburban superintendents, and 28 percent of small-town superintendents sought private political support by talking to influential locals, trying to involve specific groups in school activities, and gaining a place in a local organization. Urban areas, as opposed to suburban and small-town, tend to be more conducive to superintendents' achieving potential political support from the community. Zeigler and Jennings argue that superintendent interaction with influential leaders of the community discourages the board from opposing the superintendent. This is not true in suburban districts, however, where private support seeking is associated with a high probability of board victory. In suburban districts, the seeking of private support by the superintendent might be a sign of loss of board support, which requires the superintendent to seek other help. In small towns, the seeking of private support by the superintendent is slightly related to decreasing the possibility in any controversy of board victory over the superintendent.

The differences between urban, suburban, and small-town districts, in terms of the superintendent's use of private support against the school board is related to the power structure of the particular community. The study by Zeigler and Jennings is not helpful in this regard because they did not relate the political activities of the superintendent to particular community power structures. But one can assume, for instance, in urban areas characterized by a high degree of democratic pluralism, that private support seeking would be very important to a superintendent faced with a board that reflects many different groups and attitudes within the community. It would be essential for superintendents in these situations to build their own political power base and support system to protect themselves from the potential hostility of the board. On the other hand, in communities where the board of education represents a monopolistic power structure, support from private sources is the same thing as support from the board. In such cases the superintendent cannot use support from private sources against the board, because the board represents those private sources. Of course, it is possible that a superintendent might try to organize community support to defeat control by the monopolistic power structure.

In summary, one cannot say with certainty whether the superintendent and the professional staff wield more power over the local school district than does the elected board of education. Interconnections of power and support are too close to confirm any particular conclusion. Superintendents can use gatekeeping, agenda setting, indoctrination of new board members, and private and community support to enhance their power. But it is hard to determine whether a superintendent's strength is derived from these activities or from the silent support of the local power structure, which is given because the superintendent pursues educational policies supported by these groups.

Local Control in American Education

Any statement about local control in American education must recognize that there is almost-general agreement about the steady erosion of power in local school districts to state and federal governments and to national public and private organizations. The next series of chapters deals with these groups and their influence on local school curriculum, school organization, and student and teacher activities. In many respects, as will be shown, the United States has a national system of education, with some variation at the state and local levels.

There is still enough variation at the local level to give importance to consideration of the political power of superintendents and boards of education. The board and the school staff can determine the degree of freedom of political expression that will exist within the school, and the quality and variety of educational programs that will be offered. The actions of the local district can affect the options made available to a student and the degree of emphasis placed on vocational and academic programs. The board and the superintendent can create a tone within a school system that will either attract or repel certain types of teachers and other staff members. For instance, a school district noted for lack of toleration of nonconservative political views will not attract some teachers. Local boards also still have power with regard to local financial support of the schools and the spending of money. In one community, the board and superintendent might agree that money should be spent for new construction and expansion of the athletic program. In another community, money might be given for support of special fine-arts programs. In contrast, another board might decide it is more important to reduce taxes and, therefore, it would support the reduction of spending in certain areas.

Increasingly the major governing role of local boards and school administrative staffs is to serve as interpreters and administrators of educational policies that are dictated at the state and federal levels. This is still a very important function. For instance, the board and administrative staffs can have considerable influence on the execution of something like a desegregation order from the courts or the U.S. Office of Education. In some communities desegregation has been accomplished with a great deal of success because of the cooperation of the school board; however, in other communities exactly the opposite has occurred.

All these continuing functions of boards of education and superintendents still depend on the political structure of the local community. One generalization that can be made on a national level about members of boards of education is that they tend to be drawn from the upper social and economic groups within a community. What this means in terms of a local district depends upon the power structure within that community. The variation in power structures between communities requires that each community be studied separately to learn its particular organization. Techniques such as those described earlier in the chapter can be used by people interested in finding out about the nature of power in their local community.

The division of power and control between the board and the administrative staff will also vary from community to community. A person can look closely at the gatekeeping, agenda-setting, and political activities of the local superintendent to determine the extent and nature of their power within a particular community. One good measure of the division of responsibility between the superintendent and the board is the number of times the board and its committees meet and the range of topics discussed and acted upon. One can assume that a school board that talks only about taxes and construction and not about curriculum and teaching has relinquished most of those concerns to the administrative staff.

Another important way of determining the relationship between the superintendent and the board is to investigate how superintendents have been selected within a particular community and how people are able to get elected or appointed to the local board. Usually, some formal board-committee structure is responsible for finding and reviewing potential candidates for a superintendent's position. What one needs to investigate is the informal power structure that plays a major role in the selection. The best way of asking the question is to ask which people a candidate for the superintendent's position needs to please to get the position. One technique for finding this out is to look at the formal and informal contacts each candidate for the position must make during the interview process. For instance, does each candidate meet with certain business and civic groups? Why do some groups interview candidates and not others? In communities characterized by democratic pluralism usually there will be a large number of groups and individuals involved in the interviewing process.

Methods of election or appointment to the board of education will depend in most instances on the nature of the community power structure. For instance, in communities characterized by a monopolistic power structure there will usually be one organization or informal group of community influentials responsible for most candidates for the school board. On the other hand, in a community with democratic pluralism a number of competing groups will try to get their particular candidates on the board. One gauge of the community power structure and its relationship to the school board often is the degree of competition that is generated by board elections or appointments.

Any analysis of the educational politics in a community must include the role of the central office staff. It is extremely difficult for a person outside of the school system to determine the extent of the central office staff's power. In some school districts the central office might be just a place where older teachers from within the system are placed when it becomes difficult for them to teach or they encounter problems within the school system. Sometimes superintendents will remove people from principalships and place them in the central office as a method of opening up the position for some other person. When the central office staff is composed of persons who have been placed there for these reasons, this can be a sign of its very weak political force. But this can be deceptive, because even under these conditions there might be many members of the central office staff who have held their positions under a number of different superintendents and who thus can exercise a great deal of power based on their knowledge and on community support received as a result of length of time in the position.

On the other hand, the central office staff might be composed of people brought in from outside the school system because of their expertise. When this occurs the superintendent very often relies upon the expertise and opinions of the staff. This situation enhances the gatekeeping power of the central office staff and strengthens its position as adviser to the board of education.

One measure of the potential importance of the central office staff is to determine how many members of the staff were hired from within the school system and how many were brought in from outside the system. One can also check on the training and expertise the person in question has brought to the position. This method will not provide an absolute determination of the power of the staff but will give some indication of how staff members are viewed as experts and advisers. The image of the staff members as experts is very important in terms of their gatekeeping functions. If the board, the community, and the superintendent view the staff as being composed of education experts, they are more likely to give close attention to the information, opinions, and advice coming from this group.

The importance and size of central office staffs in local school districts has increased in the last decade because of state and federal education programs and increased regulation of the education system by the courts. The central office staff is the group that is responsible for applying for money from these programs and making sure the school system conforms to state and federal guidelines. Many members of these staffs have become education entrepreneurs who frequently travel to their state capital and to Washington, D.C., in search of new funds and to attend workshops on how their school system can conform to new guidelines and regulations.

The next series of chapters discusses the increasing role in the control of

local education by state and federal governments and other national organizations. One important idea to keep in mind when reading these chapters is that
the increasing power of these groups in local education has had two important
consequences: (1) They have decreased local control of education, and (2) they
have increased the size and importance of the central office staff. To state it
another way, decreasing local control of education has been directly linked to
increasing the importance of the local educational bureaucracy.

Exercises

1. Determine the occupations of members of a local board of education and
   compare them with distribution of local population in the different occupational categories in the U.S. census. Is the school board representative of
   the population of the community?
2. Using the methods of Nunnery and Kimbrough described in this chapter,
   determine the power structure of your local community. For practical
   reasons, you may want to limit interviews to a few leading members of the
   community.
3. Interview local board members to determine how one can get elected to the
   board. Remember, it is important to find out about the local informal
   power structure and if the backing of certain groups is required for actual
   election.
4. Interview a local school superintendent about the amount of power this
   person feels he or she has in relationship to the central office staff, the
   school board, the state, and the federal government.

Suggested Readings and Works Cited in Chapter

Borman, Kathryn, and Joel Spring. *Schools in Central Cities.* New York: Longman,
    1984. Chapters 2 and 3 of this book provide an analysis of school-board and
    administrative politics in central-city schools.
Cronin, Joseph N. *The Control of Urban Schools.* New York: Free Press, 1973. This is a
    history of the control of American schools and an exploration of the major issues
    surrounding the relationships between the public, school board members, and pro-
    fessional staff.
Davis, Lee. "The School Board's Struggle to Survive." *Educational Leadership* (Novem-
    ber 1976): 95–96. The issue of *Educational Leadership* is devoted to the politics of
    education.
Education Week. This excellent weekly newspaper contains news about local, state, and
    federal politics of education.
Gans, Herbert J. *Levittowners.* New York: Random House, 1969. This study of a com-
    munity provides a good description of school-board politics in a new suburban
    community.

Hansen, Lee H. "Political Reformation in Local Districts." *Educational Leadership* (November 1976): 90–94. An associate superintendent's view of shifts in power in local school district.

Hawley, Willis D. *Nonpartisan Elections and the Case for Party Politics.* New York: John Wiley & Sons, 1973. This is a study of the effects of nonpartisan elections.

House, Ernest. *The Politics of Educational Innovation.* Berkeley, Calif.: McCutchan, 1974. The first four chapters of this book are excellent studies of the internal politics and local school systems.

Iannaccone, Lawrence, and Frank Lutz. *Politics, Power and Policy: The Governing of Local School Districts.* Columbus, Ohio: Charles E. Merrill, 1970. This study focuses on school-board politics in a small community.

Kirby, David et al. *Political Strategies in Northern School Desegregation.* Lexington, Mass.: Lexington Books, 1973. A major study of the politics of school desegregation in northern cities.

Koerner, James. *Who Controls American Education?* Boston: Beacon, 1968. Koerner argues that professional educators control American education.

McCarty, Donald and Charles Ramsey. *The School Managers: Power and Conflict in American Public Education.* Westport, Conn.: Greenwood, 1971. A study of the different types of community power structures and the resulting style of boards of education and school superintendents.

McGivney, Joseph and James Haught. "The Politics of Education: A View from the Perspective of the Central Office Staff." *Educational Administration Quarterly* (Autumn 1972): 18–38. Another good study of the internal politics within a local school system.

Nunnery, Michael Y. and Ralph B. Kimbrough. *Politics, Power, Polls, and School Elections.* Berkeley: McCutchan, 1971. A guide to studying local politics of education and community power structures.

Zeigler, L. Harmon and M. Kent Jennings. *Governing American Schools: Political Interaction in Local School Districts.* North Scituate, Mass.: Duxbury, 1974. A major national study of local boards of education.

7

Power and Control at the State Level

By the middle of the 1980s a major change had taken place at the state level in the politics of education. In previous decades, state departments of education, state legislatures, and educational lobbying groups worked closely to shape state educational policies. Sometimes these groups were in conflict with each other but most often they played the determining role in decisions about education. The dramatic set of events that reshaped this scenario was the discovery by state governors that education makes good politics.

By the middle of the 1980s governors throughout the country were placing educational issues at the top of their political campaigns and legislative proposals. Education made good state politics because it offered easy solutions to economic problems and created a good public-relations image for political leaders. As state economies declined in the early 1980s, governors began to call for improved systems of education as a means of economic revitalization. It was argued that good school systems were needed to produce the types of workers necessary to attract high-technology industries into the various states. For governors the advocacy of better educational systems was an easy way of creating a public image of being actively involved in trying to do something about economic development.

Governors also found that education issues could be used to win political support from those citizens who were discontented with the functioning of the public school system. Feeding on this public discontent, governors began to make the improvement of the quality of teachers a central focus of their political strategy. In fact, some governors attempted to build their political careers on programs to improve the quality of teachers. These plans usually *pulls*

see gallup

185

called for changes in the salary structure and career patterns for teachers, and for competency testing of teachers. In regard to salary structure and career patterns, governors advocated different plans for career ladders, master teacher plans, and merit pay.

A major result of the increased involvement of governors in the politics of education was to increase conflict between the various political actors at the state level. This was particularly true of the relationships between the professional teachers' organizations and the governor. Teachers proved very cautious regarding career ladders and master teacher proposals. They often were strongly resistant to any proposals for merit pay and bitterly fought attempts to use competency tests to evaluate practicing teachers.

Both the involvement of governors in educational politics and the resulting political controversy made the state politics of education more exciting and important then it had been in decades. These two factors also resulted in a greater extension of state power over educational matters, which in turn heightened the already increasing antagonism between private religious schools and state control. Many religious schools and groups have traditionally complained about state-imposed school regulations interfering with their religious practices and beliefs. These groups want less, not more, state control.

One example of this occurred in 1968, when a group of Amish parents in Wisconsin was arrested for refusing to comply with the state's compulsory education law requiring the parents to enroll their children in high school. The Amish in Ohio, Pennsylvania, Iowa, and Wisconsin had fought against compulsory schooling laws for years because they believed that high schools taught values that undermined their religious and communal life-style. The Amish eventually won their case against state-imposed compulsory education (see Chapter 10 for a detailed analysis for their suit).

Another, more current issue revolves around the rapid growth of Christian fundamentalist schools, which believe that state requirements often force them to teach ideas that are contrary to their religious beliefs. These groups are opposed to both state certification of teachers and state certification of educational institutions. Thus, some of these schools have refused to comply with state regulations (again see Chapter 10 for a detailed analysis of the legal issues).

To understand these issues one must first understand the extent of state authority over education and the variety of ways states have organized to exercise this authority. After presenting descriptions of state authority and educational organization, this chapter deals with the issue of professional domination of education and the extent of state regulation of education.

State Authority over Education

The Constitution of the United States does not mention education; consequently, education is a power reserved to the states. As I will show in Chapter

8, the federal government does have other means of exercising control over state education systems. Most state constitutions give legal responsibility for local education to the state. These two conditions, in theory at least, give state governments greater authority over the education than is exercised by any other government unit in the United States. A school district, in most cases, is legally an agent of the state. Local school boards have and can exercise only those powers that are granted explicitly by the state legislature.

In the early-nineteenth century, state governments exercised very little control over local education. In the 1830s Horace Mann worked in Massachusetts for increased state involvement in education through the establishment of teacher-training institutions and by promoting good schools in local communities. Throughout the century, state departments of education remained relatively small and confined their activities to collecting statistics related to education and promoting good schools and teacher training. In the late-nineteenth and early-twentieth centuries, the states began to expand their role in education with the passage of compulsory education laws and laws requiring specific curriculum content in the schools. Compulsory education laws required expanded staffs to ensure their enforcement. Early state curriculum requirements were often the result of state lobbying by "patriotic organizations" and groups concerned about the Americanization of immigrants. Over the years these curriculum requirements have expanded in many states to cover a great deal of the course content offered in local school districts. Teacher-certification requirements have also increased and have become more complex. As a result of the enforcement requirements of these laws, state educational bureaucracies have grown steadily in the twentieth century.

The increased involvement of the federal government in education in the 1960s further extended the importance of state departments of education. Federal money was provided for the expansion of state educational bureaucracies, as a means of strengthening their role in funneling federal money and programs to local school districts. This widening of state power over education carried with it seeds of controversy. For some, an expanded state-controlled education enterprise signaled the collapse of local control of education. For others, state control of education appeared to be lost as federal money increasingly determined the functions of state education bureaucracies.

This situation began to change in the early 1980s with the election of President Ronald Reagan. President Reagan advocated the return of control and power to local governments through a block grant program, a program that helped to strengthen state departments of education in relationship to the federal government and local systems of education. This legislation will be discussed in more detail in the next chapter.

Today, most states exercise the following functions with regard to education. Most states set minimum standards for curriculum, pupil promotion, and graduation, and for specific education programs such as kindergarten, vocational education, and high school. Some states have detailed courses of study for specific subjects such as social studies and math, and adopt textbooks that are distributed to local schools. Most states have detailed regulations regarding the physical features of school buildings and the size of school libraries. States define the length of the school day and year. State regulations are very detailed with respect to requirements for the certification of teachers.

States increasingly are playing a major role in financing local schools. In some states, tax limits are set for local districts and requirements are made for certain local budget breakdowns. State financial support has varied greatly from state to state. For instance, in 1969–70 the New Hampshire state government provided 8.5 percent of the total amount of school expenditures, but the state government of Hawaii provided 87 percent. States probably will assume greater shares of education expenses as state courts rule that existing systems of financial support provide unequal educational opportunities. Court cases dealing with this issue are discussed in more detail in Chapter 10, when we examine the involvement of the courts in education.

The Organization of State Systems of Education

The broad authority that states have over education is usually exercised through a governmental system that includes the governor's office, the state legislature, a state superintendent of education, a state department of education, and a state board of education. The actual arrangement and relationship of these groups varies from state to state.

Only Wisconsin and Illinois do not have state boards of education. In the other 48 states there are three different methods of selecting members of the state board of education: (1) election by the people or representatives of the people, (2) appointment by the governor, or (3) automatic appointment as a result of holding another state office.

The selection of the state superintendent or chief state school officer also varies from state to state. In some states the superintendent is elected; in other states the person is appointed by the governor or state board of education. Table 7.1 classifies states according to their method of selecting state school board members and the chief state school officer.

The state department of education is the administrative staff of the chief state school officer or superintendent and the state board of education. The staff of the state department of education is mainly composed of professional educators, who do most of the administration and regulation of state education laws and programs. Some of the major activities of state departments of education include the actual operation of state schools for the handicapped, and involvement in the operation of vocational programs and teacher's colleges. The regulatory activities of state departments of education can extend into areas such as curriculum and teaching standards, school construction, school

H + W.

Table 7.1 Classification of States According to Method of Selecting State School Boards and Chief State School Officers

Method of Selection	States
1. State school board members	
a. Ex officio	Florida, Mississippi
b. Appointed by governor	Alabama, Alaska, Arizona, Arkansas, California, Connecticut, Delaware, Georgia, Idaho, Indiana, Iowa, Kentucky, Maine, Maryland, Massachusetts, Minnesota, Missouri, Montana, New Hampshire, New Jersey, North Carolina, North Dakota, Oklahoma, Oregon, Pennsylvania, Rhode Island, South Carolina, South Dakota, Tennessee, Vermont, Virginia, West Virginia, Wyoming
c. Elected by the people or representatives of the people	Colorado, Hawaii, Kansas, Louisiana, Michigan, Nebraska, Nevada, New Mexico, New York, Ohio, Texas, Utah, Washington
2. Chief state school officer	
a. Appointed by governor	New Jersey, Pennsylvania, Tennessee, Virginia
b. Elected by popular vote	Alabama, Arizona, California, Florida, Georgia, Idaho, Illinois, Indiana, Kentucky, Louisiana, Mississippi, Montana, North Carolina, North Dakota, Oklahoma, Oregon, South Carolina, South Dakota, Washington, Wisconsin, Wyoming
c. Appointed by state board of education	Alaska, Arkansas, Colorado, Connecticut, Delaware, Hawaii, Iowa, Kansas, Maine, Maryland, Massachusetts, Minnesota, Michigan, Missouri, Nebraska, Nevada, New Hampshire, New Mexico, New York Ohio, Rhode Island, Texas, Utah, Vermont

SOURCE: From John Thomas Thompson, *Policymaking in American Public Education* (Englewood Cliffs, N.J.: Prentice-Hall, 1976), p. 127.

buses, civil defense and fire drills, and other items specified in the state code or constitution.

In addition, most state departments of education provide consulting service to each local school district and conduct development and research activities. Members of the state department of education consult and advise groups and individuals working on education projects. They often provide in-service education for teachers or establish programs through universities to provide further training for teachers. State departments of education usually publish and distribute information to local school districts on education research and teaching aids. On top of all these activities, state departments of education administer and regulate federal programs, which are funneled through the state governments.

The sources of most of the responsibilities and power of state boards of education, departments of education, and superintendents are the state constitution and the state legislature. Most state constitutions specify the general organizational features and methods of selection of the state superintendent and board of education, and define their general responsibilities. Laws passed by the state legislature provide the more detailed and specific responsibilities of the state educational agencies.

Most state legislatures have a specific legislative committee that is responsible for proposing legislation pertaining to education, conducting hearings on proposed legislation, and recommending to the legislature the passage or defeat of specific laws affecting education. Sometimes legislation concerning education is initiated by the governor's office and is reviewed and placed before public hearings by the education committee of the state legislature. Legislation is often proposed by the state department of education and by outside lobbying groups representing professional educators. In fact, the major role of these two groups in proposing and campaigning for specific legislation has often led to the charge that professional educators dominate state educational politics.

The Structure of Power in State Education

As mentioned in the introduction to this chapter, state educational policy has become increasingly politicized as governors seek to use education as a cure for economic problems and to improve their public image. But governors present only one aspect of state educational politics. Important education decisions are made within the ranks of professional educators in state departments of education and among lobbyists for education associations. To understand the distribution of power at the state level, one has to understand the interplay between the state board of education, the state department of education, the governor, the state legislature, and educational lobbyists.

Gerald Sroufe argued, in research findings presented at the 1969 meeting of the American Educational Research Association, that state boards of education primarily function as a legitimating agency for board educational policies. The overwhelming majority of state board members in Sroufe's survey were professionals earning high salaries. This means that, like that local boards of education, the social composition of state boards of education is not representative of the total population.

Whether the state board is elected or appointed by the governor has little effect on its social composition or its involvement in education issues. In states where the board is appointed, Sroufe found that at time of appointment, board members did not have highly specific education goals, nor did they show particular education issues.

Most elections to state boards of education can be described as nonevents. Over half the elected members in Sroufe's survey reported that they did not campaign. Most candidates issue a single press release and do little to interest the public in state educational issues. Public interest in the election is minimal, and candidates receive a minimum of publicity. Sroufe argues that the "reason board members are so much alike is that no one expects the board to be very influential in formulation or implementation of state educational policy."

The reader will note the similarity between state boards of education and local boards of education in terms of involvement in educational policy. In fact, from the evidence it would appear that local boards are more active and turn less decision-making power over to the professional staff than do state boards of education. The minimal role played by state boards of education results in increased authority being given to state superintendents of education and the staff of state departments of education.

It can also be argued that state boards of education merely legitimate the actions of the department of education as long as the actions of the professional staff within that agency conform to the ideological outlook of the members of the board. This contention is based on the fact that the majority of board members are from one particular (upper) social class in the United States. The board approves the actions of educational bureaucrats as long as they reflect the members' views about education. If this is true, state board members exert influence and give approval through silence and lack of activity.

The involvement of governors in state educational policy is best exemplified by the 1983 report of the Task Force on Education for Economic Growth of the Education Commission of the States. This task force brought together the governors of 13 states and the chief executive officers of 10 of the largest corporations in the United States to discuss how education could contribute to economic development. The governors were, of course, primarily concerned about the economic development of their particular states.

The report of this task force, *Action for Excellence*, set the education and political agenda for many governors. It set the tone and general framework for the involvement of governors in educational politics. The specific proposals were designed to improve the economy through improvement of education. For governors, participation in or support of the task force's recommendations was a safe and easy way to create a public appearance of doing something about economic development.

Specifically, the task force called upon governors to assume the leadership in the development of state plans for education and economic growth, by establishing a broadly inclusive state task force. The report of the task force also called for partnerships between business leaders and the schools. In addition, the report recommended that states work to improve teaching in the schools by improving methods of recruiting, training, and paying teachers. It was specifically mentioned that states should create career ladders for teachers. It was also recommended that states develop methods of measuring the effectiveness of teachers, and examine and tighten procedures for deciding which teachers to retain and which to dismiss. And lastly, the report recommended that states increase requirements for discipline, attendance, homework, grades, and curriculum.

The recommendations of the task force have been reflected in the actions of governors throughout the United States. For instance, in 1984, the year immediately following the issuance of *Action for Excellence*, Governor James Thompson of Illinois asked the state legislature to establish master-teacher programs in every school in the state; in Pennsylvania, Governor Richard Thornburgh called the increases in state expenditures for school improvement and incentives for outstanding teachers; Connecticut Governor William A. O'Neill requested funds for developing competency requirements for new teachers and incentives for those choosing teaching as a career; and in Tennessee, Governor Lamar Alexander waged a major political battle to achieve a career ladder for teachers.

These were only some of the major actions taken by governors around the country. This new era of involvement in education by governors was not free of conflict. In fact, it often created conflict between governors and teachers' unions over merit-pay plans, the testing of practicing teachers, and various forms of career ladders and master-teacher proposals. Teachers' unions sometimes found these plans objectionable because of their threat to teacher security and the difficulty in merit-pay plans of determining merit.

A major result of this situation has been to change the traditional climate of state educational politics. Traditionally, state educational politics have tended to center around the interactions of educational lobbying groups and state departments of education. The emergence of the governor as a major actor has complicated state educational politics and increased the potential political conflict.

The increased activity of governors has been matched by increased activity by state legislatures. Prior to the 1970s, state legislatures were faced with low salaries, rapid turnover in the composition of the legislature, and lack of professional staffs to assist legislators and legislative committees. All these factors contributed to a general lack of expertise and ability to formulate educational policy.

Beginning in the 1970s, state legislatures changed dramatically with the growth of legislative staffs that allowed legislators to work independently of state departments of education. Susan Fuhrman, in her essay "State-Level Politics and School Financing," writes that "the fragmentation of the educational interests combined with the growing expertise of legislators and governors to set the stage for the eclipse of the educators and the emergence of general government, particularly the legislature, as the education policymaker."

The increased importance of the state legislature in educational policy-making has reduced the role of state departments of education in this area. In the past, state departments of education have been the prime initiators of education policy, but now state legislatures have, in many cases, taken over the leadership role. Susan Fuhrman writes, "A fifty-state study of legislative leadership...revealed that for the past fifteen years most of education policy, including finance reform, was made by a single, unusually committed group of legislators."

State educational politics now involve the concerns and interests of professional educators in state departments of education, the political ambitions and interests of governors and state legislators, and the interests of various educational lobbyists. It is within this arena of political struggle that decisions are made about school finance, teacher certification, educational standards, and curriculum requirements. Of major importance is the role of educational lobbyists.

Lobbyists and the State Legislature

Of fundamental importance for understanding the actions of state legislatures regarding educational policy is an understanding of the organization of educational lobbying groups and their influence on the state legislature.

The relationship between educational lobbyists and the state legislature varies from state to state. Lawrence Iannaccone, in his *Politics of Education*, has classified the differences in relationships into four major types. He calls his first type "local-based disparate." Within this pattern, which he describes as characteristic of Vermont, New Hampshire, and Massachusetts, state educational associations are unable to reach agreement on educational issues or present a unified set of proposals to the state legislature. The main points of contact within this pattern are between local school administrators and local state legislators who seek their advice on educational issues.

Iannaccone's second type, which he calls "monolithic," is the most common pattern among states and can be found in New York, Missouri, New Jersey, and Rhode Island. Unlike the local-based disparate pattern, the monolithic pattern has all state educational associations plus the state department of education working together to develop a legislative program and influence the state legislature. Conflicting ideas are worked out between these groups and a unified front is presented to the state legislature. The leadership of this educational monolith is usually dominated by school administrators. Education experts from universities are used to help formulate legislative proposals. These groups usually maintain close contact with certain state legislators and supply them with information. Lobbyists for these groups appear before state legislative committees to build a case for their proposals. Because a "monolithic" lobbying group contains most of the educational expertise within a state, it has a virtual monopoly over information about education received in the state legislature. Without a doubt this monolithic structure gives the greatest political influence to state educational associations.

With the third type, called the "disparate" pattern, educational associations are not united, and there is a great deal of conflict. This pattern, according to Iannaccone, can be found in California and Michigan. When this pattern appears, state legislators become very aware of the issues dividing the groups and are often forced to take sides. For instance, the Michigan Association of School Administrators is often in conflict with the National Education Association; the NEA is viewed by the state legislature primarily as a bargaining agent for teacher-welfare issues, whereas the administrative organization concentrates on local tax issues.

The fourth type is characteristic of Illinois only and is called by Iannaccone a "statewide syndical" system. Illinois has a School Problems Committee that functions like a legislative council and is composed of representatives from government and major groups having interests in educational decisions. This group has become the center of educational decision making, and most of its proposals are passed by the state legislature with a minimum of debate.

It must be remembered that Iannaccone's framework was developed in the 1960s and that patterns have changed in many states. The financial crisis in education in the 1970s probably resulted in the educational associations in many states working together for particular legislation. This would mean a broader development in most states of the monolithic pattern, and the strengthening of the power of educational lobbyists and state departments of education over legislative action. These patterns vary from state to state; each state must be analyzed separately to determine its particular pattern at a particular time.

The educational groups that have statewide lobbyists include state teachers' associations and unions, state school administrators' associations, state school board associations, and parent organizations such as the PTA. In most areas the strongest lobbying group is the state teachers' association, which in many states is an affiliate of the National Education Association. In some states, such as New York, the American Federation of Teachers has gained considerable statewide influence. (These two teachers' associations are discussed in greater detail in Chapter 9.) Paid lobbyists of state teachers' associations usually attempt to maintain close contact with the head of the legislative committee on education and with members of the state department of education. The directors of these state associations work to mobilize support within their own organizations and from the general public through the publication of newsletters and monthly journals. In a study reported by Nicholas Masters in *State Politics and the Public Schools*, he found that in the three states in his sample, legislators considered the state teachers' associations in most powerful interest groups in the state.

Throughout the states, school administrators increasingly are forming their own organizations. Administrators traditionally belong to state teachers' associations, but as militancy among teachers has grown, administrators have been forced to seek their own organizations. Although these organizations are small in size when compared to teachers' organizations, their influence has sometimes been strong because of local contact between superintendents and locally elected state legislators. Also, many superintendents of large urban areas have governmental-relations officers on their staffs to work with state and federal political and administrative personnel.

Another group that has great influence on state educational policies is state school board associations. These organizations are composed of representatives from local school boards and are often in conflict with teachers' associations and associations of state administrators. Because they usually have the support of the power structure in their local community, they have easy access to state politicians. The National School Board Association and state school board associations have traditionally fought to maintain local control of the schools. Another statewide educational lobbying group is the PTA. For many years the PTA primarily existed to provide community support for local superintendents and principals. Increasingly, members of this group have become more militant and have been placing pressure on state legislatures for support of particular educational programs.

Other state lobbying groups from time to time have had considerable influence on particular features of state educational policy. Patriotic organizations such as the American Legion have often campaigned for increased emphasis on patriotism in the schools. Farm groups have worked hard for greater support of agricultural education programs. Labor organizations have been interested in ridding the schools of antiunion bias and making sure that vocational education is not used to undermine union apprenticeship programs. Business groups such as the chamber of commerce have sought legislative support in some states for proposals that would require the teaching of a particular type of economics. One could construct an almost endless list of people and organizations that would like certain subjects and ideas made mandatory in the schools by state legislative action.

One of the major weaknesses of the lobbying activities of state educational associations is their lack of unified effort. As stated earlier, Iannaccone found that a monolithic structure of educational groups was most effective for lobbying. If the state teachers' associations, administrators' associations, school board associations, the PTA, and the state department of education are able to unite around educational programs, they can exert considerable influence on the state legislature.

While these educational lobbying groups have had considerable influence over the details of educational policy because of their frequent monopoly of information, their greatest area of weakness is in gaining financial support for school programs from state legislatures. Nothing shows more clearly that these educational groups do not have complete control of educational policy than the financial crisis of the schools in the early 1970s, when many state legislatures refused to increase state school support. The reason was that other lobbying groups had greater influence on state expenditures and tax policies. These lobbying groups include taxpayers' associations, research leagues created by various economic groups within the state, and organizations such as the chamber of commerce. These groups usually do not attack educational spending directly, but call for decreased taxes and fiscal responsibility, which usually means less money for social programs such as education.

In summary, one can make the following generalizations about the interactions between educational lobbyists and state legislators. In most states, because of the lack of large professional staffs to help state legislators and committees, legislators tend to rely on state administrative agencies and lobbying groups for information and expertise. In terms of educational policy, this means educational associations and the state department of education have considerable influence over state policy. The degree of influence on state legislative action by educational associations depends on the degree of cooperation existing between the various educational groups. The more there is unity of action, the greater the influence on the state legislature. In the area of educational finance, educational lobbyists do not seem to have as much influence as economic lobbying groups.

Business and Teachers' Unions in State Politics

Increasingly in the 1980s, the primary influences over state politicians in education matters are the teachers' unions and the business community. Sometimes the business community and the unions form alliances, and at other times they are at war.

The increasing influence of these two groups occurred as state educational policy making became concentrated at the state level and governors made education a central focus of political campaigns. As politicians, governors try to please both the teachers' organizations and the business community. To the business community, governors promise to improve the economic system through better schooling. To teachers, they promise improved salaries and a restructured profession. Sometimes governors are forced to choose one group over another. Most often the choice is the business community.

While there is a trend toward centralization and increased influence of teachers' organizations and business, there are still differences in patterns of influence between states. These differences were studied by Catherine Marshall, Douglas Mitchell, and Fredrick Wirt. These researchers synthesized previous studies of influence in state politics, and identified by order of influence the major political actors in Arizona, West Virginia, California, Wisconsin, Pennsylvania, and Illinois.

Within government, the researchers rank ordered the following in regard to influence over state education policies:

1. the state legislature
2. the chief state school officer and senior members of the state department of education
3. the governor and executive staff
4. legislative staff
5. the state board of education

Obviously, as the lawmaking body of state government, the legislature would have the most power. Within the legislature, certain legislators specialize in educational issues and guide the votes of others. In general, chief state school officers function as long-term bureaucrats who work patiently to establish educational policies. As Marshall, Mitchell, and Wirt note, governors increased their involvement in educational policy in the early 1980s. Members of legislative staffs gain their influence by being links between interest groups and members of the state legislature. At the bottom of the list are state boards of education.

With regard to the influence of groups outside of government on educational policy makers in government, Marshall, Mitchell, and Wirt found the following groups listed by order of importance.

1. education associations
2. noneducation groups (business leaders, taxpayers' groups)
3. lay groups (PTAs, school advisory groups)
4. educational research organizations
5. producers of educational materials

In the six states studied by the researchers, education associations have the greatest influence on government officials. Teachers' associations are the most influential, with a coalition of educational associations running a close second. School board associations are slightly more influential than organizations representing school administrators. The combined figures for all six states give education groups more influence than noneducation groups except Arizona, where the "Phoenix 40," a group of prestigious businesspeople that meets informally once a month, exercises strong influence over state education policy.

A major influence on the degree and type of outside influence on government officials regarding education policies is the degree of centralization. What is meant by "centralization" is the amount of control over local school districts exercised by state government. The pattern in the 1980s is increased centralization of educational policies at the state level.

With centralization there is a reduction of the number of groups and individuals influencing educational politics. Only the most powerful have meaningful influence within this reduced field of political actors, with the most powerful being the teachers' associations and the business community.

In highly centralized states the education associations protect their interests and support educational changes that will enhance their power position. On the other hand, the business community supports educational policies that serve its economic interests, which usually means assuring that the schools prepare students to meet labor needs.

Should the State Regulate Public and Private Schools?

This chapter began with two examples of protests against state regulation of public and private schools. With the rapid growth of small alternative private schools in the 1960s and the expansion of religious schools in the 1970s, this issue became a topic of major debate. Many of these schools encountered difficulty with their particular state government because they did not meet some state standard, or refused to comply because of their particular desires or needs.

The major authority states have had for exercising regulation over public and private schools has been compulsory-education laws. In most states parents can be arrested if they do not send their children to school. The state usually defines a "school" as *an educational institution that conforms to state standards and regulation, including curriculum and teacher-certification requirements.* This means that if an educational institution is not accredited by the state as complying with all state school requirements, its pupils are technically truant and their parents are liable for criminal prosecution. Without compulsory-school laws, parents would be free to send their children to educational institutions that do not conform to state regulations.

Compulsory school-attendance laws vary from state to state in their actual form and interpretation by state courts. Robert P. Baker, a lawyer, has reviewed judicial interpretations of compulsory school laws in an article titled "Status Law and Judicial Interpretations" in *The Twelve Year Sentence*, edited by William F. Rickenbacker. Baker divides compulsory-schooling laws into what he calls the "other-guy type" and the "cookie-cutter type." The argument given for the "other-guy type" of law is that although most people would educate their children without compulsory-schooling laws, there is somebody somewhere who would not educate his or her children. Compulsory school laws in this case are designed to protect children from parents who are not willing to educate them. Where adopted, the "other-guy type" of interpretation results in a compulsory-schooling law requiring no more than what most parents would do anyway.

The "cookie-cutter type" of law is based on the idea that all children should have the same experiences within the same kind of institution. The most extreme example of a "cookie-cutter type" of law was a 1920 Oregon statute that required all children to attend public schools. One purpose of the law was to close Catholic schools. The U.S. Supreme Court ruled in 1925 that the law was not constitutional. The Court stated: "The fundamental theory of liberty upon which all governments in this Union repose excludes any general power of the state to standardize its children by forcing them to accept instruction from public teachers only." But the ruling also upheld the right of the state to regulate private schools, which continued its right to enforce some form of standardization.

The differences between the "other-guy" and the "cookie-cutter" laws are best exemplified in judicial interpretations. For instance, in New Jersey in 1937 a Mr. and Mrs. Bongart were accused of being disorderly persons because they themselves were educating their children in their home. The New Jersey compulsory-schooling law required attendance at school or equivalent instruction. Education in the home was not considered equivalent instruction by the trial judge because, in his words, "I cannot conceive how a child can receive instruction and experiences in group activity and in social outlook in any manner or form comparable to that provided in the public school." This is what Baker would call a "cookie-cutter" interpretation of the law. In a similar case, a young girl in Washington state was considered a delinquent and made a ward of the court for not attending school. The trial court found that the instruction being given to the girl in her home was at least the academic equivalent of that available in the public schools. Despite this finding, the Washington Supreme Court ruled against the child and her parents, with the argument that no school existed unless instruction was being given by a teacher certified by the state of Washington.

On the other hand, the "other-guy" type of judicial interpretation can result in more flexible application of compulsory-schooling law. The most famous case was in Illinois in the 1950s in *People* v. *Levisen*, in which the parents, who were Seventh-Day Adventists, believed that educating their daughter in a public school would create an un-Christian character. The parents argued, "For the first eight or ten years of a child's life, the field or garden is the best school room, the mother the best teacher, and nature the best lesson book." Education in the parents' home was considered adequate: The father was a college graduate and the mother had received training in pedagogy and educational psychology. Unlike the New Jersey and Washington courts, the Illinois courts formulated the "other-guy" philosophy in their ruling that "the law is not made to punish parents who provide their children with instruction equal or superior to that obtainable in the public schools. It is made for the parent who fails or refuses to properly educate his child."

The interpretation and application of state compulsory-schooling laws and education regulations will vary from state to state between the "cookie-cutter" and the "other-guy" interpretations. In recent years all states have been limited in their application of the law as interpreted by the U.S. Supreme Court in the 1972 Amish case, *State of Wisconsin, Petitioner* v. *Jonas Yoder et al.*, mentioned at the beginning of the chapter. In this case the Court argued that religious freedom was more important than state compulsory-schooling laws and that state law could not abridge the practice of religion. This meant that if parents could prove in court that attending public school would interfere with the practice of their religion, they could not be forced to conform to state compulsory-schooling laws. Thus the Supreme Court recognized that public schools were not in all cases neutral in terms of religion. The social life, curriculum, and educational goals of the public schools could be in conflict with some religious customs and practices.

One of the most thorough criticisms of state regulation of education has been made by one of the participants in the Amish case. Professor Donald Erickson provided expert educational testimony defending the right of the Amish to maintain their own educational practices. Erickson summarized some of his views in *Super-Parent: An Analysis of State Educational Controls*, written for the Illinois Advisory Committee on Nonpublic Schools.

In his critique Erickson argues that two major reasons are given for state programmatic control of education. One reason is to ensure that all children have a reasonable chance to pursue happiness as free individuals. Education might be able to provide the individual with some of the intellectual tools required for autonomous behavior. The second major reason given for state control of the schools is the protection of society from unemployment, indigence, crime, juvenile delinquency, mental illness, and political strife. This reason encompass the social purposes of education discussed in the first chapter of this book.

In response to the first reason, that state-controlled education ensures autonomous individuals, Erickson points out that state-prescribed education is in direct conflict with the autonomy of all parents and does not provide the child with a model of a society of freely acting individuals. Erickson states, "In complex societies all over the world, however, state-controlled education arouses parental resistance. The reason is that child-rearing practices sponsored or required by the state in pluralistic societies are at odds with many parental views of the good life and how to prepare for it."

Erickson argues that what is essential for the development of the autonomous individual in modern society is to learn reading, writing, arithmetic, and the fundamental workings of society's political, legal, and economic institutions. But even if we agree that knowledge of these subjects is essential for autonomous action, it does not, according to Erickson, justify the maintenance of the current system of compulsory school attendance and regulations. Parents and children could be given complete freedom to decide how the specified competencies were to be learned, and the child could be required to demonstrate through a national system of tests that progress is being made. This system would require compulsory education, but not compulsory school attendance.

The distinction between compulsory education and compulsory school attendance is very important for Erickson's argument. Compulsory education without compulsory school attendance would allow for the protection of those children suffering from parental neglect, without burdening all children with attendance at a state-regulated school. If during the course of examinations the state found that a child was not learning the basics, it could prescribe some form of remedial action like required attendance at a state school.

With regard to education beyond elementary school, Erickson argues, there is no agreement among scholars about what knowledge is of most worth and what is essential for autonomous growth. This being the case, he feels that parents and children can make their own determination of what they should know and how they should learn it. Even if state officials can identify indispensable understandings and skills beyond the elementary ones described above, this does not require programmatic state regulation of schools. State intervention could be limited to those cases in which tests show that children are not making satisfactory progress toward the acquisition of required competencies.

Erickson rejects the second major reason given for state regulation of schools, which is protection of society from crime, unemployment, political strife, and other social problems. First, Erickson argues that no one knows what attitudes, understandings, and skills are truly necessary for the survival of a society. Second, no one knows how much consensus about social and political beliefs is required before that same consensus actually becomes harmful to a society by limiting the freedom to find new ideas and adapt to new situations. The reader should remember from the first chapter that the argument for the achievement of the social and political purposes of schooling centers on the development of a consensus of political and social beliefs. Erickson rejects state involvement in this process with the argument that "state officials are probably the last group we should trust to decide how much commonality is essential to the general weal. It is in the interest of these officials to discourage the dissension and diversity that may jeopardize their positions, subject them to challenge, and make public institutions more difficult to govern smoothly."

In addition, it has never been proved that a relationship exists between the amount and quality of education available in a society and a decrease in crime, unemployment, and other social, economic, and political problems. In the twentieth century the amount of education received by each person in society has steadily increased. At the same time crime has either remained the same or increased; unemployment has fluctuated with changes in the economy and labor market; indigence continues; and mental illness seems unaffected by the quantity of education. The nineteenth-century dream of schooling as a panacea for social problems does not seem to have been justified by the events of the twentieth century.

Questioning of the degree of state regulation of schools is occurring at the same time that state responsibility for education is increasing. School desegregation is resulting in the development of large school districts and more state involvement in the regulation of programs. The crises in school finance, as well as court decisions, are resulting in state governments assuming more and more of the burden for financing the schools. Probably the issue of school finances will be the most important reason for the expansion of state regulation of education.

Because of the nature of state government, and because of greater voter interest and involvement in local and national politics, the responsibility and burden of state regulation will likely continue to be mainly in the hands of professional educators within state departments of education. For many years, state governments have been neglected as public interest has been directed to the more dramatic actions of the federal government. If greater public control of education is desired, this trend must be reversed and greater attention focused on events at the state level. The other alternative is to end or limit state regulation of the schools.

Exercises

1. Interview a local representative to the state legislature about the political process as it relates to educational legislation. Inquire about the important lobbying organizations and the role of the state department of education.
2. In a discussion group or in an essay discuss whether there should be complete professional control of education.
3. In a discussion group or in an essay discuss what areas of education you think the state should regulate.
4. Contact your state department of education and find out the extent of regulation of schools in your state.
5. In a discussion group or in an essay discuss whether there should be compulsory-education laws.

Suggested Readings and Works Cited in Chapter

Education Week. Published by Editorial Projects in Education. This excellent weekly newspaper is a good source of information on state educational politics.

Erickson, Donald. *Super-Parent: An Analysis of State Educational Controls*. Written for the Illinois Advisory Committee on Nonpublic Schools. N.d. An important critique of the concept and practice of state regulation of schools.

Fuhrman, Susan. "State-Level Politics and School Financing." In *The Changing Politics of School Finance*, edited by Nelda Cambron-McCabe and Allan Odden. Cambridge, Mass.: Ballinger, 1982. An analysis of the school finance reform movement on the structure of state politics of education.

Iannaccone, Lawrence. *Politics of Education*. New York: Center for Applied Research in Education, 1967. This book classifies the major types of state lobbying groups.

Keim, Albert. *Compulsory Education and the Amish*. Boston: Beacon Press, 1975. This book provides background and discussions of *State of Wisconsin, Petitioner* v. *Jonas*

Yoder et al., the important U.S. Supreme Court decision regarding compulsory education.

Marshall, Catherine, Douglas Mitchell, and Fredrick Wirt. "The Context of State Level Policy Formation." Paper given at the American Educational Research Association Meeting in San Francisco, California, April 16–20, 1986. A study of the differing degrees of influence of government officials and lobbying groups over state education policy.

Masters, Nicholas et al. *State Politics and the Public Schools: An Exploratory Analysis.* New York: Alfred A. Knopf, 1964. An early and important work about state educational politics.

Rickenbacker, William, ed. *The Twelve Year Sentence.* Chicago: Open Court, 1974. Essays in this book discuss legal, historical, and philosophical arguments against compulsory education.

Sroufe, Gerald. "Recruitment Processes and Composition of State Boards of Education." Paper presented at the American Educational Research Association meeting in 1969. This paper provides general information about the backgrounds of members of state boards of education.

Task Force on Education for Economic Growth. *Action for Excellence.* Denver: Education Commission of the States, 1983. This set of recommendations for educational reform was written by a task force composed of governors and leading heads of corporations. It has had a major influence on recent state activities in education.

Thompson, John Thomas. *Policymaking in American Public Education.* Englewood Cliffs, N.J.: Prentice-Hall, 1976. Chapters 6, 7, and 8 provide summaries of state educational politics.

Wirt, Frederick, and Michael Kirst. *Political and Social Foundations of Education.* Berkeley, Calif.: McCutchan, 1975. Chapter 7 provides a good introduction to state educational politics.

8

Power and Control at the Federal Level

In the 1980s, the degree of federal involvement in education has become one of the major issues to divide the two major political parties. The Democrats elected to the federal government since the 1960s have sought greater federal financial support of the schools, and the shaping of educational policies to serve particular populations. On the other hand, Republicans have sought to limit the federal role and to enhance control at the state and local level. These differences in political philosophy illustrate the uneasy feeling Americans have about federal involvement in education. Some see federal involvement as destructive of the principles of free speech and thought; others see federal involvement as essential for the protection of civil rights and the public schools.

As I mentioned earlier, the U.S. Constitution makes no mention of education. This means it is a function reserved to the states. Consequently, federal involvement in education has evolved slowly over time and has often been the result of controversial issues related to education. For instance, during the 1950s the federal government began to expand its role in education because of its concern that not enough scientists and engineers were being produced to win the arms race with the Soviet Union. Also during this period, civil-rights issues related to segregated schools forced the federal government to intervene in local schools. During the 1960s the federal government launched a War on Poverty, in which educational programs were the major focus. The federal role expanded during the 1970s, as increased attempts were made to use the schools as a means of solving the problems of youth unemployment.

Federal legislation governing education must be considered in the framework of interaction between the executive and legislative branches of the federal government. Congress has the power to enact legislation related to education; the president has the power to administrate that legislation. The administration of legislation carries with it a great deal of power over the final results of laws enacted by Congress. First, there is the power of interpretation. After Congress passes a law, it is sent to the appropriate part of the executive branch. It is the job of the executive branch to interpret the intention of Congress. It is often the case that the interpretations given to legislation can have tremendous consequences. Second, the writing and enforcement of regulations pertaining to the legislation determines their ultimate impact.

Prior to 1980, the U.S. Office of Education (USOE), located in the Department of Health, Education and Welfare (HEW), had primary responsibility in the executive branch for education. Many other education programs were distributed through other parts of the executive branch. One of the goals in the establishment of the Department of Education was to consolidate the many education programs into a single departmental organization. In addition, the creation of a separate department of education meant a place in the president's cabinet for the secretary of education. It was hoped that this would give greater importance to the federal education effort.

These changes in the structure of federal involvement in education occurred during a period of widespread debate about how much control over education the federal government should have. To understand this issue one must look closely at the methods of control used by the federal government.

Methods of Control

It is important to understand that the federal government does not have the power directly to control local schools, but it does have significant indirect means of control. It is these indirect means of control that have become controversial issues between the two major political parties. The most important of these indirect means of control is the offering of financial aid if a school system adopts certain programs, materials, or curricula. Money granted for specific programs is called *categorical aid*. Whether or not federal support should be in the form of categorical aid has been a major concern of the Republican party.

Another major means of federal control is the threat to withhold federal funds if a local school district is found in violation of the civil-rights guidelines of the federal government. The major differences between the two political parties over this form of control have focused on the degree of implementation and interpretation of the civil-rights statutes. Republicans have tended to seek a narrower enforcement of the statutes, while the Democrats have pursued strong enforcement.

The third major means of control has been the funding of research and development of educational materials. The funding of research is a means of control because it shapes future knowledge and influences decision making. It is important to understand that the federal government does not support all research, but determines types of research to be supported on the basis of policy objectives. And it is precisely the issue of what types of research should be supported that has divided Democrats and Republicans.

An understanding of the political controversies surrounding these methods of control can be understood by closely examining the evolution of each means of control and the struggle over these issues in the 1980s. The issue of categorical aid first emerged in the 1950s, when educators began to seek aid from the federal government to relieve two problems caused by the post-World War II baby boom—a severe teacher shortage and a need for more school buildings. At this time, educational groups such as the National Educational Association wanted the federal government to provide general aid, to be controlled in local school districts. But during this time there existed a general sentiment against federal involvement in education. It took an international problem to finally push the federal government to action. This occurred when the Soviet Union launched the first space flight and threatened the United States' position as the world's technological leader.

The response to this crisis came in the form of the National Defense Education Act (NDEA), which was proposed and passed under the leadership of Republican President Dwight Eisenhower. The NDEA was not a general-aid package for the schools, but one that contained categorical aid for the specific purpose of improving mathematics, science, and foreign language instruction.

The National Defense Education Act linked federal support for schools with national policy objectives. This dramatically shifted part of the control of educational policy from the local to the federal level. The next major federal educational legislation, the 1965 Elementary and Secondary Education Act (ESEA), also was tied to national policy objectives and caused dramatic changes in local school systems. The ESEA, like the NDEA, was not designed to provide general aid to solve financial problems of local schools; the assistance was in the form of categorical aid given to schools as part of a broad social policy to end poverty in the United States. Like the National Defense Education Act, the Elementary and Secondary Education Act was part of a social policy in which schools were to be used as instruments to solve major social problems.

The 1965 ESEA, more than any other legislation, made categorical funding a method for shaping local educational actions according to a particular political and social philosophy. This political and social philosophy included ideas about educational and cultural deprivation that were to influence educators around the country. In other words, the legislation influenced local schools not only through direct funding of specific programs, but also by spreading a particular philosophy about poverty and the role education could play in eliminating it. The premise of this philosophy was that poverty continued in the United States as the result of a set of causal factors that were mutually interdependent. For instance, a poor education restricted employment opportunities, which caused a low standard of living and, consequently, poor medical care, diet, housing, and education for the next generation. This model of poverty suggested that one could begin at any point in the causal relationships and move around the "circle of poverty." Improving medical care for the poor would mean more days of employment and thus more money for better housing, diet, and education. Theoretically, the same chain reaction would occur if you improved any of the interrelated causal factors.

The Elementary and Secondary Education Act was the main component of the attack on poverty through improved education for the children of the poor. The most important section of the legislation was Title I, which received approximately 76 percent of the money initially appropriated for the legislation. The purpose of Title I was to provide improved educational programs for children designated as educationally deprived. Title I specifically stated that "the Congress hereby declares it to be the policy of the United States to provide financial assistance...to expand and improve...educational programs by various means...which contribute particularly to meeting the special educational needs of educationally deprived children."

At the time of its passage, the Elementary and Secondary Education Act was the most important piece of educational legislation ever passed by Congress. It strengthened Title VI of the 1964 Civil Rights Act by making available large sums of money to local schools that complied with desegregation orders. Noncompliance with desegregation orders, in other words, meant a loss of funds from the Elementary and Secondary Education Act. Desegregation of schools in the South had been progressing at a very slow rate. With the passage of this new legislation, desegregation occurred at a more rapid rate.

Because of the difficult financial situation of most public schools in the United States, there was a rush to get funds, particularly under Title I. This resulted in local schools expanding their administrative staffs to be able to apply for funds and fill out what in later years would seem like endless government forms. While the legislation claimed no federal control over local education, in reality local school administrators and boards gave up part of their local autonomy as they were forced to comply with federal standards in order to receive the funds.

As mentioned, most local school systems would have preferred general aid from the federal government. The Elementary and Secondary Education Act provided categorical aid only. Many school systems, however, needed money to support their total programs. Because of this situation, many school systems cheated and claimed the existence of large numbers of poor students in their districts in order to get federal money to support their general programs. Money designated for these nonexistent disadvantaged students made it possible for many school systems to remain in operation.

Secretary of Health, Education, and Welfare, Elliot Richardson, testified before Congress in 1972 that the major problem with the 1965 Elementary and

Secondary Education Act was the misuse of Title I funds. He told a congressional committee: "The most prevalent failing has been the use by local school districts of Title I funds as general revenue. Out of 40 states audited between 1966 and 1970, local school districts in 14 were found to have spent Title I funds as general revenue." In these cases the funds were diffused through the educational system and did not reach the educationally deprived child. He announced that the Office of Education had recently asked eight states to return $6,249,915 in misused funds and would shortly take action against approximately fifteen additional states for another $23 million.

Even though local schools needed general revenue funds in the 1960s and 1970s, Congress continued to pass legislation that designated money for specific categories of instruction. In 1966, Education of Handicapped Children, or Title VI, was added to the Elementary and Secondary Education Act. Bilingual Education Programs, or Title VII, were added in 1967, to provide financial assistance for local schools to design educational programs for children from environments where the dominant language was other than English. In 1972, a large number of "education amendments" were passed by Congress. Included in these amendments were an Emergency School Aid Act to help local schools with desegregation plans and an Ethnic Heritage Act to plan, develop, establish, and operate ethnic-heritage studies programs. Also included in the 1972 amendments was an Indian Education Act, to develop innovative and bilingual programs and provide health and nutritional services for Native American Children.

The pattern that emerged from the federal legislation of the 1960s and 1970s was one in which the federal government provided money in areas apparently neglected by local and state educational systems. The role of the federal government was not to support all schooling but only those parts of schooling that appeared not to be receiving support by the local governments. By the 1970s the American public school system was functioning under three levels of financing and control. State governments were providing regulations and requirements to local districts, which in turn were administering these regulations and requirements in terms of local needs. The federal government provided the money and planning for innovative programs such as ESEA programs under Title I and, later, ESEA amendments such as the bilingual education and ethnic heritage legislation.

The major challenge to the pattern of control represented by categorical grants came with the election of President Ronald Reagan in 1980. President Reagan wanted to reduce federal control over local school systems by giving greater administrative control of federal programs to state and local governments. The Reagan administration tried to achieve this objective through a combination of deregulation and decentralization. Deregulation involved revocation of existing rules and regulations, and reduction of enforcement. Within a year of President Reagan's election, his secretary of education, Terrel Bell, revoked 30 sets of rules governing 19 programs.

The key attack on the power of categorical grants came in the form of advocacy of block grants, which would be administered by state governments. This process of decentralization represented the first major change in federal programs in education since the beginning of categorical grants in the 1950s. It did not represent a complete abandonment of categorical aid but an attempt to give state governments more control.

The block-grant philosophy was embodied in the 1981 administration-sponsored legislation called the Education and Consolidation and Improvement Act (ECIA). Title I of the 1965 Elementary and Secondary Act of 1965 became Chapter I of the new legislation. Under Chapter I of the ECIA, requirements were simplified—administrative authority was given to the states and responsibility for program design was given to local school districts. Of major importance was the lack of detailed regulations from the Department of Education to local school districts handling program design under Chapter I.

This new legislation provided more flexibility and control at the local level, but it also raised criticisms about the use of federal money. This criticism highlighted the almost inevitable conflict between any educational legislation with a policy objective, and attempts at greater local control. The major criticism of Title I was that in its attempt to allow flexibility at the local level it was allowing opportunities for local school districts to use the money for purposes other then what was intended. In the case of Title I, it meant that funding might be used for students who were not actually the neediest within a district. This possibility meant that Title I might not achieve its policy objective of providing compensatory education while attempting to provide local control.

This problem was most evident in Chapter 2 of ECIA. Chapter 2 combined 28 categorical programs into one block grant. From the perspective of the Reagan administration, this achieved the goal of allowing greater flexibility in the use of the money at the local level. On the other hand, major objections to Chapter 2 were raised by those who wanted the money used to achieve the objectives embodied in the original categorical grants. This was particularly true of one of the categorical programs for funding desegregation that was folded into Title 2. Prior to the passage of ECIA, about 26 percent of the funding for all the programs placed in Title 2 went for desegregation aid; after Chapter 2 was introduced, only 6 percent was spent for desegregation.

The differences in money spent on desegregation before and after the passage of ECIA respresent both the hopes and the problems encountered in block-grant legislation. ECIA also provides an example of the dilemma of federal involvement in education. For those traditionally opposed to federal involvement, block grants are only a partial solution. For those believing that there exists a national interest in education and that this is best expressed by federal educational policy, block grants represent a step backward. Block grants are an unhappy compromise between these two positions.

President Reagan's administration also attempted to change the degree of control of civil rights legislation over local school systems, by reducing and limiting enforcement efforts. Federal control, through insistence on the protection of civil rights, had its origins in Title VI of the 1964 Civil Rights Act. This legislation had provided the federal government with the method and means to regulate education and protect civil rights in the schools.

Title VI established the precedent for using government money as a means of controlling educational policy. It required the mandatory withholding of federal funds from institutions practicing racial, religious, or ethnic discrimination. Title VI stated that no person, because of race, color, or national origin, could be excluded from or denied the benefits of any program receiving federal financial assistance. It required all federal agencies to establish guidelines to implement this policy. Refusal by institutions or projects to follow these guidelines was to result in the "termination or refusal to grant or to continue assistance under such program or activity."

The strength of Title VI lay in the fact that the government had extended its activities in many educational institutions around the country. Federal spending had spread to most of the educational institutions in the United States through the activities of the National Science Foundation and the National Defense Education Act. In addition, research money flowed into universities from other government agencies, including the Department of Defense. Many institutions received funds for the Reserve Officers Training Corps. Federal spending in education continued to increase in the 1960s, particularly after the passage in 1965 of the Elementary and Secondary Education Act. Title VI announced that all aid to institutions and school districts that failed to comply with federal guidelines would end. This was certainly a powerful government weapon. The most extreme concern about Title VI was voiced by Senator Sam Ervin of North Carolina, who claimed that "no dictator could ask for more power than Title VI confers on the President."

The justification for using the spending of federal money in this manner was given by Senator Hubert Humphrey during the Senate floor debate over the civil rights bill. The major concern at the time was the extent of racial segregation in educational institutions. Humphrey argued that Title VI was not designed to be punitive, but was designed to make sure that funds were not used to support segregated programs. He also claimed that Title VI did not create any new government authority. "Most agencies," he stated, "now have authority to refuse or terminate assistance for failure to comply with a variety of requirements imposed by statute or by administrative action." While Title VI represented an unquestioned power of the federal government to establish the terms under which funds shall be disbursed, Humphrey made the point that "no recipient is required to accept Federal aid."

Title VI completely reversed the relationship that had existed between the Office of Education and local and state school districts. The Office of Education had traditionally defined its constituency as local and state school officials. The doctrine of local control and opposition to federal control had resulted in most money being disbursed by the Office of Education with minimum requirements and regulation. The Office of Education was viewed as a public servant of each local and state educational system.

With Title VI, the Office of Education was forced to embark on a path that put it in an adversary position in relation to many school systems. School systems would now be required to show proof of compliance with civil rights guidelines, and the Office of Education would be placed in the position of judging the adequacy of the actions of local school systems. The Office of Education was also given responsibility for drafting guidelines that would be used in enforcing the provisions of Title VI in government educational programs. This meant the Office of Education was placed in the position of being both interpreter and enforcer of the law. An agency that had always avoided any hint of federal control was suddenly handed the problem of protecting the constitutional rights of children around the country.

The precedent for using the threat of withholding federal money as a means of protecting civil rights also provided the basis for government attempts to end sex discrimination in the schools. Title IX of the 1972 amendments to the Higher Education Act stated: "No person in the United States shall, on the basis of sex, be excluded from participation in, be denied the benefits of, or be subjected to discrimination under any education program or activity receiving Federal Assistance."

The passage of Title IX reflected over a century of struggle by women to attain equal rights in the United States. Women had traditionally been discriminated against in specific educational programs and in hiring practices in colleges and universities. In the public schools, male athletic programs often received more funding and were more varied than those provided for females. Girls were often excluded from certain vocational programs. A federal task force stated: "We believe it is not the case that opportunities exist for women which they simply decline to exercise. Rather, we find there are specific barriers which block their progress and which will not disappear without conscious effort."

Title XI expanded the activities of the Office of Education to include the writing of guidelines and the establishment of methods to determine the possible existence of sex discrimination. Women's organizations stepped up their efforts to end sex discrimination by filing complaints against educational institutions. In 1972 alone, the year of the passage of Title IX, formal charges of sex discrimination were filed against 360 institutions of higher learning.

In 1974, federal protection of civil rights in the schools was again expanded with the passage of what was known as the Buckley Amendment, named after its sponsor, Senator James Buckley of New York. The Buckley Amendment was a rider to the Educational Amendments of 1974; it stated that educational institutions would lose federal funds unless they gave parents the right to examine and challenge school records. Senator Buckley stated in an interview in the January 1975 issue of the *Nation's Schools and Colleges* that the idea for the amendment came from an article he had read in a Sunday supplement in a newspaper. The concern was that teachers and school officials often put damaging statements into student files and never provided an opportunity for children or parents to see these statements. A careless comment by a third-grade teacher calling a student a "born liar" might follow the pupil through school and affect the attitudes of other teachers and the pupil's whole educational career. Moreover, student files remain with the school through college and are sometimes referred to when students seek employment. Senator Buckley stated in the magazine interview: "When you're talking about records that affect the life of an individual, that affect decisions that are being made about him, then he has a right to see them and to determine their accuracy."

The Buckley Amendment gives parents the right to examine school records, to challenge items they feel are inaccurate, and to have misleading records changed. Parents must also give their consent before any records are shown to any individuals or groups outside the school. The same rights of inspection and challenge are given to any student 18 and over who is attending an institution of higher learning. Specifically, parents and older students are allowed to inspect and review at will "official records, files and data, including all material that is incorporated into each student's cumulative record folder." These records include, in the words of the legislation: "identifying data; academic work completed; level achievement (grades, test scores); attendance data; scores on standardized intelligence, aptitude, and psychological tests; interest inventory results; health data; family background information; teacher or counselor ratings and observations; and verified reports of serious behavior patterns."

Although civil rights actions by the federal government continued through the 1970s, there appeared a wide-ranging dissent to this type of federal involvement in school systems. President Reagan's campaign in 1980 tried to use this dissent as a means of gaining voter support. Once in office, the Reagan administration took very definite action to attempt to limit and reduce the degree of federal civil rights enforcement in education.

A good example of the Reagan administration's attempt to limit enforcement was the 1983 Supreme Court case *Grove City College* v. *Bell*. In this particular case the Reagan administration successfully argued for limiting the enforcement of Title IX to specific programs within an educational institution and not to the entire institution. Title IX's original wording stated that any "program or activity" receiving federal aid must comply with the law's anti-discrimination requirements. Traditionally, "program or activity" encompassed the entire educational institution receiving federal aid. This meant that if only one unit of an educational institution received federal money then the entire institution would have to eliminate all discrimination based on differences in sex.

In the Grove City College case, the Reagan administration argued for a narrower interpretation of "program or activity." Its argument was that the law should only be applied to the specific activity receiving money within an institution and not to the entire institution. In the Grove City College case this issue was made explicit by the fact that Grove City College did not directly receive any aid from the federal government. As a private college it had attempted to avoid any entanglement with the federal government. But some of its students received financial aid directly from the federal government. Colleges enrolling students who receive this federal money were required to sign a form stating that they would not discriminate on the basis of sex. As a reflection of its belief in the separation of school and state, Grove City College refused to sign the federal form, and a government suit was filed against the school.

The Reagan administration saw the court case as an ideal opportunity to begin limiting the enforcement of civil rights legislation. They believed that the original intention of Congress was to limit enforcement to the specific program receiving federal money. Therefore, under this interpretation federal money does not follow a student from class to class. Federal control is strictly limited to individual programs.

Another example of reduction of civil rights enforcement under the Reagan administration occurred in the area of school desegregation. Before entering office, President Reagan informed the public of his own opposition to forced busing for purposes of school desegregation. After its election in 1980, President Reagan's administration did not file a school desegregation case until January 1984. And in that suit, filed against the Bakersfield, California, School District, a negotiated settlement that emphasized voluntary forms of desegregation was reached almost immediately.

Both the immediate settlement of the suit and the desegregation plan agreed upon represented the Reagan administration's attitude toward enforcement of school desegregation issues. Rather than pursuing lengthy court battles, the administration sought an early out-of-court settlement. Second, the settlement emphasized the use of magnet schools to bring about voluntary desegregation. And, it should be emphasized, this was only the first court case pursued by the administration after almost four years in office.

It is important to understand that the actions of the Reagan administration to limit and reduce enforcement of civil rights legislation did not involve a repudiation of the laws. In fact, what the actions meant was that civil rights enforcement by the federal government would probably continue but that the degree and extent of enforcement would depend upon the attitudes of the particular administration in office. Therefore, involvement in and regulation of local schools and school systems by federal civil rights legislation will probably continue, but its importance will vary with shifting political attitudes.

The importance of political attitudes has also affected the type of control exerted by the federal government through its funding of research and of development of educational materials. The most controversial aspects of federal involvement have been in curriculum development. The federal government first became involved in the development and sponsorship of public school curricula in the 1950s. Prior to that time, the Office of Education had only printed and distributed information about new curricula and organized national and regional conferences about them. But in the late 1950s the federal government began to provide actual financial support to groups to develop new curricula, as well as to federal institutes to train teachers and distribute new materials.

Federal involvement in curriculum writing in the late 1950s represents an additional step in the establishment of national control of the educational system. It provides an example of how a national curriculum can come into existence without direct control being imposed over all schools in the United States. One of the key government agencies in this process was the National Science Foundation, established by Congress in 1950. The foundation was a product of the dreams of government scientist Vannevar Bush. In a report written in the closing days of World War II, Bush had originally called for a National Science Foundation, which would have as its objective the increase in scientific capital in the United States. This was to be accomplished, according to Bush, by improving science education in the public schools, supporting basic research in science, and providing undergraduate and graduate fellowships in science. Bush felt that the improvement of science education in high schools was imperative if latent scientific talent was to develop. There was a great danger, he felt, if high school science teaching failed to awaken interest or to provide adequate instruction. The National Science Foundation's goal to improve science instruction in the public schools paved the way for federal support and the introduction of new curricula in the public schools.

The major involvement of the National Science Foundation in curriculum writing began in 1958, when President Eisenhower proposed the National Defense Education Act (NDEA) and, at the same time, called for a fivefold increase in appropriations for the scientific education activities of the National Science Foundation. Eisenhower claimed that the scientific education programs of the foundation "have come to be recognized by the education and scientific communities as among the most significant contributions currently being made to the improvement of science education in the United States."

This major increase in funding resulting from passage of the NDEA in 1958 went immediately to support and expand projects started earlier by the National Science Foundation. Two of the major groups involved were the Physical Science Study Committee, organized in 1956, and the School Mathematics Study Group, organized in 1958. The Physical Science Study Committee was the brainchild of physicist Jerrold Zacharias of the Massachusetts Institute of Technology. He decided in the mid-1950s that one way of getting around the shortage and mediocrity of high school physics courses was through the production of teaching films and classroom equipment. A statement of purpose given at the initial meeting of the Physical Science Study Committee called for changes in the content of physical science courses as a means of finding a "way of make more understandable to all students the world in which we live and to prepare better those who will do advanced work. It is probable that such a presentation would also attract more students to careers in science."

The distribution of materials by the Physical Science Study Committee and other curriculum groups sponsored by the National Science Foundation provides an excellent illustration of the combination of methods available to the national government to influence public schooling. First, government money was channeled through the National Science Foundation to support curriculum-writing groups. Second, money was provided in the NDEA for local school districts to purchase new equipment for science and mathematics programs. Third, local school systems were heavily influenced to purchase materials developed by the curriculum groups sponsored by the National Science Foundation, because their science and mathematics teachers were being trained to use these materials in summer institutes funded by the foundation. The summer institutes were attractive to teachers because no tuition was charged, and participants often received some form of monetary compensation for attending. In addition, many institutes gave academic credit for attendance. To most teachers, this meant a move up on the pay scale in their local school district.

This whole process was aided by the development of a national textbook market. Certainly one of the most important influences on the content of teaching in the public schools is the textbook. By the late 1950s fewer than 100 textbook companies were in the public-school textbook market. Approximately one-half of these companies concentrated on elementary-school textbooks; the rest published high-school texts. Almost all textbooks were distributed on a national basis and had to conform to state statutes that covered such things as the physical appearance of the book and marketing procedures. Textbook prices were essentially nationalized in 1934, with the passage of an Ohio law which stated that the price for any textbook sold in Ohio could not exceed the lowest price for the textbook sold anywhere else in the country. A majority of states followed the example of Ohio, with the result that textbook prices became a matter of nationwide competition. Added to these factors was the fact that the similarity of state and local study guides influenced the content of textbooks.

One result of the concentration of textbook publishing and the national market was the virtual creation of a national curriculum. A person could travel from Maine to California and find a similar lessons being taught in schoolhouses across the nation. In other words, the textbook industry had the ability to influence curriculum nationally by changing the nature and content of textbooks.

Textbook companies have not been in the business of sponsoring curriculum development and have had to rely on outside groups for new ideas and materials. The curriculum-study groups supported by the federal government provided new materials that could be incorporated into the textbooks in the national school market. The control of the textbook market became a very important strategy of the School Mathematics Study Group.

The School Mathematics Study Group combined influence over the textbook industry with federal funding and summer institutes from the National Science Foundation to spread the "new math" throughout the country like a rapidly burning brushfire. The initial writing session of the group began during the summer of 1958, with 21 participants drawn from college departments of mathematics and 21 from high schools. During this writing session an outline was developed for a series of textbooks in mathematics for grades 9 through 12 and for the writing of a series of units on specific topics for students in grades 7 and 8. The goal of the second summer writing session in 1959 was to carry out the actual writing of 6 textbooks and 6 teachers' manuals in a 9-week period. At the close of the summer's work there was a complete set of textbooks covering grades 7 through 12. During the fall of 1959 the new textbooks were tested in experimental centers around the country. The final revision of the textbook series took place during the summer of 1960. During the 1960–61 academic year the Yale University Press printed and sold 130,000 of the textbooks, with sales increasing to 500,000 the following year. Within four years of the organization of the School Mathematics Study Group, its material was being used by 20 percent of its intended market.

The tremendous success of the School Mathematics Study Group in being able to develop and market a textbook series in such a short period of time was a result of both its high level of federal funding and its sophisticated dealings with book publishers. In terms of the publishing industry, a committee was established by the study group after the textbook series was completed; each year the committee was to review all mathematics textbooks on the market to determine if texts comparable to those of the School Mathematics Study Group were available, and if so, to remove the study group's text that was in competition with the commercial publication. The procedure was designed to put competitive pressure on the textbook industry. This pressure forced publishers to begin marketing similar textbooks in 1961 and 1962.

In terms of federal funding, the School Mathematics Study Group began with an initial grant of $100,000 in 1958; during the summer months it received another $1.2 million. In 1960 it received another $2.8 million. During the late 1950s, given the value of the dollar, this was a considerable sum to finance a project.

The Physical Science Study Committee and the School Mathematics Study Group were landmarks in new curriculum developments of the late 1950s and early 1960s. Their work became models for many other areas of the school curriculum. In 1959 the American Institute of Biological Sciences Curriculum Study received a grant from the National Science Foundation and began working on a new curriculum for the public schools. Between 1960 and 1963 the Chemical Education Material Study produced a text, a laboratory manual, a teachers' guide, a set of motion pictures, and supplementary equipment.

The science and mathematics curriculums of the late 1950s and early 1960s represent one method the federal government has used to develop and distribute a national curriculum. Another method is exemplified by the career-education movement of the early 1970s. In this case, the program was initiated and financed through the Office of Education. In 1971 and 1972, Commissioner of Education Sidney Marland began to earmark discretionary funds provided by Congress to the Office of Education for the development of career-education models. Projects using these funds were begun in Arizona, California, Georgia, Michigan, and New Jersey. In addition, funds were made available to states through the Office of Education for the development and operation of career-education programs. As money started to flow from the federal coffers, educators began to jump on the bandwagon of career education. During the first two years, $100 million in discretionary funds went into the program. Commissioner Marland was able to announce in 1972–73, one year after the beginning of the program, that 750,000 young people had participated in career-education demonstrations and models supported by funds from the U.S. Office of Education, and that five state legislatures had been persuaded to approve funds to launch career education. He also reported that the Dallas public school system had been completely restructured around the concept of career education.

The power of the federal government to influence curriculum development and distribution of materials was fairly well established by the early 1970s. Its primary means of influence was the availability of money to finance these projects. Local and state governments provided either nothing or minimal amounts of money for new curriculum projects. Private foundations were sometimes a source of research and development funds. But none of these sources could really match the spending power of the federal government or the contacts the Office of Education had with local school administrators.

In the middle of the 1970s a controversy broke out about a social studies curriculum called *Man: A Course of Study* (MACOS). This turbulence seemed to indicate that the federal government would, in the future, restrict its activities to noncontroversial areas. Developers of MACOS received $2,166,900 in grants from the National Science Foundation to write, promote, and market a course designed to introduce students to anthropology and crosscultural studies. The course first presented animal behavior and then focused on a Canadian Eskimo group. In March 1975 the controversy exploded. Members of Congress attacked the curriculum for presenting allegedly "lurid examples of violence and sexual promiscuity." One unhappy congressman was critical that schoolchildren were being exposed to "human characteristics" such as adultery, cannibalism, incest, infanticide, murder, robbery, wife swapping, and sexual promiscuity.

The MACOS controversy made federal agencies wary not only of getting involved in controversial areas of the curriculum but also of distributing materials directly to the schools. It will be remembered that the National Science Foundation had used competitive techniques to influence publishers to produce similar materials for the schools or else had turned over the material directly to the publishers. In the case of MACOS, the National Science Foundation funded the publication and marketed the materials. Congressman Albert H. Quie, in an interview in the November 1976 issue of *Educational Leadership*, stated that one of the major problems with MACOS was that the "National Science Foundation went contrary to its traditional manner.... It did not make MACOS available to publishing firms. It published the program and made it available to schools themselves. And, that is where the NSF made the mistake."

Congressman Quie predicted in the interview that the federal government would probably continue federal development of curriculum, especially in vocational education and the physical sciences. "When you get into the social sciences, then I think we'll not see the federal government actually distributing curriculum [materials]." He went on to state that to "the extent that it finances the research, it will find some point short of directing the use of that curriculum by school systems."

The controversy over MACOS did not end federal involvement in curriculums. In 1980 a new controversy broke out over the regulations for bilingual education issued by the Department of Education. In a court case described in more detail in Chapter 10, it was ruled that local school systems had to provide special help to students who did not use English as their first language. The courts did not specify what program school systems had to provide to meet the special needs of these students.

In 1980 the Department of Education issued a set of regulations to bring school systems into compliance with the court decision. The problem that occurred with the regulations was that they specified a particular remedy. The regulations called for the establishment of bilingual education courses and detailed the manner in which local school systems were to respond to the special needs of children with language problems. The immediate reaction of local school systems and national organizations such as the American Federation of Teachers was that the federal government had overstepped the limits of its power. The complaint was that the courts had required some remedy to the situation but had not specified a particular remedy. The Department of Education, by calling for a particular remedy, was mandating a national curriculum in bilingual education.

The controversy was resolved in 1981, after the election of Ronald Reagan. The Department of Education, shortly after his inauguration, withdrew the bilingual regulations. One important lesson that can be learned from these events is the real power of the presidential office to control and shape education policies. Congress can pass legislation, and the courts can make decisions regarding education, but how that legislation is carried out and how the court decisions are applied depend on the actions of the executive branch of the federal government.

Support of educational research has also been affected by changes in the political climate. The major involvement of the federal government in educational research came with the passage of the 1965 Elementary and Secondary

Education Act, which provided legislative and financial support to the idea of government-sponsored research and development in education. It is important to understand that the sponsorship of research-and-development activities was considered to be a method to indirectly control the actions of local school systems. In this particular case, the concern about control was voiced in terms of educational change; educational research was to be the means of changing the actions of local school systems.

This argument was specifically stated by a government planning group, the Gardner Task Force, which was responsible for the research section of the Elementary and Secondary Education Act. The report of the Gardner Task Force declared: "We must overhaul American education." The key to this overhaul was to be the educational language, the report stated: "We now know, beyond all doubt, that educationally speaking, the old ways of doing things will not solve our problems. We are going to have to shed outworn educational practice, dismantle outmoded educational facilities, and create new and better learning environments."

The result of the research finds provided under the Elementary and Secondary Education Act was to make the federal government the major supporter of educational research. Educational research was further highlighted in the early 1970s, during the administration of President Richard Nixon, with the establishment of the National Institute of Education (NIE). The primary argument for the establishment of the NIE was that past educational policy and programs had failed because research had not been conducted before implementation. The purpose of NIE was to determine through research the best methods of achieving particular goals of educational policy.

The organizational structure of the NIE allowed for policy and politics to control research: In organizational terms the NIE followed the typical pattern of educational institutions, with an elite governing board and a bureaucratic structure that makes most of the decisions. It is important to keep in mind, as organizational features are reviewed here, that the NIE's major concern is the control of education by the channeling of research interests into particular fields, which is accomplished by making available government funds for certain areas of research. The NIE, by designating priority areas for research, creates a potential situation wherein the production of knowledge about education is guided, by the means of attracting researchers into desired areas with offers of monetary support.

The group responsible for formulating general policies for the NIE is the National Council of Educational Research. The original membership of the council was a combination of elites from the education community and the business community. This group established the original research priorities—these were essential skills, productivity, education and work, problem solving, and diversity. It is important to keep in mind that these research priorities might change with changing administrations.

This is precisely what did happen in the early 1980s. Once he assumed office, President Reagan appointed to the NIE a series of new directors whose research agendas were clearly conservative. Of major importance was the funding of research to investigate vouchers and tuition tax credits. Tuition tax credits had been the most important part of President Reagan's political platform for education. The dramatic shift in research emphasis in the NIE that took place with the election of President Reagan highlights the political nature and political uses of educational research.

Even with the political controversies surrounding federal educational policy, the methods of federal control over education had become established by the middle of the 1980s. The patterns of control were very complex because of the lack of direct Constitutional provision for federal involvement in education. Although many objected to federal involvement, it appeared by the 1980s that the federal government was permanently in the schools.

The methods and the degree of control will continue to be related to the political ideology of the administration in control of government. Whether federal funding should be primarily categorical, or in the form of block grants and general aid, will depend on the particular administration's view of the proper relationship between the federal government and local governments. In the same manner, the enforcement of civil rights legislation and research policy will continue to shift with administrations. What is clearly evident is that federal involvement has made education both a benefactor and victim of national politics.

The Politics of Education at the National Level

The importance of education in politics at the national level has increased with federal involvement in education. Prior to the 1950s, education played a minor role in national politics. But with increased federal involvement in education and the growing political activity of organized educational interest groups, education became a major political issue by the 1980s. One example of this has been the growing importance of educational issues in the mind of the voter. In a 1983 poll conducted for *Time* magazine by Yankelovich, Skelly, and White, voters were asked how much influence a presidential candidate's stand on a particular issue would have on a decision to support that candidate. Education ranked third, after inflation and unemployment (it was tied for third place with the issue of relationships with the Soviet Union). A poll conducted by the Gallup Organization for *Newsweek* in 1983 asked a similar question and found the issue of "the quality of public education" to be second in importance to the highest-ranking issue of "economic conditions in the country."

The growth as a national political issue of voter concern over education parallels the rise of education issues as a national compaign issue. In the 1950s and 1960s education was not a major campaign issue, but the topic grew in importance due to presidential politics. President Eisenhower used his advocacy of federal involvement in education through the National Defense Education Act as a means of answering the political problems created by the Soviet Union's early advances in technology related to space travel. In the same manner, President Johnson, in the 1960s, used education as a political tool in his war against poverty. One result of the actions of both of these presidents was that educational interest groups turned to the federal government for increasing financial support for the public schools and for maintaining existing programs. As the federal government became the focus of these groups, others who were critical of federal involvement and of the public schools also began to organize to influence politics at the national level. The result of the political activity of these groups was that education became a major issue in national politics.

The 1980 presidential election ushered in the new era of national educational politics. The incumbent, President Jimmy Carter, tried to win votes and build a strong campaign by gaining the support of major educational organizations. During the 1976 campaign President Carter had promised the National Education Association (NEA), the largest teacher organization, that a separate Department of Education would be established. This proposal was bitterly opposed by a rival teacher organization, the American Federation of Teachers (AFT), out of fear that the NEA would dominate the new department. In the 1980 campaign the NEA supported President Carter; the AFT supported Senator Edward Kennedy during the presidential primaries and only reluctantly supported Carter after Kennedy was unable to gain the Democratic party nomination.

President Carter gave the NEA and the newly appointed Secretary of Education, Shirley Hufstedler, a significant place in his 1980 campaign strategy. When Ms. Hufstedler was appointed as secretary, there was considerable concern in the education community about her lack of background in education. Most commentators felt that President Carter planned to make her the first woman to sit on the U.S. Supreme Court.

One thing was certain during the 1980 campaign: Ms. Hufstedler spent more time campaigning for President Carter than she did organizing the new Department of Education. Part of the campaign strategy was for Secretary Hufstedler to speak before local chapters of the NEA, portraying President Carter as the champion of the public school and urging members to hit the campaign trail and get out the vote for the incumbent.

President Carter's opponent, Ronald Reagan, appealed to a constituency different from that of the professional education organizations. Reagan attacked the federal government's role in education and called for the abolition of the Department of Education. His campaign platform included a proposal for tuition tax credits for parents choosing to send their children to private schools. This won the support of private-school interests, particularly parochial schools, and of that section of the public dissatisfied with the public schools. Reagan's proposal for tuition tax credits was vehemently attacked by the NEA and the AFT.

After President Reagan was elected in 1980 he continued to emphasize education as part of his political strategy. His major problem was his inability to get Congress to pass proposals to abolish the Department of Education, and to establish tuition tax credits and school prayer. Therefore, before the impending 1984 election, Reagan found himself being criticized by his original supporters for being ineffective and by the public-school establishment for his apparent lack of support of public education. To counter this situation President Reagan tried to use a report, *A Nation at Risk*, issued by his administration in 1983—one year before the 1984 election—as a politically safe method of trying simultaneously to project an image of himself as a friend of public education without alienating his original educational constituency.

President Reagan's use of the *Nation at Risk* report presented a political dilemma. Obviously, there could be no proposal for increased federal involvement in education. Also, President Reagan could not stress increased state academic requirements, because of the possible alienation of his original supporters, which included major opponents of all state standards over education. He thus faced the political problem of deciding which parts of the report to support in his effort to project a public image of concern with social issues and the public schools. The solution was to focus on that section of the report dealing with teachers and, for very specific political reasons, to concentrate on the issue of merit pay. Reagan's attempt to shine the public spotlight on this issue made 1983 into what can be called the "year of the teacher."

Reagan's support of merit pay immediately involved him with the two teachers' unions. In one sense he hoped to divide the two unions over the issue and hopefully gain some support from at least one of the unions during the 1984 campaign. Initially, Albert Shanker, president of the American Federation of Teachers, showed some sympathy and willingness to support the merit-pay concept. This show of sympathy gave Reagan an ideal opportunity to try and divide the educational community. In June 1983, Reagan invited Albert Shanker along wih other education officials to the White House to discuss merit pay. Of major importance was the fact that the National Education Association was not invited.

Education Week described this meeting in the following manner:

> Mr. Reagan, according to other sources, was also commencing a "divide-and-conquer" strategy to gain the support of most of the education community as the 1984 Presidential campaign begins, while excluding the NEA. The strategy, the sources said, involves generating education and public support for teacher-pay reforms, while portraying the NEA and the Democratic candidates seeking its endorsement as being on the wrong side of the issue.
>
> "It is clear that one of the things the administration is thinking about is how merit pay divides our community." said one education lobbyist.

In the end, Reagan's attempt to divide and conquer provided few political gains from the educational community. The AFT continued to attack the Reagan administration's policies and to back Democratic candidates. By December

1983, at a meeting in Indianapolis that was staged by the commission that had issued *A Nation at Risk*, Reagan emphasized school discipline and stressed that the federal government should not provide more money for education. This speech indicated that Reagan was less confident of this ability to win votes from the educational community and was instead appealing to the general public.

President Reagan's brief attempt to court the AFT and develop a broader base of educational support prior to the 1984 elections indicates the importance that education had attained as a national political issue. His actions also highlight the nature of national educational politics. Politicians must try to win support from educational organizations and reflect public attitudes about educational issues. Obviously, a candidate for office cannot represent every organization or individual. For instance, President Reagan sought support from a constituency composed of critics of public schooling, moral reformers, the Christian school movement, and supporters of private schools. On the other hand, his opponents have often sought support from teachers' unions and other organized supporters of public schools.

The conservative nature of Reagan's education policies were apparent in his appointment in 1985 of William Bennett as secretary of education. With the appointment of Bennett, the report of the Moral Majority, a conservative religious group, announced in headlines, "Finally a friend in Education." During the Reagan years the Moral Majority gained strength in the Department of Education. For instance, in 1985, Thomas Tancredo, Department of Education's Region VIII representative in Denver, distributed at government expense a speech written five years previously by the then-executive-director of the Moral Majority, Robert Billings. The speech declared that "godlessness has taken over America." President Reagan appointed Billings to direct the Department of Education's ten regional offices.

During confirmation hearings before the Senate Committee on Labor and Human Resources, Bennett, under oath, admitted he was screened for the position of Secretary of Education by 12 conservative organizations meeting under the umbrella of the Committee for Survival of a Free Congress. He claimed that pressure from the White House forced him to attend the meeting. Bennett told the Senate committee that he received a call from Ms. Lynn Ross Wood of the Office of Presidential Personnel. "The advice to me," he said, "was to attend the meeting, that they requested that I should attend this meeting."

Education can also play a role in congressional election campaigns. There are a small number of congressmen who do attempt to build their political reputation on educational issues. One example is given by Jack H. Schuster in his article, "An 'Education Congressman' Seeks Reelection," in Harry L. Summerfield's *Power and Process*. The case described in the article concerns Representative John Brademas, who was seeking reelection in a highly contested congressional district that included South Bend, Indiana. An important part of Brademas's strategy was to win support from educational groups in the area, which included Notre Dame University. Brademas had sponsored some education-related legislation and had won awards from education groups.

Brademas attempted to use his involvement in education in a number of ways to win votes in the election. Five days before the election, a representative of the National Education Association gave Brademas its Distinguished Service Award. Brademas's staff arranged for this award to be presented at the Faculty Club of Notre Dame University and invited local school and university educators to attend. A top-ranking official of the Department of Health, Education, and Welfare who was interested in Brademas's reelection was also on hand to make kind comments about Brademas. During the award presentation a letter was read from the Indiana affiliate of the NEA praising Brademas's work in Congress.

Teachers in South Bend were represented by the American Federation of Teachers. A telephone call from the national organization stimulated the local organization to support Brademas. A group of 18 teachers volunteered to canvass for Brademas under the banner *Teachers for Brademas.* Brademas's staff helped train the teachers for door-to-door campaigning.

Written support for Brademas's campaign was given by the Department of Audio-Visual Instruction of the National Education Association in letters sent to members residing within the congressional district. Other aid came from two officials of the Department of Health, Education, and Welfare. One official made kind remarks at the awards ceremony and then attended a meeting of local workers and officials of the Democratic party to give a pep talk for Brademas's reelection. The other official wrote letters of solicitation to 50 or 60 possible contributors to Brademas's campaign. A "Dear Educator" letter was mailed to 9,000 school and college personnel within Brademas's congressional district. In this letter Brademas urged their support because of his sponsorship of educational legislation. In addition to all these activities, a group of faculty wives from Notre Dame contacted college teachers for contributions and for permission to use their names in a newspaper advertisement which, when it appeared, proclaimed in banner headlines: *350 College and University Educators from the Third Congressional District Endorse Congressman John Brademas's Bid for Reelection.*

A national campaign to gain support for Brademas's reelection was organized under a National Friends of John Brademas Committee, whose membership included a former dean of Harvard's Graduate School of Education and a former commissioner of education. Under a special letterhead, this group mailed 25,000 letters praising Brademas's educational activities. A slightly different version of the letter was mailed to Americans who had attended Oxford University, where Brademas had been a Rhodes Scholar. These efforts were directed at gaining financial support for the campaign.

Shortly before the election, Brademas, in cooperation with the Department of Education at Notre Dame, organized a conference on "Major Tensions in American Education: Shaping Policies for the '70's." Attending the conference and providing support for Brademas were a former commissioner of education, the president of the Ford Foundation, the director of the teacher corps, and the superintendent of the Cleveland public schools. Several thousand invitations to the meeting at Notre Dame were mailed to school administrators and teachers throughout northern Indiana.

How much did this effort to enlist the support of the education community contribute to Brademas's victory in the election? And of even greater importance, can members of Congress build their political support on issues related to education? Schuster's study of the Brademas campaign is inconclusive on these questions. Schuster states: "On balance, then, the efforts made to harness educators at the local and national levels yielded visible but modest results. A cost-benefit analysis might well indicate that Brademas should have invested much of that campaign energy in ways other than those calculated to win minds, money, and manpower from within the education community."

The President and the Congress

A great deal of the activity of the federal government in education since the 1950s can be explained in terms of presidential politics. Traditionally, American presidents have not given a great deal of attention to educational matters because education has been considered a state and local matter and because other domestic and foreign problems have taken precedence over educational issues. But, beginning in the 1950s, American presidents have been forced to confront educational problems directly, as a result of national and international events. For instance, President Eisenhower, during the early years of his administration, did not make education a focus of his administration. In fact, he refused to discuss the 1954 decision (*Brown* v. *Board of Education of Topeka*) on school desegregation. In his autobiography, *Waging Peace, 1956–1961*, he stated that he felt the civil rights campaign was an attempt to cause him to lose political support in the presidential election of 1956.

All of this changed in the fall of 1957, when Governor Orval Faubus took action to block the integration of schools in Little Rock, Arkansas, by ordering the National Guard into the area. When black students attempted to enroll in the previously all-white high school in Little Rock, they found the doors of the schoolhouse blocked by the National Guard and were informed that the school was off limits to "colored" students. Such an open and flagrant violation of the Supreme Court decision forced Eisenhower to take action. He federalized the Arkansas National Guard and sent federal troops into the city. He then went on national television to explain the involvement of the federal government in local desegregation matters.

During President Eisenhower's administration, the civil rights movement and the National Defense Education Act of 1958 made education an important factor in presidential politics. John F. Kennedy became the first president to make aid to education a major part of his domestic program and give it vigorous personal support. President Johnson, under pressure from the civil rights movement, made education a central part of his War on Poverty. In many ways, President Johnson wanted to be known as the "education president." Richard Nixon made opposition to busing for desegregation an important item in his 1972 campaign. Both the 1968 and 1972 presidential campaigns included major discussions of school desegregation. During the 1976 campaign, busing and school desegregation were not major items discussed by Gerald Ford or Jimmy Carter, one reason being that school desegregation had become such an explosive issue that both candidates seemed to feel it was better avoided as an issue.

One of the important powers presidents have had with respect to education has been the power to propose educational legislation, such as President Johnson's important Elementary and Secondary Education Act. Another and somewhat more negative power has been the power to withhold money from the financing of educational legislation. This became one of the hallmarks of President Nixon's administration. The Nixon administration adopted a method of budgeting called the "full-employment budget," in which the amount of federal spending is determined by economic conditions. James Guthrie argues (in an article on "The Flow of Federal Funds for Education" in Harry Summerfield's *Power and Process*) that under full-employment budgeting, where federal expenditures are "speeded up, slowed down, delayed, or drawn out, education expenditures tend to be among the first affected. This is so because dollars for school-related programs represent one of the few places in the budget where the president has a degree of discretion." Yet another important power of the president is to withhold money appropriated by Congress for particular legislation. This occurs when presidents are not willing to veto entire appropriations bills, but object to parts of the legislation. Richard Nixon used his executive prerogative freely against education legislation. Guthrie claimed that "between 1969 and 1973, it is likely that the Nixon administration forestalled or forbade the spending of approximately $1 billion in education funds."

The president can exert direct pressure upon educational policies. A classic example of this, described by Gary Orfield in his study, *The Reconstruction of Southern Education: The Schools and the 1964 Civil Rights Act*, occurred in 1965, when the USOE decided to apply Title VI of the 1964 Civil Rights Act to northern school districts. The USOE first took action against Chicago and announced that $32 million was being withheld from the Chicago public school system pending investigation of alleged racial segregation. At the time, Chicago had one of the best-documented cases of racial discrimination in the North. Black students in Chicago attended segregated, overcrowded schools on a double-shift basis. As a result, black students spent less time in school than white students.

The attempt by the USOE to withhold funds from Chicago was almost immediately stopped by Lyndon Johnson because of pressure from Chicago's Mayor Richard Daley and from congressional leaders from Illinois. Johnson quickly let it be known that he wanted the funds to begin flowing to Chicago. After the Chicago incident, the major thrust of Title VI under the Johnson administration was directed at the South.

The example just cited demonstrates the way in which presidents can use the regulatory power of the Department of Education, and education spending, to improve their political positions and pay off political debts. Obviously, Republican presidents will tend to be more sympathetic toward Republican mayors and governors and Democratic presidents to members of their party. For instance, under Republican administrations in the 1970s, the USOE did apply title VI in Chicago, but not in notoriously segregated Cleveland, where the mayor was a Republican.

Presidential power and the power of federal agencies such as the Department of Education all function within the framework of legislation passed by Congress. When the president impounds money, it is money appropriated by congressional legislation. When the president pressures agencies to act in certain ways and appoints particular people to those agencies, it is mainly in terms of influencing how congressional legislation is interpreted and executed. The Constitution invests in Congress "all legislative powers." In addition, Congress participates in the overseeing of the administration of policies by administrative agencies.

The majority of congressional activity takes place within a committee system. Committees can propose, review, hold hearings, and recommend action on particular legislative items related to the work of a particular committee. The committee in the House of Representatives responsible for educational legislation is the Committee on Education and Labor, in the Senate it is the Committee on Labor and Public Welfare. Education is not the primary concern of either of these committees, however. Their primary concern usually is legislation affecting labor, and selection to the committees is therefore usually based on a member's attitude toward labor.

Membership on these two congressional committees is not highly prized because the committees deal with emotional issues that have little payoff in terms of furthering political careers. Since membership on these committees is not considered as prestigious as other committee assignments, there tends to be a high rate of turnover. Because of the lack of stability of committee membership, plus the fact that the primary interest of the committee is labor, relatively little educational expertise is to be found among committee members.

The result of this relative lack of congressional expertise in education, and the lack of major interest in educational legislation, is similar to the situation in state legislatures; in both cases there is a heavy reliance on expert knowledge and on opinion from government agencies and outside lobbying groups. The one major difference between members of Congress and most state legislators is that members of the Senate and House have staffs that can be used to investigate issues surrounding legislation. This reduces part of the dependence on outside groups.

As the 1980s began, the mood of the majority of Americans seemed to be opposed to federal intervention not only in education but in many fields. The expanded role of the federal government in education in the 1950s and 1960s seemed to have produced no substantial improvements in the quality of education. Complaints about deteriorating standards in schools and the poor quality of public-school graduates seemed not to have been answered by federal intervention. Civil rights and quality of educational opportunity certainly have increased since the 1950s, but this was not because of actions by the president and Congress. These improvements were primarily the work of the courts in protecting the civil rights of citizens.

The expansion of the role of the federal government in education did result in increased bureaucratic structures at the state and local levels and an increased politicalization of education. Anyone who saw the size of the office staffs in state departments of education and local boards of education prior to the 1960s would have to be amazed at their increased size during the 1960s and 1970s as personnel were hired to deal with federal programs and grants.

Another result of the expanded federal role in education was to make education a factor in national presidential politics. As discussed earlier in this chapter, the 1984 national campaign contained a great deal of rhetoric concerning education and significant attempts to win various educational constituents. National educational politics has also increased lobbying by educational interest groups. As discussed in the next chapter, these groups have increasingly used lobbying techniques to influence legislation and the Department of Education.

Exercises

1. Compose a list of the educational goals and concerns of the president of the United States. What other groups in the United States share these goals and concerns?
2. Contact a local member of Congress and ask what she or he thinks are the most important educational issues for the federal government. Ask if educational issues are important in her or his campaigning for Congress.
3. Investigate what percentage of financial support in local schools is received from the federal government.
4. Contact an official of a local school system and ask him or her the current requirements and guidelines of the federal government for compliance with the demands of federal legislation.

Suggested Readings and Works Cited in Chapter

"Education and Politics: A Sample of Public Opinion," *Education Week* 3, no. 22 (February 29, 1984). This "Databank" section of *Education Week* contains polls by

Time/Yankelovich, Skelly, and White, and *Newsweek*/Gallup, ranking public opinion on the subject of the importance of education in decisions made by voters.

Education Week. This weekly newspaper is one of the best sources of information on national educational politics.

Hearing Before the Committee on Labor and Human Resources, United States Senate, 97th Congress, First Session on William J. Bennett, of North Carolina, To Be Secretary, Department of Education, January 28, 1985. This congressional hearing contains evidence of the conservative influence within the Department of Education during the Reagan administration.

Orfield, Gary. *The Reconstruction of Southern Education: The Schools and the 1964 Civil Rights Act.* New York: Wiley-Interscience, 1969. A study of the effects of the 1964 Civil Rights Act on the desegregation of southern schools.

Spring, Joel. *The Sorting Machine: National Educational Policy Since 1945.* New York: Longman, 1976. A history and analysis of federal educational policy since World War II.

White, Eileen. "Reagan, Four Education Officials Meet; N.E.A. Left Out of Talk on Teachers." *Education Week* 2, no. 38 (June 15, 1983): 1. The news story about President Reagan's attempt to capture the support of the AFT.

9

Teachers' Organizations and Other Interest Groups

Educational interest groups in America have had important lobbying functions at state and national levels in terms of being sources of information and initators of educational proposals. Programs appearing in educational legislation usually originate in the work of these educational interest groups. In addition, some interest groups attempt to influence legislative candidates. The campaign of John Brademas discussed in the last chapter is an example of this type of activity. Some educational groups, particularly private foundations, also provide money for educational research and for programs that often become sources of innovative ideas in education. The ability of these private foundations to determine what programs and research to support sometimes gives them powerful influence over educational policy.

Other private groups influence educational policy by the very nature of their activity. Educational Testing Service indirectly controls the admissions policies of many institutions of higher education through the administration of tests such as the Scholastic Aptitude Test and the College Entrance Examination Board. Educational Testing Service has developed a further major gatekeeping function through the administration of entrance examinations to many professional and graduate schools. Independent agencies that accredit secondary schools and institutions of higher education directly affect the curriculum and organization of those schools through their particular standards for accreditation.

Two of the interest groups to be discussed in this chapter are the largest organizations of teachers, the National Education Association (NEA) and the

American Federation of Teachers (AFT). The major difference between these two groups is the AFT's affiliation with an organized labor group, the AFL-CIO. The NEA claims that its strength is in its size and its independence from organized labor. The *NEA Handbook 1980–81* listed its total membership at 1.6 million, while the AFT publication, *American Teacher*, gave its 1981 membership as 580,000. The NEA claims that its larger membership and its professionalism gives it superior ability to represent American teachers. On the other hand, the AFT claims that its affiliation with organized labor provides its members with a broad base of support in terms of people in the labor movement and the financial resources of organized labor.

The AFT's affiliation with organized labor has contributed to its image as the more militant of the two organizations. Today, some observers say there is little difference between the organizations. For instance, the AFT, taking its cue from organized labor, pioneered in the use of the strike and collective bargaining techniques as ways of improving education and protecting teachers. During the 1960s, however, the NEA began to use similar tactics; and in the 1970s it became associated with the Coalition of American Public Employees (CAPE), which represents roughly four million public employees. Currently, the major objective of CAPE is to achieve collective bargaining legislation for all public employees. In the 1970s the NEA essentially became an organized professional union, but one without affiliation with the AFL-CIO.

For many years the AFT displayed broader social and political concerns than the NEA. In the middle of the 1970s the NEA's image changed when it endorsed and campaigned in 1976 for the election of President Jimmy Carter. By the middle of the 1980s the NEA had become so politically active that the AFT was accusing it of trying to be a political "kingmaker." In fact, the AFT claimed it had more interest in educational standards than the NEA. What these accusations meant was that both the NEA and AFT had become full-fledged unions with concerns that extended beyond the schools to other social and political issues.

The National Education Association (NEA)

The NEA was formed in 1857 as part of an attempt to bring together a variety of educational associations that had developed in the United States. The original letter calling for the first meeting stated: "The eminent success which has attended the establishment and operations of the several teachers' associations in the state is the source of mutual congratulations among all friends of popular education." The letter went on to state the goal of nationalizing the efforts of state associations: "Believing that what has been accomplished for the states by state associations may be done for the whole country by a National Association, we, the undersigned, invite our fellow-teachers throughout the United States to assemble in Philadelphia. . . ."

The 1857 meeting in Philadelphia gave birth to an organization that in the nineteenth and early-twentieth centuries had major influence over the shaping of American schools and contributed to the nationalizing of the American school system. From the platform of its conventions and the work of its committees came curriculum proposals and policy statements that were adopted from coast to coast. Until the 1960s the work of the NEA tended to be dominated by school superintendents, college professors, and administrators. These educational leaders would take the proposals of the NEA back to their local communities for discussion and possible adoption. The NEA thus had an important nationalizing function through the sharing of information between school leaders from different parts of the country and through its recommendations and proposals.

Examples of the work of the NEA include its major role in the shaping of the modern high school. In 1892 the NEA formed the Committee of Ten on Secondary School Studies, under the leadership of Charles Eliot, the president of Harvard University. The Committee of Ten appointed 9 subcommittees with a total membership of 100 to determine the future of the American high school. The membership of these committees reflected the domination of the organization by school administrators and representatives of higher education: Fifty-three were college presidents or professors, 23 were headmasters of private schools, and the rest were superintendents and representatives from teacher-training institutions. The work of the Committee of Ten set the stage for the creation in 1913 of the NEA Commission on the Reorganization of Secondary Education, which in 1981 issued its epochmaking report, *Cardinal Principles of Secondary Education*. This report urged the creation of comprehensive high schools offering a variety of curricula, as opposed to the establishment of separate high schools offering single curricula such as college preparatory, vocational, and commercial. This report became the major formative document of the modern high school.

The NEA also had a major influence on the standardization of teacher training in the United States. The Normal Department of the NEA began surveying the status of institutions for teacher education in 1886, and debates began within the organization about the nature of teacher education. The official historian of the NEA, Edgar B. Wesley, stated in this *NEA: The First Hundred Years*: "By 1925 the training of teachers was rather systematically standardized." The work of the Normal Department of the NEA can claim a large share of the credit for this standardization.

NEA conventions and meetings also became a central arena for the discussion of curriculum changes in elementary and secondary schools. During the 1920s and 1930s large numbers of surveys, studies, yearbooks, and articles were published. In 1924 the Department of Superintendence began issuing what were to be successive yearbooks on various aspects of the curriculum at various grade levels. In 1943 the Society for Curriculum Study merged with the NEA Department of Supervisors and Directors of Instruction to form an enlarged department called the Association for Supervision and Curriculum Development (ASCD). ASCD is still recognized as the major professional organization for the discussion of curriculum issues.

After the passage of the National Defense Education Act in 1958, the NEA's leadership role in the determination of national educational policy was greatly reduced as the federal government became the major springboard for national policy. As we shall see later in the chapter, during the 1960s and 1970s the NEA became an organization whose central focus was teacher welfare and government lobbying. This shift was a result of several developments: the emergence of the leadership role of the federal government, demands within the NEA for more emphasis on teacher welfare, greater democratic control of the organization, and the success of the AFT in winning collective bargaining for its members (thus serving as a model for the NEA).

To appreciate these changes in the role of the NEA, one must understand some of the traditional criticisms of the organization. No one has denied the important leadership role of the NEA, but the organization has been attacked in past years for its close association with the American Legion, its early bias against women, its lack of concern about teacher welfare, and its control by educational elites. Except the NEA's continued association with the American Legion, these other problems are no longer major issues within the NEA. Understanding how these problem issues have evolved in the NEA helps in understanding the difference between the NEA and the AFT.

The NEA and the American Legion formed an alliance in 1921 around mutual interests in the Americanization of aliens and the teaching history, citizenship, and patriotism. American Legion speakers began to appear on programs at NEA conventions, and both organizations sponsored teaching booklets and an annual American Education Week. The right-wing bias of the American Legion and its concern about subversion of America by left-wing radicals resulted in conflict between the two organizations in the 1950s. In 1952 an article titled "Your Child Is Their Target" appeared in the June issue of the *American Legion Magazine*. The article claimed that a subversive movement had existed in the teaching profession for 30 years. Members of the NEA denounced the article as containing misinformation and as being hostile to teachers and the schools. Some members of the NEA tried to get a resolution passed by the annual convention denouncing the American Legion. When the resolution failed, the next step by the NEA was to submit an answering article for publication in the *American Legion Magazine*. The Legion refused to publish the article but did agree to prepare a second article on the subject and submit it to the NEA for criticism. This major confrontation between the two organizations did not result in the breakdown of their association. The American Legion and the NEA have continued to sponsor American Education Week.

An early criticism of the NEA concerned the second-class role of women within the organization. The original 1857 constitution of the NEA limited membership to "gentlemen." This wording was not changed until 1866, when women within the organization demanded that "gentlemen" be changed to "persons." After 1866 women began to attain some offices within the organization, but never in proportion to their numbers within the profession. Although after the Civil War women outnumbered men in the teaching profession, men outnumbered women in administrative positions and offices held in organizations such as the NEA. Not until 1910 was a woman, Ella Flagg Young, elected NEA president. Even though Young had been a teacher, principal, district superintendent, professor of education, and superintendent of the Chicago schools, it still required a great deal of struggle by her supporters to get her elected president of the organization. After Young's election, a struggle continued within the organization for equal representation for women; it was resolved in 1917 when a tradition began of alternating between men and women in elections to the presidency.

The traditional image of the NEA as an organization dominated by school administrators and college professors is a product of its early organization. As mentioned, these groups did dominate the policy-making committees and offices within the organization. This situation began to change in the early part of the twentieth century as women more actively sought offices within the organization. Until 1921, control of the NEA was in the hands of the business meeting of members. What this did was create a situation of local control, in which those in attendance at the national conventions composed the business meeting of members. The reason Ella Flagg Young won the presidency of the organization in 1910 in Boston was because numbers of women came for the sole purpose of voting for her. In 1921 large groups of women again attended the convention in an effort to elect Grace Strachan. In reaction to the growing militancy of women and the ability of groups to capture national meetings, it was proposed that the NEA change to a system of representative control. Under the representative plan, individuals would attend and vote at conventions as elected representatives of local and state education associations. When this organizational plan was adopted by the NEA in 1921, it was an attempt to curb the growing power of women and classroom teachers against the traditional leaders of the NEA, but at the same time it reduced the power of national leadership by giving power to local and state groups to elect representatives.

The current organization and control of the NEA reflects the increased power gained by classroom teachers in the twentieth century, particularly during the militant years of the 1960s. According to the *NEA Handbook 1981–82*, the Representative Assembly consists of some 7,200 delegates of state and local affiliates, student NEA chapters, retired teachers, school nurses, and higher-education and educational-support members. The Representative Assembly is the primary legislative and policy-making body of the organization. The board of directors consists of one director from each state affiliate and from the Student NEA, plus an additional director for each twenty thousand active NEA members within each state affiliate and an additional director for every twenty thousand members of the Student NEA. The democratization of control of the NEA is reflected in the 1981–82 membership of the board of directors. All of the 110 regular members of the board of directors are classroom teachers. The three at-large directors are public-school administrators. The NEA can no longer be accused of being an organization dominated by administrators and college professors.

One of the things that accompanied the development of teacher control of the NEA was its increased concern with teacher welfare. It should be remembered that the NEA was originally organized to provide a national platform for developing ideas in education, and not to deal with teacher welfare issues such as salaries, working conditions, and teachers' rights. It was not until 1905 that the NEA conducted its first survey of teachers' salaries, and only in the 1920s did it begin advocating both higher salaries and tenure laws. Teacher tenure became a major issue in the 1920s when, under the pressure of the Red Scare of the early years of that decade, many teachers lost their jobs because of their political beliefs. Tenure was considered a means of protecting the freedom of speech of teachers.

Wesley's *NEA: The First Hundred Years* claims that the NEA's advocacy of teacher welfare resulted over the years in major improvements for teachers and administrators. The word "claim" is used because the NEA did not use any direct pressure such as the strike or collective bargaining before the 1960s. Whether the improvements were actually the result of the advocacy of the NEA is therefore difficult to determine. What the NEA claims to have achieved is the increase in average salaries of classroom teachers, the establishment of tenure laws in 32 states, and the establishment of teacher-retirement plans. It is probably true that the lobbying activities of the state affiliates did contribute to the passage of both tenure and retirement laws.

In 1962, the activities of the NEA underwent a dramatic transformation, when it launched a program for collective negotiations. This meant that local affilates would attempt to achieve collective-bargaining agreements with local boards of education. This development completely changed the nature of local organizations and required a rewriting of local constitutions to include collective bargaining. Up to this point in time, many local education associations had been controlled by the local administrators, who used the local organizations to convey policies determined by the board and administration. Collective bargaining reversed this situation and turned the local affiliates into organizations that told boards and administrators what teachers themselves wanted.

The NEA's early approach to collective bargaining differed from that of the union-oriented AFT, which had pioneered collective bargaining in education. The NEA claimed it was involved in professional negotiating and not in union collective bargaining. Professional negotiation, according to the NEA, would remove negotiation procedures from labor precedents and laws and would resort to state educational associations, rather than those of labor, to mediate or resolve conflicts that could not be settled locally.

All pretense of the NEA not being a union ended in the 1970s, when the NEA joined the Coalition of American Public Employees (CAPE). CAPE is a nonprofit corporation composed of the National Education Association; American Federation of State, County, and Municipal Employees, AFL-CIO; National Treasury Employees Union; Physicians National Housestaff Association; and American Nurses Association. As mentioned, these organizations represent about four million public employees. The stated purpose of CAPE is "to provide a means of marshalling and coordinating the legislative, legal, financial, and public relations resources of the member organizations in matters of common concern." The most important of these matters "is supporting legislation to provide collective-bargaining rights to all public employees, including teachers."

By the 1980s, support of collective-bargaining legislation became one of many legislative goals of the NEA; the organization by this time was also directing a great deal of its energies to lobbying for legislation and support of political candidates. The turning point for the NEA was its endorsement of Jimmy Carter in the 1976 presidential election. This was the first time the NEA had supported a presidential candidate. After this initial involvement, the NEA expanded its activity to support candidates in primary elections. In 1980, the NEA worked actively in the primaries to assure the victory of Jimmy Carter over Edward Kennedy for the Democratic nomination. In 1984, the NEA commited itself to the support of Walter Mondale for the Democratic-party nomination.

The NEA's support of "pro-education" political candidates began in the early 1970s. For instance, in 1974 the NEA claimed that of the 310 congressional candidates endorsed by the NEA, 81 percent were elected. The methods used by the NEA to support candidates include identifying pro-education candidates by keeping a tally of their voting records in Congress, distributing information about how candidates vote, maintaining state political-action committees, and maintaining liaison with major political parties to influence their actions with regard to educational issues.

The major political organization in the NEA is the National Educational Association Political Action Committee (NEA-PAC). The funds for this organization are obtained through voluntary contributions from teachers. As stated in the *NEA Handbook 1981–82*, the objective of NEA-PAC is "to help elect to federal office those candidates who support federal legislation consistent with the policies established by the NEA Representative Assembly." The methods of support involve giving "federal candidates who are friends of education...a financial contribution to the candidate's campaign."

Being identified as a "friend of education" is dependent upon support of the NEA's legislative agenda. For example, in 1982 the NEA established a three-tier agenda for legislative action. The first tier was called priority legislation, which was to be given continuous political support. The first tier of priority legislation included legislation for the federal government to provide one-third of the funding for local school districts, and federally guaranteed collective-bargaining legislation. The second tier involved current congressional issues identified as being of major importance to the NEA. There were 11 different legislative issues listed for the second tier. These issues ranged from continued support of the Department of Education to opposition to tuition tax credits and vouchers. The third tier involved four different areas of continuing concern to the NEA—adequate support of existing federal legislation regarding education, improving the welfare of retired NEA members, protection of civil and human rights, and support for equal-education opportunities.

The NEA's support of political candidates and legislation represents a major break with its origins in the nineteenth century and portends a possible important role for it in American politics. Both its size and the orientation of its membership make it an organization that any political candidate must respect. By its support of legislation and candidates, the NEA has forced the political spotlight to shine on educational issues.

The American Federation of Teachers (AFT)

Unlike the NEA's origins as a national policy-making organization, the American Federation of Teachers (AFT) began in the struggle by female grade school teachers for an adequate pension law in Illinois. The first union local, the Chicago Teachers Federation, was formed in 1897 under the leadership of Catherine Goggin and Margaret Haley. Its early fights centered on pensions and teacher salaries. As a result of its success in winning salary increases, its membership increased to 2,500 by the end of its first year. In 1902, with the urging of famous settlement-house reformer Jane Addams, the Chicago Teachers Federation joined the Chicago Federation of Labor, which placed it under the broad umbrella of the American Federation of Labor (AFL).

From its beginnings, the AFT placed teacher-welfare issues and improving public education in the more general context of the labor movement in the United States. In an interview titled "The School-Teacher Unionized" in the November 1905 issue of the *Educational Review*, Margaret Haley declared: "We expect by affiliation with labor to arouse the workers and the whole people, through the workers, to the dangers confronting the public schools from the same interests and tendencies that are undermining the foundations of our democratic republic." Those "same interests" referred to in Haley's speech were big business organizations, against whom Haley felt both labor and educators were struggling. The early union movement believed there was unity between the educators' struggle to gain more financial support for the schools from big business, and labor's struggle with the same interests to win collective bargaining rights. Haley went on to state, "It is necessary to make labor a constructive force in society, or it will be a destructive force. If the educational question could be understood by the labor men, and the labor question by the educators, both soon would see they are working to the same end, and should work together."

Margaret Haley's comments during the interview reflected ideas about what were thought to be mutually supportive roles between teachers and organized labor. On the one hand, teachers were to work for the interests of workers by fighting for better schools and working to remove antilabor material from the classroom. In other words, teachers would fight to provide the best education for workers' children. Organized labor, on the other hand, would provide the resources of its organization to support the teachers' struggle for improved working conditions and greater financial support for the schools. In addition, the type of education received by children in the schools would provide children with the economic and political knowledge needed to continue the work of the union movement, and teachers could also share their knowledge with the adult members of the labor movement. Teachers would also increase their political and economic knowledge through their association with the labor movement.

The early work of the Chicago Teachers Federation reflected its commitment to these ideals. It is credited with being an important force behind the passage in 1903 of the Illinois Child Labor Law. During the same period, Margaret Haley found that one of the serious financial handicaps of the Chicago school district was caused by the failure of three large corporations to pay their taxes. With the cooperation of a former Illinois governor, John Altgeld, the federation entered into litigation against People's Gas, Light and Coke Company, the Chicago Telephone Company, and Edison Electric Light Company and successfully forced these corporations to pay $249,554 in taxes due to the Board of Education.

Another of the early goals of the AFT was increased participation of teachers in the decision making of local school districts. Support for this issue came from Ella Flagg Young, who was appointed superintendent of Chicago's schools in 1909. She instituted a system of teachers' councils that allowed the teachers to assist in formulating educational policy. Ella Flagg Young's support of the early efforts by teachers for more democratic control of the schools is one reason why Margaret Haley provided support for her election to the presidency of the NEA. It should be noted that not until the 1920s did the AFT consider itself a rival of the NEA. During these early years it viewed itself as something of a radical segment of the NEA.

Concern about teacher participation in the control of the schools was one of the major elements in the organization of a teacher's union in New York City in 1912. The statement calling for the organization of teachers in New York declared: "Teachers should have a voice and a vote in the determination of education policies.... We advocate the adoption of a plan that will permit all teachers to have a share in the administration of the affairs of their own schools." It should be pointed out that the early demands by teacher's unions did not involve collective-bargaining rights, but administrative rearrangements that would allow for greater teacher participation.

In December 1912, the newly established magazine of the union movement, the *American Teacher*, issued a statement of the beliefs of the growing union movement in education. First, the statement argued that the improvement of American education depended on arousing teachers to realize that "their professional and social standing is far too low to enable them to produce effective results in teaching." Second, it was necessary for teachers to study the relation of education "to social progress, and to understand some of the important social and economic movements going on in the present-day world." Third, it was believed that teachers could use their experience in teaching to adjust education to the needs of modern living. Fourth, in one of the earliest declarations for the end of sexism in education, the statement called for high-quality teaching "without sex-antagonism."

In 1915, union locals from Chicago and Gary, Indiana, met and officially formed the American Federation of Teachers. In 1916 this group, along with locals from New York, Pennsylvania, Oklahoma, and Washington, D.C., were accepted into the American Federation of Labor as the American Federation of Teachers. At the presentation ceremony, the head of the AFL, Samuel Gompers, welcomed the AFT to "the fold and the bond of unity and fraternity of the organized labor movement of our Republic. We earnestly hope... that it may...give and receive mutual sympathy and support which can be properly exerted for the betterment of all who toil and give service—aye, for all humanity."

The platform of the newly organized AFT called for improved teacher welfare and security through a program of tenure, increased salaries, teacher-exchange programs, and sabbatical-leave plans. In addition, the AFT opposed overcrowding in the schools and called for a decrease in class size. The platform condemned the movement at that time toward compulsory military service. In terms of educational programs, the AFT called for special programs for the gifted child and the development of an experimental pedagogy, and expressed hopes for a scientific basis for education. This platform remained relatively unchanged from 1916 to 1929.

The AFT did not grow at a rapid rate; in fact, it proved very difficult during the 1920s to organize new locals. One of the more interesting experiments of the AFT during the 1920s was the establishment of the Brookwood Labor College and the Manumit school for workers' children. Both were established in reaction to what was believed to be the conservative economic and political philosophies of American colleges and public schools. There was particular concern about the domination of boards of education and boards of trustees of colleges by big business and professionals. The Manumit school was an experiment to see if the labor movement could establish its own system of schooling as an alternative to the public schools. The Manumit school was operated as an industrial democracy, with students exercising control through democratically run meetings. The attempt to develop Brookwood and Manumit as an alternative system of education for the labor movement ended in the later part of the 1920s, when the AFL charged Brookwood with Communist leanings and expelled the school from the federation.

Activity within the AFT increased rapidly during the depression years of the 1930s, in response to cutbacks in teacher salaries and increased support for the public schools. At its annual convention in 1931, the AFT called for replacement of the property tax with a graduated income tax, the establishment of federal unemployment compensation, government planning of public works, and a shorter work week. In 1933, twenty-eight thousand teachers and their sympathizers marched through the streets of Chicago to protest being paid in scrip. The march tied up traffic in the downtown area for several hours, during which time groups of teachers attacked local banks. It should be noted that none of the activities of the AFT up to this point involved the use of the strike or the development of a collective-bargaining agreement with a school system.

The major educational philosophy to dominate the AFT during the 1930s was called "social reconstructionism." Social reconstructionism called upon American education to create a new social order in which depressions, such as that facing people in the 1930s, would not be allowed to occur. This new social order was to replace economic competition with cooperative and national economic planning. Teachers, through the AFT, were to use the schools as a means of spreading social reconstructionism. It was hoped that, in this manner, teachers would be at the vanguard of social change.

The social reconstructionist philosophy of the AFT in the 1930s had little impact on the schools because teachers could not exercise any organizational control over local school systems. This situation began to change in 1944 when the American Federation of Teachers local in Cicero, Illinois, signed the first collective-bargaining contract with a board of education. The form of the contract was that of a regular labor-union contract. It recognized the local as the sole bargaining agent of the teachers and listed pay schedules and grievance procedures. At the annual convention of the AFT in 1946 a committee was assigned to study collective bargaining and its application to school management. In addition, material was to be collected from trade unions on the education of shop stewards and union practices. With the introduction of collective bargaining, the AFT centered a new stage in its development.

The new involvement of the AFT in collective bargaining led naturally to the question of teacher strikes. Since its founding, the AFT had had a no-strike policy. In 1946 the use of the strike as a means of supporting teachers' demands became a major issue at the annual convention. Those supporting the use of the strike argued it was the only means available to arouse an apathetic citizenry to the problems in American education. It was also the only meaningful leverage teachers had against local school systems. AFT members who favored retention of the no-strike policy argued that teachers were in a public service profession and that work stoppage was a violation of public trust. In addition, it was argued that a strike deprived children of an education and was counter to the democratic ideal of a child's right to an education.

The AFT maintained its no-strike policy in the face of growing militancy among individual locals. In 1947 the Buffalo Teachers Federation declared a strike for higher salaries. The strike was considered at the time the worst teacher work stoppage in the history of the country. Other local unions supported the strikers, with local drivers delivering only enough fuel to the schools to keep the pipes from freezing. The Buffalo strike was important because it served as a model for action by other teachers around the country. School superintendents, school board associations, and state superintendents of education condemned these actions by local teachers. The national AFT maintained its no-strike policy and adopted a posture of aid and comfort but not official sanction. As William Edward Eaton states in his *The American Federation of Teachers, 1916–1961,* "Even with a no-strike policy, the AFT had emerged as the leader in teacher work stoppages."

The event that sparked the rapid growth of teacher militancy in the 1960s, and contributed to the NEA's rapid acceptance of collective bargaining, was the formation of the New York City local of the AFT, the United Federation of Teachers (UFT). The formation of the UFT provided the opportunity for the rapid rise to prominence of Albert Shanker, who first served as the local's secretary and later as president of the organization. In 1974 Albert Shanker became president of the national AFT.

In the late 1950s the AFT decided to concentrate on organizing teachers in New York City and to provide special funds for that purpose. After the organization of the UFT in 1960, there was a vote for a strike over the issues of a dues check-off plan, the conducting of a collective-bargaining election, sick pay for substitutes, 50-minute lunch periods for teachers, and changes in the salary schedules. On November 7, 1960, the UFT officially went on strike against the New York City school system. The union declared the strike effective when 15,000 of the city's 39,000 teachers did not report to school and 7,500 teachers joined picket lines around the schools. In the spring of 1961 the UFT won a collective-bargaining agreement with the school system and became one of the largest and most influential locals within the AFT.

During the 1960s teachers increasingly accepted the idea of collective bargaining and the use of the strike. This was reflected in the rapid growth of membership in the AFT. In 1966 the membership of the AFT was 125,421. By 1981 the membership had more than quadrupled to 580,000. This increased membership plus the increased militancy of the NEA heralded a new era in the relationship between American teachers' organizations and the managers of American education. With the coming of age of the strike and collective bargaining, teachers in the NEA and AFT proved themselves willing to fight for their own welfare and the welfare of American public schools.

Shanker's rise to power in the AFT during the 1970s represented not only the strength of the New York local within the AFT, but also a certain acceptance of Shanker's concepts of what the goals of the union should be. Prominent among Shanker's early goals for American education was what he called "Educare." Educare was made a national priority of the AFT at its 1975 national convention. As officially explained by the AFT, Educare's lifelong-education program was based on the idea that education should not be limited to one period of life. The goal of Educare was to provide cradle-to-grave educational opportunities, including expanded preschool programs and increased support for elementary and secondary schools. In addition, Educare would include programs for school dropouts; for senior citizens; for those in need of career training and retraining; for people undergoing long-term institutionalization in hospitals, nursing homes, and prisons; for workers wanting to take a sabbatical to improve their skills; and for enrichment programs to pursue self-growth interests.

By the early 1980s, the AFT had become more concerned about the survival of public schools than with broader social and economic goals. The election of President Reagan meant not only that a presidential candidate supported by the AFT lost the election, but also that the new president supported tuition tax credits. The AFT had spent considerable money and time lobbying against tuition tax credits during the years of the Carter administration. Tuition tax credits would allow parents a greater choice in determining whether their children would attend public or private schools. In addition, Reagan's victory was considered part of a general revolt against federal intervention in the schools and increased rates of taxation.

In December 1980 Albert Shanker met with President Reagan's transition team. As reported in the February 1981 issue of *American Teacher*, Shanker told team members that the increased public sentiment against public schools and for tuition tax credits resulted from declining educational standards and from violence and a lack of discipline in the schools. If these problems could be solved, he argued, there would be greater public support for the public schools. Greg Humphrey, director of the AFT legislation department, blamed actions of the federal government for part of the swing in sentiment away from the public schools. Humphrey told the president's transition team that "many federal mandates and initiatives in education, in their attempt to deal with specific problems such as segregation, access and equity, have the unfortunate result of appearing, in the minds of many parents, to produce a school system that is unattractive."

Although all major goals of the AFT are linked to general school policy or to the national economy, they are also designed to protect and improve teachers' salaries and welfare and to increase teacher control of education. The proposed Educare programs were designed to promote lifelong learning. Expanded education programs would employ more teachers, which would, of course, mean a larger union, as well as jobs for the surplus of teachers caused by fewer children now in the schools. Concerns about methods of school financing are related to the union's interest in collective bargaining, and public school control of early-childhood education provides an easy method for including early-childhood educators in local unions.

By the middle of the 1980s, the AFT was embroiled in national discussions about the reform of teaching. In 1983, when President Reagan announced his support of merit pay for teachers, the AFT appeared more sympathetic to the idea than the NEA. Delegates to the 1983 AFT convention were forced by the political pressures coming from the federal government, and the actions of state governors, to define a clear position on merit pay, career ladders, and master teachers. The convention resolution on merit pay carefully tried to avoid complete rejection of the idea. The convention report in the September 1983 issue of the AFT newspaper, *American Teacher*, reported that according to the convention statement, merit pay was not the "most important cure for what ails the teaching profession." But the official statement went on to say, "While merit pay is not AFT policy, under certain circumstances state federations and locals may need to negotiate such plans."

Therefore, the climate of the times forced the union to focus on teacher-reform issues. The 1983 convention established a series of guidelines for discussions by state and local affiliates. The first item in the guidelines urged that any new compensation plan include substantially higher pay for all teachers. The purpose of this item was to assure that master-teacher or merit-pay plans would not be used as an inexpensive method of raising teacher salaries by limiting wage increases to a select few. In addition, the guidelines urged that any evaluation procedures to be used for determining merit pay or choosing master teachers be negotiated by the local union and school district, to avoid subjective evaluations by administrators or the influence of local school politics. For those teachers not selected for extra compensation, it was recommended that an appeal-and-review procedure be established, and that no sanctions be used against those teachers. In addition, the convention statement concluded that "any financial rewards offered must be part of a plan committed to improving the conditions and pay of teachers who function in the classrooms, and not simply result in adding new layers of administration."

The flexibility of the AFT about reform plans for teachers reflected its concern that unions and teachers convey to the public an image of willingness to reform. Albert Shanker warned the 1983 convention that, "Even with issues that we strongly disagree with, we have to ask ourselves what the consequences are of fighting against them. We have to carefully weigh every decision that we make and every action that we take and ask ourselves if it's going to bring about support for public education." Shanker feared that if public education, and teacher unions, were seen as huge bureaucracies unwilling to change, public support would shift to private schools. This fear was placed against a background of concern about public support for tuition tax credits and vouchers.

Shanker let it be known in the same speech that the AFT had a long record of support for what were currently being identified as reform issues. He listed AFT's continuing support of tougher entrance exams for new teachers, tougher curriculum standards, removal from the classroom of students with discipline problems, formation of coalitions with business and other groups, and increases in teacher salaries. He warned convention delegates that governors throughout the country were announcing plans that included many of these items. "Remember," Shanker told the convention delegates, "if the country is moving in that direction, in some situations it may not be whether we have a plan or no plan, it may be whether we have a better plan or a worse plan."

AFT's focus on teacher-reform issues reflected a shift in its general concerns. Certainly, these issues have always been a major concern of the AFT, but the political pressures of the 1980s forced the AFT to concentrate on them. The union's more general concerns about representing organized labor in the classroom faded into the background as teacher-reform issues moved to center stage. In the past, one often thought of the AFT as being the more socially minded of the two teacher organizations. But under Shanker's leadership and the political pressures of the 1980s the AFT narrowed its concerns, and the NEA began to emerge as the more socially minded. Nothing better exemplifies the changes in these two organizations than the controversy over the NEA's promotion of a curriculum guide on nuclear war.

Prior to the 1980s, one would have assumed that the AFT would have advanced a curriculum supporting nuclear disarmament. This would have fit the AFT's image as supporter of liberal causes. But it was the NEA that supported the guide developed by the Union of Concerned Scientists. The curriculum tried to give students a realistic view of the dangers of nuclear war. For instance, one illustration in the guide showed the MX missile and noted that each of the 10 warheads in the missile was 25 times stronger than the Hiroshima bomb. The AFT attacked this particular illustration in its September 1983 issue of *American Teacher* on the grounds that it was biased, because it did not mention that the MX missile is only a fraction of the size of the Soviet-built SS18. The 1983 convention passed a resolution criticizing the guide. This resolution contains a statement that probably would have stunned the early, labor-minded leaders of the AFT: "A political organization of teachers is confusing the promotion of its own political positions with teaching a particular view of these in the classrooms."

These shifts in political and social concerns can make it difficult for a teacher to choose between the two organizations. But the primary concerns of most teachers joining a union are wages, benefits, and working conditions. Both unions are constantly competing for membership and making claims that they will provide the best representation. Before choosing either of the unions, the teacher should investigate the performance of the local affiliate and decide which union reflects his or her own educational, political, and social philosophy.

The goals of the AFT, compared to those of the NEA, appear to be broader and more inclusive. This is partly because of the AFT's affiliation with the AFL–CIO and party because of the small size of the AFT membership compared to the membership of the NEA. The NEA's size and diversity make it difficult for that organization to achieve a consensus on political and economic issues. It is hard to imagine the NEA stating, as did the AFT, that national economic planning is the only solution to unemployment. A teacher who joins the AFT is making a commitment to support the goals of the American labor movement. Such political and social commitment is not asked of the teacher who joins the NEA. The AFT claims that its strength grows out of its association with the American labor movement. The NEA claims that its strength is a product of its size and its independence from any union.

Private Foundations

In the United States, private foundations are established as philanthropic institutions by possessors of great wealth. Some of the largest foundations include the Ford Foundation, the Rockefeller Foundation, the Lilly Endowment, the W. K. Kellogg Foundation, and the Carnegie Corporation of New York. The names of the foundations indicate the sources of the fortunes that went into the establishment of these charitable organizations.

Because of their resources, private foundations have been able to provide large sums of money to support studies, research, and organizations. These foundations have had a major impact on social policy in the United States. The broad scope and variety of activities sponsored by the foundations has led to their activities being attacked by both the political left and the political right in the United States. Right-wing groups have attacked foundations as instruments of large corporate wealth designed to promote a social policy that works against the interests of smaller industrial groups. In other words, right-wing groups see foundations as restricting competition and supporting monopoly control of the marketplace through their funding of particular organizations and policies. In a similar fashion, left-wing political groups have been concerned about the foundations exerting control over American social policy.

The real power of foundations lies in their ability to influence or control the areas in which they choose to spend money. Until the recent expansion of the federal government in the funding of research and social-action projects, foundations were the main source of funds for these activities in the United States. In many ways, the decisions of the boards of directors of these foundations about the type of research, social projects, and organizations to be funded have determined the evolution and direction of scientific and social research, as well as social policy in the United States.

The influence of foundation spending can most clearly be seen in the field of education. Foundations have supported particular projects that have influenced the basic structure of American education. Foundations have also funded research and studies that have had influence over major court decisions related to education and national educational policy decisions. Foundation funds have been used to support particular educational interest groups and thus influence directly the control of American education by particular organizations. All these influences on American education can be best understood by specific examples of the means and kinds of influence that foundations have had over American education.

A good example of how foundation support of particular projects affected the basic structure of American education can be seen in the rise of segregated, vocational education for blacks in the South after the Civil War. As Henry Bullock explains in his prizewinning book, *A History of Negro Education in the South*, money from large foundations made possible the implementation of segregated, vocational education designed to train a labor force for the emerging industrial South in the early part of the twentieth century. Money for the support of segregated education came from the Peabody Fund, the General Education Board of the Rockefeller Foundation, the Slater Fund, and the Rosenwald Fund. One of the concerns of this group of philanthropists was the development of a nonimmigrant and nonunion labor force for the new industrial South. It was believed that freed black people, if given adequate vocational education, could provide this labor pool.

Evaluation of the deeds of philanthropy in the South reveals one of the basic dilemmas in the historical role of private foundations in a democratic society. On the one hand, the power of philanthropic aid can be criticized because it supported a segregationist educational structure and reflected the self-interest of the donors in providing a controllable industrial workforce. On the other hand, there might not have been any large-scale development of schools for blacks in the South if the money had not been given by these large foundations. In other words, the foundations can be credited with providing money that was not available from other sources. In either case, the private foundations had a tremendous influence on the development of segregated education in the South.

Another example of how foundation action resulted in shaping educational policy through particular projects was the Ford Foundation's support of the Mobilization for Youth program in the late 1950s. As Peter Marris and Martin Rein describe it in their *Dilemmas of Social Reform*, the Ford Foundation had previously used two approaches in granting aid to solve urban problems. One of these promoted the establishment of metropolitan governments that would reintegrate the central cities with the suburbs. The other promoted urban renewal, which was designed to attract prosperous residents and business back to the central city. Dissatisfied with both these approaches to reform, the Ford Foundation in the late 1950s backed Mobilization for Youth, which had community action as a central feature. The basic assumptions of community action were the existence of the poverty cycle and the lack of opportunity for the poor. It was believed that existing social-service agencies, such as those for education, medical care, and welfare, were making the poor dependent rather than self-reliant. The goal of community action was to make the poor self-reliant through their participation in the management and policy decisions of these agencies. This idea was incorporated in the Economic Opportunity Act of 1964 in the form of a requirement that all programs sponsored by the legislation have maximum feasible participation. Because the Head Start program for early-childhood education resulted from this legislation, community participation became one of its features.

Community-action programs resulted in a great deal of political controversy. Some people charged that it led to conflict between elected local officials and groups sponsored through community-action programs. Other groups charged the program with sponsoring local radicals who tried to take over special agencies. What it did accomplish in the 1960s was to increase community participation in the schools and establish school advisory committees.

Foundations have sponsored research projects and major social studies that have had a profound impact on American schools. One of the most famous and important studies sponsored by the Carnegie Corporation contributed to the U.S. Supreme Court decision ending school desegregation in the South. The subject of the study was American blacks. It began in 1938 under the leadership of Swedish social scientist Gunnar Myrdal. World War II slowed down the work, and the final study, *An American Dilemma: The Negro Problem and American Democracy*, was published in 1944. It was this study, cited in the 1954 Supreme Court case ending school desegregation, that was a main component of the social-science evidence demonstrating that segregated schools were inherently unequal.

During the 1950s the Carnegie Corporation sponsored James Conant's influential study, *The American High School Today*. The study was conducted at a time when there was strong public criticism of the failure of the schools to produce enough scientists and engineers. One of the major recommendations of the Conant study was that high schools should consolidate so that a wider range of programs could be offered to students. It was believed that in small high schools students could not be properly differentiated into programs geared toward their future social roles. The Conant report's recommendations for larger high schools resulted in a national movement to consolidate high schools.

Foundations also have helped to strengthen and establish organizations that have had a direct influence on educational policy. In this 1976 article in the *History of Education Quarterly*, "Private Foundations and Public Policy: The Case of Secondary Education During the Great Depression," Charles Biebel states that during the 1930s John D. Rockefeller's General Education Board reorganized and supported the American Council of Education as a vehicle for instituting the General Education Board's own plans to restructure American secondary education. In addition, the General Education Board established the American Youth Commission and provided money to the National Education Association to establish the Educational Policies Committee. All these groups were extremely influential in the formulation of secondary-school policy.

An extremely important organization that the Carnegie Corporation helped to found in 1947 was the Educational Testing Service (ETS). Most college students and candidates for professional schools in recent times have taken some test administered by ETS. The two major testing enterprises originally brought together in ETS were the Scholastic Aptitude Test (SAT) and the College Entrance Examination Board (CEEB). Over the years ETS has expanded its testing activities to become one of the major gatekeepers to the professions and to institutions of higher learning. By the 1970s consumer advocate Ralph Nader criticized ETS for its almost monopolistic control of testing and for the high cost of taking ETS examinations.

Because of the controversial nature of foundation activity in the United States, and the criticism of its activity from every part of the political spectrum, it is difficult to make any single general judgment about the role of foundations in American education. Any person interested in the workings of a particular foundation must ask certain questions.

The most important question is about the social composition and political views of the members of the board of directors of the foundation. This is important because it is usually this group that establishes the guiding philosophy for determining the projects to be funded. It should be remembered that where the money is spent can have a tremendous influence over shaping educational institutions and policy.

The next important question is about the relationship between foundation staff and the community. The informal activities of the staff can result in the solicitation of particular proposals for funding and for certain information being received by the board of directors. Very often the major contact of staff members and boards of directors is with social elites within communities. This might not be true if the foundation were to aggressively pursue broader contacts within the community.

A third important question is whether or not the past record of foundation activity reflects any particular social or political philosophy. Sometimes the answer to this question is to be found in those groups the foundation refused to support. If, for instance, a foundation has provided money to support particular organizations and not others, the question must be asked, why? The same question must be asked of research and projects funded by foundations. Very often a careful reading of statements by foundation officials about what they think is a good education or a good society will give clues to the general social and political philosophy behind foundation activity.

Foundations will continue to have an important impact on American society and education. It is only through regulatory legislation that the general public can directly control the activities of foundations. Local groups can indirectly place pressure on foundations by surveying their activities, writing letters of praise or criticism to local newspapers, and seeking other public forums for discussion of foundation influence over community life. A combination of these approaches should be used by those interested in public control of the influential power of these tremendous foundations of private wealth.

Washington Lobbyists

According to the estimates of Stephen K. Bailey, in his *Education Interest Groups in the Nation's Capital*, there are between 250 and 300 educational organizations located in or near Washington, D.C. All these organizations purport to speak for some interest group in American education. They vary in the scope of their concerns from general organizations, such as the American Council on Education, to more specific groups, such as the Music Educators' National Conference. Their activities range from organizing conferences and publishing research bulletins for their particular constituents to organizing lobbying activities.

Bailey divided these education interest groups into 10 categories. The first category he calls "umbrella" organizations, which are broad-based organizations with institutional and associational memberships. One organization in this category is the American Council of Education, which does not have persons as members but is a conglomerate of institutions and associations. For instance, the inner group of higher-education members (Group A) includes the American Association of Community and Junior Colleges, the American Association of State Colleges and Universities, the Association of American Universities, and five other major higher-education associations. In addition, the American Council of Education has a Group B membership of 60 associations, such as the American Association of Colleges for Teacher Education and the American Library Association. The American Council on Education claims a total membership of 14,000 institutions representing nearly all universities in the United States, most four-year colleges, and one-third of the accredited community and junior colleges.

The second category of interest groups includes institutional associations, many of whom are members of the American Council on Education. These are associations of institutions, such as the American Association of Community and Junior Colleges and the Association of American Universities.

The third category is made up of the teachers' organizations described earlier in this chapter. Also included in this category with the NEA and the AFT is the American Association of University Professors (AAUP).

The fourth category of interest groups contains groups structured around a professional field or subject-matter discipline—for instance, the National Council of Teachers of Mathematics, the Journalism Education Association, and the Home Economics Education Association. Most of these organizations are affiliated with either the National Education Association or the American Council on Education.

Some of the most influential associations compose the fifth category of interest groups. These are the groups interested in books and in supplying educational materials and technology. Many of these are private industrial groups and book publishers who have an economic stake in educational legislation. Book publishing and educational technology are big business in the United

States. Two of the major interest groups in this category are the National Audio-Visual Association and the Association of American Publishers. The membership of the National Audio-Visual Association is composed primarily of private manufacturers and dealers who sell equipment to the schools. The Association of American Publishers represents about 275 publishing firms, with the major control of the organization in the hands of the large publishers that have substantial interests in text and reference works.

The sixth category includes organizations with a particular religious, racial, or sex-based interest in education. Religious organizations, such as the National Catholic Educational Association, represent powerful religious interests in educational affairs. The National Association for the Advancement of Colored People (NAACP) is an example of one group dedicated to ending racial discrimination in education. The American Association of University Women has worked for years for women's rights in education.

The seventh category includes what is called the "liberal-labor" lobby in education. The primary work in this category is done by the Legislative Department of the AFL-CIO. This work is of course done in cooperation with the AFT.

The eighth category includes particular institutions and institutional systems, such as Pennsylvania State University and the New York State Education Department. Increased federal funding in the 1950s and 1960s resulted in many institutions of higher education having their own representatives in Washington, D.C; their purpose is to find out where money will be available and to lobby for research proposals and other funding proposals from their particular institutions.

The ninth category includes influential groups of educational administrators. There are four major associations of elementary and secondary school administrators: the Council of Chief States School Officers, representing superintendents and commissioners in the states and territories; the American Association of School Administrators, representing local and district school superintendents; the National Association of Elementary School Administrators; and the National Association of Secondary School Principals. There are also a variety of groups representing administration in higher education. Finally, there is the National School Boards Association, representing about 84,000 members of local school boards.

The tenth category is composed of miscellaneous educational interest groups. The National Committee for Citizens in Education is primarily concerned about the welfare and rights of students and parents. The Council for Basic Education has been concerned since the 1950s about scholars, as opposed to professional educators, gaining control of American education. In addition, a range of Washington attorneys represents a variety of educational clients.

As the reader can imagine from this survey of the various educational interest groups, there is a certain amount of conflict between the groups, and they do not work in harmony for common goals. For instance, the NEA does not support the goals of the Council for Basic Education for reduced professional control of education. The American Library Association and the Association of American Publishers are not always in agreement over such issues as copyright laws. Each educational interest group has its particular profession and goals to protect. Agreement often occurs between the groups, however, when it comes to the issue of increased funding for education.

The Committee for Full Funding of Education Programs is an umbrella organization of education interest groups bound together by a common concern for the level of federal appropriations for education. As Stephen Bailey describes its history in *Education Interest Groups in the Nation's Capital*, the organization was formed in 1969 by the NEA, the AFL-CIO, and the National School Boards Association and now claims a membership of 50 to 60 associations and institutions. The committee was originally created in response to the growing difference between educational legislation and congressional appropriations to support that legislation. This problem increased during the Nixon and Ford administrations, when not enough money was appropriated by Congress and the administration, moreover, refused to spend all the money that was appropriated.

In addition to time spent on this concern about increased educational funding, a great deal of the time of educational interest groups is spent protecting their own particular profession from possible harm from federal legislation. Very often harm occurs as an indirect and unforeseen consequence of legislation. Legislation affecting fiscal policy, military policy, manpower policy, and a score of other areas always has some potential consequence for education. The same is true of any changes in policies and regulations from federal agencies. Interest groups must keep a watchful eye on all government actions to protect their own interests.

For example, a 1973 price freeze issued as part of President Nixon's anti-inflation program had the potential for creating chaos for summer school tuitions, which had been set by state legislatures only weeks earlier. In another case, the National Audio-Visual Association had to fight the concept of "central purchasing" of audiovisual equipment because of a fear that such a policy would put its members out of business. The National Association of Elementary School Principals, the National Association of Secondary School Principals, the American Association of School Administrators, and the other major government groups in education have resisted and protested for many years the requirements in federal legislation for local advisory groups and community-action groups, because of the potential threat to their own ability to govern at the local level. The list of examples of what interest groups must watch for in agency and congressional action could take up several volumes. It seems likely that if government continues to expand and become more complex, this will continue to be a major function of these organizations.

To protect the interest of their members and help shape legislation and agency regulations, interest groups rely on control of information and a symbiotic relationship with government agencies. One of the problems educational groups encounter in their lobbying activities is the Internal Revenue Code, which permits an organization to have tax-exempt status if substantial parts of its activities are not devoted to propaganda or to trying to influence legislation. Because of this code, most education associations attempt to influence without lobbying, and to provide information without it being propaganda. The NEA has attempted to avoid these problems by registering as a "business league organization" and creating a foundation called the National Foundation for the Improvement of Education, which can accept tax-exempt gifts from other foundations. This allows the NEA to function openly as a lobbyist while maintaining part of its operation in a tax-exempt foundation. Most education associations attempt to avoid the problem by claiming they are providing Congress and agencies with "data" and not "propaganda." Also, they claim to provide information to their members but not to force their members to pressure their congressional representatives.

The major power of education associations is in their central location as intermediaries in an information network that provides federal agencies with feedback about their programs and about the profession, and provides members of the association with information about federal programs. Because of this information network, agencies and educational groups tend to need each other. Federal agencies need to get information about new programs and regulations to those who will be affected. Newspapers, radio, and television cannot possibly relay the constant flow of information emanating from federal offices. Newsletters from educational associations are the major channel of information about educational policies and programs. In turn, agencies often depend on associations for information they can use as guides for implementing new programs. Associations also supply agencies with data about membership reaction to new programs and their apparent effectiveness.

If one were to evaluate the overall impact of these education interest groups, one would have to consider as most important the relationship between these groups and federal agencies. As described in Chapter 8 on the role of the federal government in education, only in a few cases in the past have educational groups had a significant impact in electing congressional representatives or presidents. This, of course, might change in the future. Until now, the more significant role for educational interest groups has not been in influencing the passage of educational legislation, but in influencing the agencies that administer the legislation. Like the influence of private foundations, this influence and relationship exists outside the control of the general public.

Accrediting Associations

Accrediting associations are nongovernmental professional organizations that establish standards and criteria for educational institutions. Six major regional agencies accredit institutions of higher education and secondary schools in the United States. The 6 range in size from the North Central Association of Colleges and Secondary Schools, with 500 institutions of higher education and nearly 4,000 secondary schools on its accredited list, to the Northwest Association of Secondary and Higher Schools, with fewer than 100 institutions on its list.

Accrediting agencies originally developed to deal with the problem of admission of students from high schools into colleges. In the nineteenth century this was a major problem for many high schools because each college and university had its own admission examination and requirements. This sometimes meant that high schools would have to prepare students differently, depending on the particular college they planned to attend. Two kinds of institutions developed to deal with this problem. One was the testing organization, which developed common tests to be used for admission to a variety of colleges. The College Entrance Examination Board (CEEB) was established for this purpose. The other organization was the accrediting association, whose accrediting activities ensured that students would be admitted to college if they graduated from an accredited high school. This is still true in many states, where graduation from an accredited high school guarantees admission to a state university or college. Most institutions of higher education now use a combination in their admissions requirements of attendance at an accredited institution and test scores.

Accrediting agencies can exert a great deal of influence over secondary education. The standards of judgement established by these agencies touch almost every aspect of school life. They range from administration to relationships with the community to the curriculum and extracurricular activities. Periodic inspections by accrediting agencies require schools to compile answers to long lists of questions and to undergo several days of on-site inspection. Visiting accrediting teams usually conclude their visits with an evaluative statement about the school's performance and a list of recommendations for improvements and changes.

A major critic of accrediting is James Koerner, past president of the Council for Basic Education. One of Koerner's complaints is that accrediting groups have tended to perpetuate mediocrity in education. Since institutions are not rated in terms of one institution being superior to another, the only real function of accrediting is to deny accreditation to borderline institutions. This means that simply because an institution is accredited does not guarantee that the institution has a high-quality program.

Koerner also criticizes accrediting practices because they destroy a certain amount of local control over education. This is one of Koerner's major concerns in his book, *Who Controls American Education?* Koerner believes that local control of the schools has been replaced by the control of professional educators. From his perspective, accrediting associations are one more group of professional educators imposing outside standards over local schools. As he states in his book: "These agencies can therefore bring irresistible pressure to bear on institutions to force them to conform to what people outside the institutions think are desirable practices in matters of faculty, budget, instruction, facilities, or most other matters of moment in education."

Some of Koerner's major criticism is directed at the National Council for Accreditation of Teacher Education (NCATE), which accredits programs in professional education. NCATE is one of the largest and most powerful of the professional agencies that accredits particular subjects and degrees. One reason for this is that teacher education is one of the larger areas of higher education, in terms of numbers of undergraduates and graduate programs for teachers, school administrators, and future professors of education.

Koerner's concern about NCATE is "its monopolistic power and narrowness of its policies, but mostly because it was an organization of, by and for the professional establishment." This statement from *Who Controls American Education?* articulates the recurring argument that it is the professionals who control education, and that accrediting agencies are merely one part of the network of professional control. In addition, Koerner complains about the failure of NCATE to rate teacher education and provide some means of judging the superiority of one institution over another. Koerner feels that NCATE contributes, in the same way as the accrediting agencies for secondary schools, to maintaining a level of mediocrity in teacher education around the country.

Koerner does admit that there is a great deal of value in having accrediting associations to assure that some standard of education is maintained in secondary schools and institutions of higher education. There is also value, in his opinion, in providing the general public with information about which institutions attain certain standards. The major issues with regard to accrediting agencies are who should control them and how extensive their rating of institutions should be. Should there be public control rather than professional control of accreditation? Should accrediting institutions inform the public about which high schools are superior to other high schools? Should teacher education be rated? If, in the future, the answer to these questions is yes, it would mean more influence and power for accrediting associations.

A Theory of Conflict in American Education

The discussion in the last several chapters has been about the control of American education at the local, state, and national levels. Two theories about the control of American education have woven their way through these discussions. One theory is that economic and political elites control education at the local, state, and national levels. The other theory is that professional educators have actual control at these levels.

The theory I propose here is that no single group controls American education, but that there is competition for control between these two major power groups. This competition does not always occur, however. At times, there is a harmony of interests between the two groups. For instance, at the local level, community elites often have a major role in the selection of local school administrators. Because these administrators act in accordance with the desires of the community power structure, they are allowed to exercise major control over the local educational system. The same argument can be made about the state and national levels.

But this harmony of interests between elites and professional educators is not constant. Educators develop their own sets of interests, which are sometimes in conflict with those of elite groups. Teachers, school administrators, college professors, and leaders of major educational interest groups have their own economic stakes in education. Their stakes include job protection, higher salaries, and expansion of the educational system. This is not to imply that educators act primarily out of personal greed. Most teachers and school administrators believe in the importance of schooling for all people and devote a great deal of their lives to trying to improve educational institutions. Nevertheless, the combination of idealism and an economic stake in education often results in conflict between the interests of professional educators and the interests of elite groups.

The major area of conflict is over school financing. Educators have a major economic and professional stake in obtaining more money for the schools. The NEA and the AFT have consistently fought at every level of government for increased spending for the schools. Often the major groups resisting increased spending for the schools are local industrialists and taxpayers' associations. But at the state and federal levels, professional educators exert little influence over appropriation committees. In fact, the major evidence that professional educators do not control the schools is the fact that throughout the twentieth century, American schools have consistently lacked adequate financial support. If educators controlled the system, there would not be school closings and overcrowded classrooms in most of the school systems in the United States.

Also, professional educators do not seem to have major control over educational policy. As noted earlier in this chapter, private foundations have had an important influence over major educational policy in the twentieth century. In terms of the federal role in national educational policy since 1945, educators have consistently fought for general aid while the federal government has provided categorical aid. The categorical aid, moreover, has been primarily determined by groups other than professional educators. For instance, the National Defense Education Act received its major support from the military-industrial complex, whereas the basic philosophy of the Elementary and Secondary Education Act has grown out of the work of private foundations.

Where professional educators have the major power is in influencing the actions of state and federal educational agencies and in implementing policy. It should be recognized that average classroom teachers do not feel they have direct influence over the action of state and federal agencies. It is their representatives in teachers' organizations and other educational associations who have this influence. The control of information, the network of personnel that moves between educational groups and government agencies, the influence over the administration of legislation, and the administration of local school systems are the areas of major control by professional educators.

The increased political militancy of the NEA and the growth of the AFT might result in greater power for professional educators over school financing and educational policy. But this will not occur without increased and continued conflict with local and national power structures. In the interest of American education, the American teacher must not only labor in the classroom but must also struggle in the political arena.

Exercises

1. Contact local members of the AFT and NEA about current goals and issues in local school districts. Inquire about the lobbying activities of both organizations at the state and national level. If possible, organize a class debate between representatives of both organizations.
2. In a group discussion or essay, discuss the current goals of the AFT and NEA. These goals can be found in the current NEA handbook and the most-recent September issue of the AFT's *American Teacher.*
3. Contact local members of boards of education about their views concerning collective bargaining with the NEA and AFT. Ask what they think should be the role of teachers' organizations in American education.
4. If a private foundation operates in your local area, investigate the social composition of its board of directors and the kinds of projects and organizations it sponsors. Try to determine what effect it might have over local social and educational policy.
5. Ask a university official about the lobbying activity and lobbying organizations the university sponsors.
6. As a way of understanding accreditation, ask to see the NCATE evaluation of your department or college of education.

Suggested Readings and Works Cited in Chapter

The best sources of current information about the NEA and AFT are the NEA *Handbook* and the AFT's *American Teacher.* Contact local offices of these organizations for more information about them.

Aronowitz, Stanley. *False Promises: The Shaping of American Working Class Consciousness.* New York: McGraw-Hill, 1973. An important book for understanding why professionals, including teachers, are rapidly joining the union movement.

Bailey, Stephen. *Education Interest Groups in the Nation's Capital*. Washington, D.C.: American Council on Education, 1975. A survey of the educational lobbying groups in Washington.

Biebel, Charles. "Private Foundations and Public Policy: The Case of Secondary Education During the Great Depression." *History of Education Quarterly*, Spring 1976. Provides good examples of foundation influence over educational policy and organizations.

Bullock, Henry. *A History of Negro Education in the South*. New York: Praeger, 1970. Chapter 5, "Deeds of Philanthropy," shows the influence of foundations on southern educational policy.

Cardinal Principles of Secondary Education. Washington, D.C.: Bureau of Education, 1918. The major policy statement of the NEA about the goals of the comprehensive high school in the twentieth century. This policy statement had a major impact on shaping the modern high school.

Conant, James B. *The American High School Today*. New York: McGraw-Hill, 1959. The Carnegie-funded study of the American high school. This study is discussed in more detail in Chapter 1 of this text.

Eaton, William. *The American Federation of Teachers, 1916–1961*. Carbondale, Ill.: Southern Illinois University Press, 1975. A history of the AFT. Much of the information in this chapter on the history of the AFT was taken from this study. Quotations in this text from articles by Margaret Haley were taken from Chapter 1 of Eaton's history of the AFT.

Koerner, James. *Who Controls American Education?* Boston: Beacon, 1968. Koerner argues that professional educators control American education.

Marris, Peter, and Martin Rein. *Dilemmas of Social Reform*. Chicago: Aldine, 1973. Reading this book will give you an understanding of the influence of foundations over American social policy.

Myrdal, Gunnar. *An American Dilemma: The Negro Problem and Modern Democracy*. New York: Harper & Brothers, 1944. A Carnegie-sponsored study that has had a major influence on race relations in the United States.

Nielsen, Waldemar. *The Big Foundations*. New York: Columbia University Press, 1972. A survey of the origins and activities of the major foundations in the United States.

Wesley, Edgar. *NEA: The First Hundred Years*. New York: Harper & Brothers, 1957. The main source of information, in addition to original sources, about the early years of the NEA. The controversy about the American Legion article is discussed on pages 316–18.

10

The Courts and the Schools

During the last three decades courts have increasingly been forced to decide on issues that touch every aspect of schooling. One reason for increasing court involvement in the schools has been complaints about the violation of constitutional rights. These complaints have ranged from issues involving student and teacher rights to school finances. A result of this development has been a greater involvement of the courts in the control and regulation of the schools.

The reader of this chapter must be cautioned that only a limited number of constitutional issues involving the school are discussed here. Court decisions are being made every day, and legal issues are daily becoming more complex. Anyone planning a career in teaching should make a full investigation of the rights and responsibilities of both teachers and students. Education law is at present a whole field of study, and many lawyers are becoming specialists in education issues as school systems spend increasing amounts of time in the courts.

In terms of constitutional issues, the majority of court cases have been decided by invoking the First and Fourteenth Amendments to the U.S. Constitution. As mentioned in Chapter 8 on the federal control of education, there is nothing in the federal Constitution regarding education, which means that education is a power reserved to the states. But the Fourteenth Amendment does say that states cannot take away any rights granted to an individual as a citizen of the United States. This means that although states have the right to provide schools, they cannot in their provision of schools violate citizen rights granted by the Constitution. The wording of Section 1 of the Fourteenth

Amendment has been extremely important in a variety of constitutional issues related to education:

> All persons born or naturalized in the United States, and subject to the jurisdiction thereof, are citizens of the United States and of the State wherein they reside. No state shall make or enforce any law which shall abridge the privileges or immunities of citizens of the United States; nor shall any State deprive any person of life, liberty, or property without due process of law; nor deny to any person within its jurisdiction the equal protection of the laws.

These few lines have a great deal of meaning for state-provided and state-regulated schools. For instance, "no state shall make or enforce any law which shall abridge the privileges or immunities of citizens of the United States" means that the courts can protect the constitutional rights of students and teachers particularly with regard to freedom of speech and issues related to religion. The line that reads, "nor shall any State deprive any person of life, liberty, or property without due process of law" has been used in cases involving student suspensions and teacher firings. Since states provide schools to all citizens, they cannot dismiss a student or teacher without due process. As we shall see later in this chapter, the courts have established guidelines for student dismissals.

All the protections of the Fourteenth Amendment depend on the states' making some provision for education. Once a state government provides a system for education, it must provide it equally to all people in the state. Thus, under the Fourteenth Amendment, the state cannot "deny to any person within its jurisdiction the equal protection of the laws."

This part of the Fourteenth Amendment has been central in cases involving school segregation, non-English-speaking children, school finance, and children with special needs. The reader will recall from an earlier chapter that the famous *Brown* v. *Board of Education of Topeka* decision in 1954 centered on whether segregated schools were "equal." Prior to that decision, the Supreme Court had ruled that segregated schools were constitutional as long as they offered an equal education. The importance of the 1954 case was the decision that segregated schools were *inherently* unequal.

As one can see from the preceding discussion, the Fourteenth Amendment allows for constitutional protection in the schools. What has been of considerable importance, and has caused controversy, has been the protection of the rights granted in the First Amendment:

> Congress shall make no law respecting an establishment of religion, or prohibiting the free exercise thereof; or abridging the freedom of speech, or of the press; or the right of the people peaceably to assemble, and to petition the Government for a redress of grievances.

The section of the First Amendment dealing with the establishment of religion has played an important role in decisions regarding school prayer and religious exercises in the schools. The section dealing with laws prohibiting the free exercise of religion has been important when religious groups have claimed that public schools have interfered with their religious practices or that the public schools have taught something that is offensive to their religious beliefs.

There has always been a thin line between not allowing the establishment of religion and interfering with the free exercise of religion. For instance, as we shall see later in this chapter, the U.S. Supreme Court has prohibited school prayer because it involves the government in the establishment of religion. On the other hand, groups defending school prayer claim that the Court's decision interferes with their free exercise of religion.

The same problem plagues the issue of freedom of speech. On the one hand, the courts recognize the importance of protecting the free speech of students and teachers; on the other hand, the courts recognize the necessity for maintaining order in the schools and for school boards to exercise control over teachers. This dilemma also has existed in the interpretation of the Eighth Amendment, which reads: "Excessive bail shall not be required, nor excessive fines imposed, nor cruel and unusual punishments inflicted." But when does punishment of a student become "cruel and unusual" punishment? This, as we shall see later in the chapter, became a major issue in court cases dealing with corporal punishment.

The often thin line of interpretation involved in many court decisions has resutled in a great deal of controversy. Probably the two most explosive court decisions were those banning school segregation and school prayer. These two decisions forced some members of society to act contrary to their personal values.

Compulsion, Religion, and the Schools

A major area of conflict in American education has been the relationship of the public schools to established religions. The First Amendment to the U.S. Constitution states that "Congress shall make no law respecting an establishment of religion, or prohibiting the free exercise thereof." The problem with this amendment is that many religions believe education cannot be separated from religion. Both education and religion are concerned with the moral and social development of the individual. Religion, education, and the First Amendment come into conflict when certain religious groups are forced to send their children to school and conform to the practices of the school, and when religious groups demand that the schools engage in certain religious practices, such as school prayer. In the first case, forced attendance and compliance with school regulations can be an infringement on an individual's right to practice religion, if school practices conflict with religious beliefs. In the second case, religious activities in public schools can mean that the government is giving support to particular religious practices.

The first major U.S. Supreme Court case related to the conflict between compulsory schooling and religious freedom was *Pierce* v. *Society of Sisters* (1925). The case originated in 1922 when Oregon passed the Compulsory Education Act, which required every parent, guardian, or other person having control or charge or custody of a child between 8 and 16 years of age to send the child to a public school. The act was clearly an attempt to close parochial schools by forcing all children to attend public schools. Two private schools in Oregon immediately obtained injunctions against Governor Pierce and Oregon state officials.

The First Amendment was not directly involved in the case because the law affected both religious and nonreligious private schools. The Supreme Court did indirectly support the guarantee of religious liberty, however, by maintaining the right to choose a religious school in preference to a public school. The Court stated in its decision that the "fundamental theory of liberty upon which all governments in this Union repose excludes any general power of the State to standardize its children by forcing them to accept instruction from public teachers only."

The Supreme Court ruling in *Pierce* v. *Society of Sisters* was based on an earlier ruling that involved a Nebraska law requiring that all subjects in private and public schools be taught in the English language. The purpose of the law was to curb a feared growth of nationalism during World War I by limiting the use of foreign languages. The Court in its ruling *Meyer* v. *Nebraska* (1919), which declared the law unconstitutional, recognized the right of the teacher "to teach and the right of parents to engage him so to instruct their children." The importance of the *Meyer* decision was the recognition of the parental right to direct the upbringing of their children within the reasonable limitations of the law.

In *Pierce* v. *Society of Sisters* these rights were again confirmed in declaring the 1922 Oregon law unconstitutional. The Court stated: "Under the doctrine of *Meyer* v. *Nebraska* . . . we think it entirely plain that the Act of 1922 unreasonably interferes with the liberty of parents and guardians to direct the upbringing and education of children under their control." But the Court did not recognize the complete control of the parents and guardians over the education of their children. The Court very clearly defined the power of the states with regard to education.

Probably the most important part of the *Pierce* decision, besides declaring that children coud not be forced to attend public schools, was the recognition of the power of the state to regulate education and compel students to attend school. The Court stated: "No question is raised concerning the power of the State reasonably to regulate all schools, to inspect, supervise and examine them, their teachers and pupils; to require that all children of proper age attend some school." Besides recognizing the right of regulation and requirements to attend, the Court also recognized the right of the state to certify teachers and regulate the curriculum with regard to citizenship studies. The Court stated that the state had the right to require "that teachers shall be of good moral character and patriotic disposition, that certain studies plainly essential to good citizenship must be taught, and that nothing be taught which is manifestly inimical to the public welfare."

These qualifications to the *Pierce* decision placed important limitations on the right of parents and guardians to direct the education of their children. The state had the right to force attendance at an educational institution that met state requirements with regard to teachers, curriculum, and other reasonable standards. The only right recognized for parents was the choice between public and private schools, and this right was limited by the ability to pay for private schooling. The unresolved issue was what would happen if the state standards used to regulate public and private schools were in conflict with religious practices and the state required attendance at a state-accredited school. This is the problem that the Amish encountered.

The Amish are a subgroup of the Anabaptist-Mennonite tradition that has refused to be assimilated into the mainstream of American society and the modern urban and industrial world. They first came to America in the eighteenth century and settled in eastern Pennsylvania in compact communities. They retained in America their original European dress style of men wearing black clothes and wide-brimmed hats and women wearing capes and aprons. In areas of Pennsylvania, Ohio, Indiana, Iowa, and Wisconsin, communities of Amish continue to exist with traditional religious practices, clothes, and community living. The Amish continue to use horse-and-buggies for transportation and avoid the use of electricity and telephones.

One of the major threats to the Amish way of life has been the public school and compulsory education. The public school threatens the destruction of the Amish community by the teaching of values contrary to its traditions and by the introduction of the children to modern styles of life. For the Amish, this threat can occur in areas that might seem unimportant to other people. For instance, one objection of Amish parents to compulsory high school attendance is the requirement that girls wear shorts for physical education, which is in serious violation of Amish beliefs. In the nineteenth century the Amish began to object to the rise of public schools. In an article entitled "From Erlanback to New Glarus" in a book he edited titled *Compulsory Education and the Amish*, Albert N. Keim quotes a nineteenth-century Amish leader: "The righteousness that counts before God is neither sought nor found in the public or free schools; they are interested only to impart worldly knowledge, to ensure earthly success and to make good citizens for the state."

The Amish particularly objected to the public high school because of its broader curriculum and preparation for a vocation or college. The Amish do their own vocational training within their communities. In addition, the Amish objected to what was considered the modern education of the twentieth century. Amish education stresses following instructions, respecting authority, and mastering basic information. The Amish disapprove of education that stress critical thinking and asking questions. Obedience to authority and tradition are seen as essential for the survival of the community.

New Glarus, Wisconsin, was the scene of the final confrontation between the Amish and compulsory education laws. In 1968 public school authorities insisted that the Amish community comply with a Wisconsin law requiring school attendance until 16 years of age. The county court upheld the school authorities. The Amish appealed the case to the Wisconsin Supreme Court, which rejected the lower court's decision and ruled that compulsory schooling of Amish children beyond the eighth grade was a violation of the free exercise of religious rights. In 1972 the U.S. Supreme Court in *State of Wisconsin, Petitioner* v. *Jonas Yoder et al.* upheld the Wisconsin Supreme Court decision.

In the *Yoder* decision the U.S. Supreme Court placed some limitations upon the right of a state to compel school attendance, as recognized in *Pierce* v. *Society of Sisters*. The Court stated that in the *Pierce* decision there was recognition given that the "values of parental direction of the religious upbringing and education of their children in their early and formative years have a high place in our society." In addition the Court argued that a state's interest in universal education should not be at the sacrifice of other rights, specifically those of the First Amendment. In the words of the Court: "We can accept it as settled, therefore, that however strong the State's interest in universal compulsory education, it is by no means absolute to the exclusion or subordination of all other interests."

The *Yoder* decision also placed limitations on state educational requirements. The Court stated that there were two primary arguments for maintaining a system of compulsory education. One argument was the necessity for citizens to be prepared to participate intelligently in an open political system. The other argument was that education was necessary to prepare people to be self-reliant and self-sufficient in society. The Court clearly stated with regard to these two arguments: "We accept these propositions." The Court then went on to argue that the requirement that the Amish attend school beyond the eighth grade did not aid in the achievement of the above educational goals. The Court stated that the Amish community was a highly successful social unit and its members were productive and law-abiding. Education within the community therefore appeared to fulfill the state interests in education.

The importance of the 1972 *Yoder* decision is in the placing of First Amendment religious freedoms above those of the state's interest in education. This would mean that in the future any conflict between religious practices and compulsory schooling would be decided in favor of individual religious freedom. The decision also requires that, in any future cases dealing with compulsory schooling, the state must show some relationship between its educational requirements and standards and its interest in educating self-sufficient and intelligent citizens. State standards cannot be arbitrary and unrelated to these objectives.

The U.S. Supreme Court has also protected First Amendment rights when required practices in the schools came into conflict with religious beliefs. This decision was made with regard to the objections of the Jehovah's Witnesses to saluting and pledging allegiance to the flag. The case began in the early 1940s, when the West Virginia Board of Education ordered that the flag salute become a regular part of the school program and that all teachers and pupils be required to salute the flag and say the Pledge of Allegiance. Refusal to participate was to be viewed as an act of insubordination, and pupils who failed to conform were to be expelled from school. Pupils expelled from school were considered delinquent and could possibly be sent to juvenile reformatories.

The Jehovah's Witnesses objected to the flag ceremony because they believed that the obligations imposed by the law of God were superior to the laws of government. One of the laws of God taken literally by Jehovah's Witnesses is, "Thou shall not make unto thee any graven image, or any likeness of anything that is in heaven above, or that is in the earth beneath, or that is in the water under the earth; thou shalt not bow down thyself to them nor serve them." Jehovah's Witnesses believe that the flag is an image and refuse, for religious reasons, to salute it.

The U.S. Supreme Court ruling in *West Virginia State Board of Education* v. *Barnette* declared the West Virginia School Board ruling unconstitutional because of its abridgment of First Amendment freedoms. In its decision the Court went beyond the issue of protection of religious practices to the issue of protection within public schools of all constitutional privileges. The Court argued: "That they are educating the young for citizenship is reason for scrupulous protection of Constitutional freedoms of the individual, if we are not to strangle the free mind at its source and teach youth to discount important principles of our government as mere platitudes." Within the same framework, the Court emphasized that patriotic exercises should not be made compulsory. In the words of the Court: "To believe that patriotism will not flourish if patriotic ceremonies are voluntary and spontaneous instead of a compulsory routine is to make an unflattering estimate of the appeal of our institutions to free minds."

Another major area of controversy has been the issue of religious practices in the schools. There has been a great deal of pressure to introduce religious practice into the schools in the form of Bible reading, prayer, and released time from school classes for religious instruction. All three practices have become issues before the courts and have generated a great deal of public controversy.

The U.S. Supreme Court has ruled with regard to released time for religious instruction that this is permissible as long as the religious instruction does not take place within the public-school building. The decision of the Court against allowing religious instruction within school buildings during released time from the regular school day was made in *Illinois ex rel. McCollum* v. *Board of Education* (1948). In this case the Champaign, Illinois, school system permitted religious teachers employed by private religious groups to come weekly into school buildings during regular school hours. For a period of 30 minutes they were allowed to teach their particular religious beliefs. These religious classes were composed of students whose parents had signed printed cards requesting that their children be permitted to attend. The classes were taught by Protestant teachers, Catholic priests, and a Jewish rabbi. Students who did not attend the religious classes were required to leave their classrooms and go to some other part of the building to study regular school subjects.

The Court ruled against the practices of the Champaign school system because the state's compulsory school system was being used to aid and promote the work of religious groups. The Court stated: "Pupils compelled by law to go to school for secular education are released in part from their legal duty upon the condition that they attend the religious classes. This is...a utilization of the...public school system to aid religious groups to spread their faith." The Court made it clear that, in its opinion, the First Amendment "erected a wall between Church and State which must be kept high and impregnable."

A different plan for released time was developed by New York City, a plan that the U.S. Supreme Court in *Zorach* v. *Clauson* (1952) decided was constitutional and not in violation of the First Amendment. The New York City program released students during the school day and allowed them to leave the school grounds to attend religious centers for instruction. Students were released only on written request from the parents. The religious centers made weekly attendance reports to the schools by sending a list of students who had been released from school but had not attended religious instruction. Students who were not released from school for religious instruction were required to remain in their classrooms.

The Court argued in its decision that the New York City release-time plan did not involve the violation of the free exercise of religion. The Court stated, "No one is forced to go to the religious classroom and no religious exercise or instruction is brought to the classrooms of the public schools. A student need not take religious instruction." The decision recognized the constitutional importance of maintaining separation of church and state but also argued that this did not mean that the state was to be hostile to religion. For instance, the Court stated that students might request permission from the school to attend religious ceremonies of their particular faith. If the school denied permission to attend, this would be interference with the free practice of religion. In the same manner, denying a student the right to attend religious instruction outside the school might be considered a denial of the right to practice religion. The government cannot, the Court declared, "coerce anyone to attend church, to observe a religious holiday, or to take religious instruction. But it can close its doors or suspend its operations as to those who want to repair to their religious sanctuary for worshop or instruction."

The school-prayer decision in *Engel* v. *Vitale* (1962) has been one of the most controversial religious rulings of the U.S. Supreme Court. The decision denied the right of a public school system to conduct prayer services within school buildings during regular school hours. Those groups of people who have been angered by the decision have argued that it has made education godless, and have sought an amendment to the Constitution that would allow for prayer ceremonies in the school. The Court decision against school prayer was primarily based on the argument that school prayer involved the state in the establishment of religion. This was viewed as a violation of the First Amendment.

The school-prayer case began in New York when a local school system was granted the right by the New York Board of Regents to have a brief prayer said in each class at the beginning of the school day. The prayer, considered to be denominationally neutral, read: "Almighty God, we acknowledge our dependence upon Thee, and we beg Thy blessings upon us, our parents, our teachers and our country." The New York courts granted the right of local school systems to use this prayer. The one requirement was that a student could not be compelled to say the prayer if the student or parents objected.

It was this decision of the New York courts against which the U.S. Supreme Court ruled in *Engel* v. *Vitale*. One of the major objections of the Court was the fact that government officials had written the prayer. This seemed to put the government directly in the business of establishing religion. The Court stated that "in this country it is not part of the business of government to compose official prayers for any group of the American people to recite as a part of the religious program carried on by government." The Court reviewed the early history of the United States, and the struggle for religious freedom and the ending of government support of churches. The Court argued: "By the time of the adoption of the Constitution, our history shows that there was a widespread awareness among many Americans of the dangers of a union of Church and State." The writing of a prayer by government officials ran counter to this long-standing struggle in the United States.

The Court rejected the argument that the school-prayer law did not violate any rights because it did not require students to recite the prayer and the prayer was nondenominational. The Court argued that this confused the right of free exercise of religion with the prohibition against the state establishing and supporting religion. Excusing students from reciting the prayer might protect their free exercise of religion, but the very existence of the prayer involved the establishment of religon. In the words of the Court: "The Establishment Clause, unlike the Free Exercise Clause, does not depend upon any showing of direct governmental compulsion and is violated by the enactment of laws which establish an official religion whether those laws operate directly to coerce nonobserving individuals or not."

The Court applied the same reasoning to the issue of Bible reading in the public schools. One of the cases to come before the Court, *Abington School*

District v. *Schempp* (1963), involved a Pennsylvania law that permitted the reading of 10 verses from the Bible at the opening of each public school day. The verses were to be read without comment, and any child could be excused from reading the verses or attending the Bible reading, upon the written request of the parents or guardians. Like the school-prayer issue, the Court felt that a Bible-reading service of this type involved the state in the establishment of religion. The Court made it clear that it did not reject the idea of Bible reading as part of a study of comparative religion or the history of religon. Nor did the Court exclude the possibility of studying the Bible as a piece of literature. What the Court objected to was the reading of the Bible as part of a religious exercise.

The U.S. Supreme Court cases dealing with religion and the schools have touched upon one of the most difficult aspects of establishing a public school system in a country with a great deal of cultural diversity and a wide variety of religions. Most religious groups believe that religious instruction should be a part of the education of children and adolescents. But the public schools cannot open their doors to religious groups because not all religious groups are in agreement about basic beliefs and what should be taught. In addition to the practical problem of antagonistic religious beliefs in the schoolhouse, there are clear constitutional prohibitions against state support of religion and interference with religious practices.

But recognizing the practical problems and the constitutional prohibitions does not solve the problem for people who believe that religious instruction should be a part of education. The *Pierce* decision provides some relief by allowing parents to send their children to private schools. Private schools can conduct religious services and provide religious instruction. The major limitation on this right is that the family must be able to afford the cost of private schooling. If families cannot afford private schooling, and if they believe their children should be given a particular religious instruction, then their rights are limited by the fact that state-provided public schools offer the only free education that is available. The state cannot provide support to private schools, particularly religious schools, because for them to give financial support to religion would be a violation of the First Amendment.

Those who want religion to be a part of education have been put in a bind because of the constitutional prohibition against religious services and instruction in the public schools, and the prohibition against state support of private religious schools. There have been several attempts to provide indirect means to support private schools. The one method through which indirect support for private school students has been provided is called the "child-benefit theory."

The child-benefit theory was articulated by the U.S. Supreme Court in *Cochran* v. *Louisana State Board of Education* (1930). At issue in this case was a Louisiana law that permitted the purchase and distribution of textbooks to all schoolchildren. Under this law textbooks were provided to children attending private religious schools. The U.S. Supreme Court affirmed the Louisiana Supreme Court ruling that the law did not sanction the support of religious schools. Taxpayers' money was spent to purchase books that went directly to schoolchildren. The law existed for the benefit of children, not for the support of religious institutions.

The same reasoning was involved in the U.S. Supreme Court decision *Everson* v. *Board of Education* (1974), which allowed public support of school transportation for parochial students. In this case the support again went directly to the child and not to a religious institution. The Court stated: "We cannot say that the First Amendment prohibits...spending tax-raised funds to pay the bus fares of parochial school pupils as a part of a general program under which it pays fares of pupils attending public and other schools."

In a surprise decision in 1983, the U.S. Supreme Court made it possible for states to allow deductions in 1983, the U.S. Supreme Court made it possible for states to allow deductions from state income taxes for educational expenses including tuition, textbooks, and transportation. In the past, similar laws had been found to violate the Establishment Clause of the First Amendment. What was different in this particular situation was that the law recognized expenses for both public and private schools.

The decision, *Mueller* v. *Allen* (1983), concerned a Minnesota law that allowed state taxpayers to take deductions from gross income for expenses incurred for "tuition, textbooks, and transportation" for dependents attending elementary and secondary schools. The law allowed a $500 deduction for each dependent attending elementary schools and a $700 deduction for those attending junior and senior high schools.

The U.S. Supreme Court provided several reasons for its decision that the law did not violate the Establishment Clause. First, the Court argued that the deductions were only one among many deductions. For instance, Minnesota law allowed taxpayers to deduct for medical expenses and charitable contributions. The Court stated, "The Minnesota legislature's judgement that a deduction for education expenses fairly equalizes the tax burden of its citizens and encourages desirable expenditures for educational purposes is entitled to substantial deference."

Second, and more important, the Court believed that the inclusion of public schools in the allowance for tax deductions avoided the pitfalls of previous attempts by states to provide aid to private schools. For instance, in *Committee for Public Education* v. *Nyquist* (1973) the Court found a New York law in violation of the Establishment Clause because it provided tuition grants only to parents of children in nonpublic schools. In the case of the Minnesota law, the Court noted, "Most importantly, the deduction is available for educational expenses incurred by *all* parents, including those whose children attend public schools and those whose children attend nonsectarian private schools or sectarian private schools." The fact that the law benefited a broad spectrum of groups, the Court felt, meant that it had a primarily secular effect.

Mueller v. *Allen* is important because it makes it possible for states to provide an indirect means of support to private schools. It also has important implications for state funding of public schools. It opens the door for local public-school systems to charge students for tuition and textbooks, with reimbursement for parents through state tax deductions. In some states this might be limited by state constitutions that require provision of free public education. The decision also might make it possible for the federal government to provide vouchers or tuition tax credits if they apply to both private and public schools.

Secular Humanism and the Religion of Public Schooling

One of the most interesting sets of court cases to develop in the 1970s involved claims that the public schools taught a religion, *secular humanism*, which could be a violation of the rights of those not subscribing to secular-humanist values. The issue arose over state regulation of private schools. During the latter part of the 1970s and into the 1980s, the fastest-growing private schools were those identified as "Christian." These usually were associated with a fundamentalist Christian organization. At first, people outside the movement assumed the growth of Christian schools was a result of "white flight" from desegregated school systems. But when Christian schools began to multiply in rural areas of Wisconsin and Alaska, where segregation was not an issue, it became evident that the movement was a result of strongly held religious values.

Problems began in the Christian-school movement when state authorities demanded that the schools conform to state minimum educational standards. Most state minimum standards are not a small list of requirements but a vast set of statutes and regulations covering everything from the design of the water fountain to the curriculum. Christian schools did not have any problems with regulations related to the safety of school buildings, but they did object to curriculum requirements that interfered with the Christian objectives of their schools.

Of primary concern were state regulations that required the schools to teach ethical values that the Christian schools called *secular humanism*. The simplest definition of secular humanism is that it comprises a set of ethical standards that place primary emphasis on a person's ability to interpret and guide his or her own moral actions. This is in opposition to the Christian-fundamentalist viewpoint, which holds that the source of ethical and moral values should be the Bible and God. Secular humanism relies on the authority of human beings, while Christian fundamentalism relies on the authority of the Scriptures.

One of the earliest and most famous cases dealing with the issue was decided by the Ohio Supreme Court in 1976 in *State* v. *Whisner*. The case originated when Levi Whisner opened the doors of the Tabernacle Christian School in Bradford, Ohio, in 1973. The issue for Pastor Whisner was not whether the school met minimum state standards, but whether he should even apply for a charter from the state. The reader should keep in mind the fact that compulsory-education laws in most states require attendance at a school approved by the state. If the student does not attend an approved school, the student can be considered truant and the parents and student held liable for the truancy.

James Carper of Tulane University reported in a paper delivered at the 1980 meeting of the American Educational Studies Association, that after reading the 149-page *Minimum Standards for Ohio Elementary Schools, Revised 1970*, "Whisner and the governing board of the school concluded that as a matter of religious principle they could not conform to all of the standards and, therefore, decided not to initiate the prescribed procedures for obtaining a charter." The consequence of that action was immediately felt by the parents and their children when, within a month of the school's opening, the local probation officer sent out letters informing the parents that if their children did not attend a school that met minimum standards, a complaint against the parents would be filed in the local juvenile court. In November, two months after the opening of the school, 15 parents were indicted by the country prosecutor's office for not sending their children to school. After some negotiation, the trial date was set for May 7, 1974.

Professor Carper wrote: "The trial court proceedings revealed again that to the state the primary issue was non-compliance with state law while the defendants believed that free exercise of religion was at the heart of the matter." One point revealed in the first trial was that the Ohio Department of Education required total compliance with state minimum standards and that one of those standards was a written statement of philosophy of education. The interesting question raised by this standard was how conflicts between a school's statement of philosophy and other department standards would be resolved. It was revealed during the trial that "if the statement of a school's philosophy of education, a mandated standard, ran counter to other minimum standards and made it impossible to fully embrace them, the department would not approve the school."

In August 1974 the trial court found the 15 parents guilty; after an appeal, the Supreme Court of Ohio agreed to hear the case in October 1975. On July 28, 1976, the Supreme Court of Ohio reversed the lower court's decision and argued that Pastor Whisner and the appellants had "sustained their burden of establishing that the 'minimum standards' infringe upon the right guaranteed them by the First Amendment to the Constitution to the United States, and by Section 7, Article of the Ohio Constitution, to the free exercise of religion."

This decision gave legal recognition to the argument that the state minimum standards did require the teaching of a philosophy, secular humanism, which was in conflict with the religious values of the appellants. To understand this conflict it is best to review some of the specific points in the state's minimum standards objected to by Pastor Whisner.

Alan Grover, in his book *Ohio's Trojan Horse: A Warning to Christian Schools Everywhere*, provides a detailed summary of Whisner's objections to the minimum standards. For our purposes, I will deal with only a few of these objections, as a means of highlighting the issue of secular humanism. In Grover's words, "The 'Minimum Standards' philosophy points to the wisdom and self-sufficiency of man in finding solutions to all of society's problems." This, of course, is contrary to the belief that humans need the Scriptures and God to deal with social problems. As examples of the Ohio minimum standards' emphasis on the wisdom and self-sufficiency of humans, Grover cited the following statements from the standards:

> Problems are solved by group discussion and decision. Man's comprehension of the present and his wisdom in planning for the future depend upon his understanding of the events of the past and of the various forces and agencies in society that influence the present. Through all time and in all regions of the world, man has worked to meet common basic human needs and to satisfy common human desires and aspirations. The health of the child is perhaps the greatest single factor in the development of a well-rounded personality. [The objection to this is the belief that the spiritual condition of the individual is more important.]

All statements quoted above were taken from the curriculum section of the state standards. What should be remembered is that the state required compliance with all standards and, consequently, Pastor Whisner considered compliance a violation of his religious beliefs. This particular case has opened the door to similar cases in other states and has made it possible to argue that compulsory attendance at a public school might be violation of religious freedom. And it was certainly clear in the mind of Pastor Whisner that the public schools taught the religion of secular humanism.

In 1986, two other cases dealing with secular humanism received wide publicity. The first was brought by a group of parents against the Hawkins County School District in Tennessee for requiring students, on threat of suspension, to read from the Holt, Rinehart & Winston basic reading series. The fundamentalist parents claimed that the textbook series contained explicit statements on secular humanism and taught values contrary to the religious beliefs of their children. In the words of presiding U.S. District Judge Thomas Gray Hull, "The plaintiffs believe that, after reading the entire Holt series, a child might adopt the views of a feminist, a humanist, a pacifist, an anti-Christian, a vegetarian, or an advocate of a 'one-world government.'"

In the decision, *Mozert et al. v. Hawkins County Public Schools* (1986), Judge Hull argued that the beliefs of the defendants were sincere and that by suspending the students the school district was denying them a right to an education because of the exercise of free speech. In addition, the school district provided no evidence of a compelling reason for requiring students to read the textbook series. In fact, the judge dismissed as bureaucratic the school district's argument that it was necessary for classroom instruction to require all students to use the same textbooks.

Consequently, he required the school district to allow students who were offended by the material in the textbook series to not participate in reading instruction. In his words, "During the normal reading period, the student-plaintiffs shall be excused from the classroom and provided with suitable space in the library or elsewhere for a study hall."

The *Mozert* case is being appealed in higher courts as I write, so the final outcome is still uncertain. But the case is an example of the difficulty courts face in dealing with charges that the contents of particular textbooks violate the free exercise of religion.

A second case, decided in 1987 by U.S. District Court Judge W. Brevard Hand, is also still in the appeal process. As I write, it seems unlikely that Judge Hand's decision will survive in the higher courts. But the case, *Smith* v. *School Commissioners*, raises a prospect even more interesting than the *Mozert* case: that the U.S. courts will recognize secular humanism as a religion.

The *Smith* case originated in a complaint by 624 teachers, parents, and students in Mobile, Alabama, that "the curriculum used in the school system unconstitutionally advanced the religion of humanism, unconsititutionally inhibited Christianity. . . ." At issue were 44 different textbooks that the plaintiffs, mainly fundamentalist Christians, claimed taught the values of secular humanism.

The argument here was unique. The plaintiffs claimed not that the textbooks violated the free exercise of students' religious values, but that the school system itself was violating the Establishment Clause of the First Amendment of the Constitution by teaching a religion—the religion of secular humanism. The problem for the plaintiffs, then, was convincing the court that secular humanism was in fact a religion. The judge, after reviewing the intellectual origins and organizational features of secular humanism, declared, "For the purposes of the First Amendment, secular humanism is a religious belief system. . . [it] is not a mere scientific methodology that may be promoted and advanced in the public schools." Using this reasoning, the judge ruled that the textbooks in question were in violation of the Establishment Clause because they promoted the religion of secular humanism.

In another interesting twist in the case, Judge Hand found that the majority of the textbooks omitted the significant role of religion in American life. Judge Hand argued that this was in violation of the First Amendment because "the Supreme Court has recognized a right to not be prevented from learning material if it was excluded for religious reasons and there is a legitimate secular or nonreligious reason for teaching the material." In this situation the judge argued that religious material was excluded from textbooks because of the tenets of secular humanism and that it was legitimate to include material on the role of religion in American life in public school education.

While the final outcome of cases dealing with secular humanism is unknown at the time of this edition, it is clear that the struggle over the values taught will continue in the public schools. It is difficult to imagine how the public schools can meet the conflicting demands of differing religious and ethical systems.

The Academic Freedom of Teachers and Students

During the nineteenth and early-twentieth centuries, schoolteachers were expected to be models of purity of the community. Pressure was placed on teachers to be circumspect outside the school with regard to dress, speech, religion, and types of friends. Within the school, a teacher's freedom of speech was abridged at the whim of the school administrator. Some school administrators allowed teachers to discuss controversial topics freely within the classrooms; others fired teachers who spoke of things within the classroom that were not approved by the administration. Very often, teachers were fired for their political beliefs and activities.

During the last several decades, court actions, the activities of teachers' associations, and state laws granting teachers tenure have expanded academic freedom in the public schools and have protected the free speech of teachers. The expansion of academic freedom in the United States first took place at the college level and later in elementary and secondary schools. The concept of academic freedom was brought to the United States in the latter part of the nineteenth century by scholars who had received their training in Germany. The basic argument for academic freedom was that if scientific research was to advance civilization, scholars had to be free to do research and to lecture on anything they felt was important. The advancement of science depended on free inquiry. In Germany this was accomplished by appointing individuals to professorships for life.

The concept of academic freedom was not immediately accepted in institutions of higher education in the United States. Many professors were fired in the late-nineteenth and early-twentieth centuries for investigating certain economic problems and for backing reforms such as child labor laws. College professors found it necessary to organize the American Association of University Professors (AAUP), to fight for academic freedom. The major protection of academic freedom in American universities is provided by tenure. The idea behind tenure is that after individuals prove they are competent as teachers and scholars, they are guaranteed a position until retirement, as long as they do not commit some major act of misconduct.

Tenure and academic freedom have been promoted by the NEA and AFT as ways of protecting the free speech of public-school teachers. Many states have adopted tenure laws for the express purpose of protecting the rights of teachers. Court decisions have also played an important role in extending academic freedom. But there have been major differences between the way academic freedom has functioned at the university level and how it functions at the secondary and elementary levels. The organizational nature of public schools and the age of children in them have placed some important limitations on the extent of teachers' academic freedom.

Before they teach in the public schools, it is important for teachers to understand their rights and the limitations of their rights. There are three major types of rights about which teachers must be concerned. The first deals with the rights and limitations of speech and conduct of teachers in relationship to administrators and school boards. The second deals with rights and limitations of the speech of teachers in the classroom. And the third deals with the rights of teachers outside the school.

The most important U.S. Supreme Court decision dealing with the rights of teachers in relationship to school boards and administrators was *Pickering* v. *Board of Education of Township High School* (1967). The case involved an Illinois schoolteacher dismissed for writing a letter to the local school board criticizing the district superintendent and school board for the methods being used to raise money for the schools. The letter specifically attacked the way money was being allocated among academic and athletic programs, and stated that the superintendent was attempting to keep teachers from criticizing the proposed bond issue. In court it was proved that there were factually incorrect statements in the letter.

The U.S. Supreme Court ruled that teachers could not be dismissed for public criticism of their school system. In fact, the Court argued in *Pickering*: "Teachers are, as a class, the members of a community most likely to have informed and definite opinions as to how funds allotted to the operation of the schools should be spent. Accordingly, it is essential that they be able to speak out freely on such questions without fear of retaliatory dismissal." In this case, the participation of teachers in free and open debate on questions put to popular vote was considered "vital to informed decision-making by the electorate."

The Court also did not consider the factual errors in the public criticism grounds for dismissal; it did not find that erroneous public statements in any way interfered with the teacher's performance of daily classroom activities or hindered the regular operation of the school. "In these circumstances," the Court stated, "we conclude that the interest of the school administration in limiting teachers' opportunities to contribute to public debate is not significantly greater than its interest in limiting a similar contribution by any member of the general public."

The *Pickering* decision did place some important limitations on the rights of teachers to criticize their school system. The major limitation was on the right to criticize publicly immediate superiors in the school system. In the words of the Court, immediate superiors were those whom the teacher "would normally be in contact with in the course of his daily work." The

Court, however, did not consider the teacher's employment relationship to the board of education or superintendent to be a close working relationship. One could imply from the decision that teachers could be dismissed for public criticism of their immediate supervisor or building principal. But what was meant by "close working relationship" was not clearly defined in the decision. The Court stated in a footnote: "Positions in public employment in which the relationship between superior and subordinate is of such a personal and intimate nature that certain forms of public criticism of the superior by the subordinate would seriously undermine the effectiveness of the working relationship between them can also be imagined."

There is a possible procedural limitation on a teacher's right to criticize a school system if the school system has a grievance procedure. This issue is dealt with in a very important book on teachers' rights published under the sponsorship of the American Civil Liberties Union (ACLU). The question is asked in David Rubin's *The Rights of Teachers*: "Does a teacher have the right to complain publicly about the operation of his school system even if a grievance procedure exists for processing such complaints?" The answer given by this ACLU handbook is "probably not." The handbook states that this issue has not been clarified by the courts, but there have been suggestions in court decisions that if a formal grievance procedure exists within the school system, a teacher must exhaust these procedures before making any public statements.

The Rights of Teachers also argues that a teacher is protected by the Constitution against dismissal for bringing problems in the school system to the attention of superiors. But, again, the teacher must first exhaust all grievance procedures. The example in the ACLU handbook was of a superintendent who dismissed a teacher because her second-grade class wrote a letter to the cafeteria supervisor asking that raw carrots be served rather than cooked carrots, because of the higher nutritional value of the raw vegetable. In addition, when the drinking fountain went unrepaired in her classroom, her students drew pictures off wilted flowers and of children begging for water, and presented them to the principal. The ACLU handbook states that the court decision found "the school policy was arbitrary and unreasonable and in violation of...First and Fourteenth Amendment rights of free speech and freedom peaceably to petition for redress of grievances."

The U.S. Supreme Court has not ruled directly on the issue of teachers' freedom of speech in public-school classrooms. The Court has ruled with regard to academic freedom in colleges and universities in *Sweezy* v. *New Hampshire* (1957). In this case the attorney general of New Hampshire subpoenaed Sweezy and questioned him about lectures he had given at the state university. He refused to answer and was jailed for contempt. The Court stated in this case that the content of classroom lectures was shielded from legislative investigation. The Court agreed that the right to lecture was a constitutionally protected freedom. The Court proclaimed its support of the concept of academic freedom. The Court stated:

> To impose any strait jacket upon the intellectual leaders in our colleges and universities would imperil the future of our Nation. No field of education is so thoroughly comprehended by man that new discoveries cannot yet be made. Particularly is that true in the social sciences, where few, if any, principles are accepted as absolutes. Scholarship cannot flourish in an atmosphere of suspicion and distrust. Teachers and students must always remain free to inquire, to study and to evaluate.

The *Sweezy* decision does not provide an exact guide for teachers in public elementary and secondary schools. The ACLU handbook, *The Rights of Teachers*, argues that the decisions of lower courts have provided some guidelines with regard to public-school teachers. These guidelines should not be considered law or as final interpretations of the Constitution. All the guidelines can do is to help teachers understand what types of arguments might be used in court in class involving free speech in the classrooms of public elementary and secondary schools.

One of the most important things for public elementary and secondary teachers to know is that the courts seem to recognize certain limitations on freedom of speech in the classroom. One of the things the courts appear to consider is whether or not the material used in the classroom and the statements made by the teacher are appropriate for the age of the students.

An example of the courts giving consideration to the age of the students, given by the ACLU in *The Rights of Teachers*, was a case in Alabama where a high school teacher had been dismissed for assigning Kurt Vonnegut's "Welcome to the Monkey House" to her eleventh-grade English class. The principal and associate superintendent of the school called the story "literary garbage," and several disgruntled parents complained to the school. School officials told the teacher not to use the story in class. The teacher responded that she thought the story was a good literary work and felt she had a professional obligation to use the story in class. The school system dismissed her for insubordination. The first question asked by the court was whether the story was appropriate reading material for eleventh-grade students. In its final decision, the court found that the teacher's dismissal was a denial of First Amendment rights, since it had not been proved that the material was inappropriate for the grade level or that the story disrupted the educational processes of the school.

Another important issue that the courts seem to consider is whether the classroom statements of a teacher are related to the subject matter being taught. One example given in *The Rights of Teachers* was of a teacher of a basic English class making statements about the Vietnam War and anti-Semitism, although the lessons dealt with language instruction. The court found that his remarks had minimum relevance to the material being taught, but might have been appropriate in courses such as current events and political science. What is important for teachers to know is that their freedom of speech in the classroom is limited by the curriculum and subject being taught.

Whether the method used by the teacher is considered appropriate by other members of the teaching profession appears to be another consideration of the courts. In a case in Massachusetts, an eleventh-grade English teacher wrote an example of a taboo word on the board and asked the class for a socially acceptable definition. The teacher was dismissed for conduct unbecoming a teacher. The teacher went to court and argued that taboo words were an important topic in the curriculum and that eleventh-grade boys and girls were old enough to deal with the material. The ACLU handbook states that the court ruled that a teacher could be dismissed for using in good faith a teaching method "if he does not prove that it has the support of the preponderant opinion of the teaching profession or of the part of which he belongs."

In summary, one can say that teachers do not lose their constitutional rights when they enter the classroom, but that their employment does put certain limitations on those rights. It would appear that before introducing material and speaking in the classroom, teachers must consider the ages of the students, the relevance of the material to the prescribed curriculum and subject matter, and the opinion of other members of the profession.

Another major concern with regard to a teacher's rights is activity outside the school. One of the most controversial issues has been whether a teacher's membership in a radical political organizations is grounds for dismissal or denial of employment. The two most important U.S. Supreme Court decisions on this issue both originated in cases resulting from New York's Feinberg Law. The Feinberg Law was adopted in New York in 1949, during a period of hysteria about possible communist infiltration of public schools. The law ordered the New York Board of Regents to compile a list of organizations that teach or advocate the overthrow of the U.S government by force or violence. The law authorized the Board of Regents to give notice that membership in any organization on the list would disqualify any person from membership or retention in any office or position in the school system.

The first decision concerning the Feinberg Law was given by the U.S. Supreme Court in *Adler* v. *Board of Education of New York* (1952). This ruling upheld the right of the state of New York to use membership in particular organizations as a basis for not hiring and for dismissal. The Court argued that New York had the right to establish reasonable terms for employment in its school system. The Court also recognized the right of a school system to screen its employees carefully because, as stated by the Court, "A teacher works in a sensitive area in a schoolroom. There he shapes the attitude of young minds toward the society in which they live. In this, the state has a vital concern." The Court went on to state that not only did schools have the right to screen employees with regard to professional qualifications but, also, "the state may very properly inquire into the company they keep, and we know of no rule, constitutional or otherwise, that prevents the state, when determining the fitness and loyalty . . . from considering the organizations and persons with whom they associate."

The *Adler* decision underwent major modification when the Feinberg Law again came before the U.S. Supreme Court 15 years later in *Keyishian v. Board of Regents of New York* (1967). In this case a teacher at the State University of New York at Buffalo refused to state in writing that he was not a communist. This time the Court decision declared the Feinberg Law unconstitutional, on the grounds that mere membership in an organization "without a specific intent to further the unlawful aims of an organization is not a constitutionally adequate basis for exclusion from such positions as those held by appellants." The reasoning of the Court was that membership in an organization did not mean that an individual subscribed to all the goals of the organization. The Court stated: "A law which applies to membership, without the specific intent to further the illegal aims of the organization, infringes unnecessarily on protected freedoms. It rests on the doctrine of guilt by association which has no place here."

The *Keyishian* decision did not deny the right of school systems to screen employees or to dismiss them if they personally advocated the overthrow of the U.S. government. What the *Keyishian* decision meant was that mere membership in an organization could not be the basis for denial of employment or for dismissal.

Whether a teacher's private life can be a basis for dismissal from a school system has not been clearly defined by the U.S. Supreme Court. The American Civil Liberties Union argues in *The Rights of Teachers* that courts have been increasingly reluctant to uphold the right of school authorities to dismiss teachers because they disapprove of a teacher's private life. Examples given by the ACLU include an Ohio court ruling that a teacher could not be dismissed for using offensive language in a confidential letter to a former student. The Ohio court ruled that a teacher's private actions are not the concern of school authorities unless they interfere with the ability to teach. The California Supreme Court ruled that a teacher could not be dismissed because of a homosexual relationship with another teacher. The court could not find that the relationship hindered the ability to teach.

It would appear that the major concern of the courts is whether teachers' private lives interfere with their professional conduct as teachers. But the difficulty of establishing precise relationships between private actions and ability to teach allows for broad interpretation by different courts and school authorities. Teachers should be aware that there are no precise guidelines in this area. The best protection for teachers is to develop some form of agreement between their teachers' organization and their school district with regard to the use of private actions as a basis for dismissal and evaluation.

One of the limiting conditions applied by the U.S. Supreme Court to the actions of teachers and students is whether the activity interferes with normal school activities. For instance, in *Board of Education* v. *James* (1972) the U.S. Supreme Court upheld a lower-court ruling that a teacher could not be dismissed for wearing an armband in class as a protest against the Vietnam War. The lower court had reasoned that the wearing of the armband did not disrupt classroom activities and therefore there was no reason for school authorities to limit a teacher's freedom of expression. The reasoning in this case was similar to that in the landmark case dealing with the rights of students, *Tinker* v. *Des Moines Independent School District* (1969).

The *Tinker* decision is considered one of the most important cases in the area of students' rights. The case originated when a group of students decided to express their objections to the war in Vietnam by wearing black armbands. School authorities in Des Moines adopted a policy that any student wearing an armband would be suspended. When the case was decided by the U.S. Supreme Court, clear recognition was given to the constitutional rights of students. The Court stated that a student "may express his opinion, even on controversial subjects like the conflict in Viet Nam. . . . Under our Constitution, free speech is not a right that is given only to be so circumscribed that it exists in principle but not in fact."

One extremely important condition was placed on the right of free speech of students and that was the possibility of disruption of the educational process. The Court did not provide any specific guidelines for interpreting this condition and limitation. What it meant was that school authorities had an obligation to protect the constitutional rights of students and, at the same time, an obligation to assure that there was no interference with the normal activities of the school.

The *Tinker* decision was a major step in recognizing students' rights. Later court cases dealing with student rights were argued in terms of students having a property interest in public education and a right to attend public schools. A student's "property interest" in education is the result of a state statutory entitlement to a public education. The right to attend public schools is usually conferred on children by state law. This law, of course, can vary from state to state.

Property interest and the right to an education were major considerations of the U.S. Supreme Court in dealing with due process and suspensions from school in *Goss* v. *Lopez* (1975). This case dealt with suspensions from school of junior and senior high school students. The Court ruled that due process "requires, in connection with a suspension of 10 days or less, that the student be given oral or written notice of the charges against him and, if he denies them, an explanation of the evidence the authorities have and an opportunity to present his side of the story." The Court based its decision on "legitimate claims of entitlement to public education" as given in state law. What this meant was that a student's right to an education could not be taken away in an arbitrary manner.

The *Goss* decision established a precedent that due process is required before a school-dismissal decision. R. Lawrence Dessem, in a 1976 article in the *Journal of Law and Education*, "Student Due Process Rights in Academic Dismissals from the Public Schools," argues that in the future the due-process requirement might be applied to cases involving dismissal from school for academic reasons. The *Goss* decision dealt only with suspension for disciplinary reasons. In either case there seems to be a clear obligation upon school authorities to guarantee due process for all students.

Dessem outlines in his article the basic procedures that must take place to assure due process for students. First, there must be an attempt to make all decisions on the basis of fact. Second, there must be some provision to guarantee future review of any decisions. And third, just procedures must be followed in reaching any decisions.

In practice, these three procedures mean very specific things. A student must be provided with a notice detailing the charges, and the notice must be received in sufficient time for the student to prepare answers to the charges. A student must be given the chance to present answers to the charges in a hearing before an unbiased group. Dessem argues that schools cannot be required to have groups outside the school conduct the hearings because of the expense. Dessem states: "A hearing before a panel of disinterested teachers and school administrators would seem to strike an acceptable balance between the right of the student to an impartial arbitrator and the school's interest in keeping the expense and inconvenience of such hearings to a minimum." Students do have a right to have the decision based only on the evidence presented.

In *Goss*, the U.S. Supreme Court did place a limit on the procedural elements of due process by refusing to require that students be given the right to call witnesses and have legal counsel. "The Supreme Court's rationale," states Dessem, "for refusing to mandate this and several other procedures was that since 'brief disciplinary suspensions are almost countless, to impose in each such case even truncated trial type procedures might well overwhelm administrative facilities in many places.'"

One of the more complicated First Amendment cases to be decided by the U.S. Supreme Court involved balancing the right of students to books in the school library with the right of the school board to decide which books should be in the school library. The case, *Board of Island Union Free School District* v. *Steven A. Pico* (1982), involved the removal of books from the school library by the board of education because the content of the books was considered unsuitable for high school students. The issue originated when several members of the board of education attended a conference of a politically conservative organization of parents concerned with educational legislation in the state of New York. While they were at the conference the board members received a list of books considered morally and politically inappropriate for high school students. Upon returning from the conference the board members investigated the contents of their high school library and discovered nine books that had been on the list. Subsequently, the board ordered the removal of the books from the library shelves. The books included: *Best Short Stories of Negro Writers*, edited by Langston Hughes; *Down These Mean Streets*, by Piri Thomas; *The Fixer*, by Bernard Malamud; *Go Ask Alice*, of anonymous authorship; *A Hero Ain't Nothin But A Sandwich*, by Alice Childress; *Naked Ape*, by Desmond Morris; *A Reader for Writers*, by Jerome Archer; *Slaughter House-Five*, by Kurt Vonnegut Jr.; and *Soul on Ice*, by Eldridge Cleaver.

In rendering its decision the Supreme Court gave full recognition to the power of school boards to select books for the school library, and to the importance of avoiding judicial interference in the operation of local school systems. On the other hand, the Court recognized its obligation to assure that public institutions do not suppress ideas. In this particular case, there was a clear intention to suppress ideas by making decisions about book removal based upon a list from a political organization.

The Supreme Court's method of handling the above dilemma was to recognize the right of the school board to determine the content of the library, as long as its decisions on content were not based on partisan or political motives. In the words of the Court, "If a Democratic school board, motivated by party affiliation, ordered the removal of all books written by or in favor of Republicans, few would doubt that the order violated the constitutional rights of the students denied access to those books." In another illustration, the Court argued, "The same conclusion would surely apply if an all-white school board, motivated by racial animus, decided to remove all books authored by blacks or advocating racial equality and integration." Or, as the Court more simply stated, "Our Constitution does not permit the official suppression of ideas."

On the other hand, the Court argued that books could be removed if the decision were based solely on their "educational suitability." The Court also limited its decision to apply only to books removed from school library shelves, not to decisions about books added to the shelves. In summary, the Court stated, "We hold that local school boards may not remove books from school library shelves simply because they dislike the ideas contained in those books and seek by their removal to prescribe what shall be orthodox in politics, nationalism, religion, or other matters of opinion."

The *Tinker* decision has provided some protection for the freedom of speech of students in public schools, and the *Goss* decision has provided protection from arbitrary dismissal of students from public schools. Both decisions represent the continuing expansion of civil liberties granted under the Constitution of the United States. Teachers and other school authorities have a duty and an obligation to ensure that these rights are protected. Teachers also have an obligation to protect their constitutional rights, thereby serving as models for students and setting an example for interpreting the meaning of civil liberties in the United States.

Do School Authorities Have the Right to Beat Children?

Readers are asked to consider and offer their opinions in the following situations and compare their opinions with the decisions of the courts. Assume the following set of circumstances: The family of a child cannot afford private schooling. Due to compulsory education laws, the family is forced to send the child to a local public school where the primary means of discipline is corporal punishment. The parents do not believe in the use of physical punishment, have never used physical punishment at home, and do not want the public school to use physical punishment on their child. In this situation, can school authorities spank the child? In other words, can the child be forced to attend an institution that gives its personnel the right to use physical punishment, contrary to practices in the child's home?

Part of the answer to these questions was given in the U.S. Supreme Court decision *Ingraham* v. *Wright* (1977). A junior high school student, James Ingraham, in Dade County, Florida, refused to let the principal of his school, Willie Wright, paddle him for not leaving the stage of the school auditorium promptly. (Ingraham claimed that he had left the stage when requested by the principal.) When Ingraham refused to be paddled, Principal Wright called in his two assistant principals, who held Ingraham's legs and arms. The student was hit 20 times on the buttocks with a two-foot-long wooden paddle. His mother examined him when he arrived home and immediately took him to a local hospital, where the doctor prescribed pain pills, ice packs, and a laxative, and recommended that Ingraham stay home for a week.

At a Florida trial court hearing, many other students complained about beatings at the school. Children described being pushed up against urinals in the boys' bathroom and being beaten on the legs, back, and across the neck. One boy described how he refused to take a whipping because he felt he was innocent, and was beaten with a board across the head. Within a few days of the beating, the student underwent an operation to have a lump removed from his head; he claimed a subsequent loss of memory.

After a week-long trial, the Florida court granted the defense a motion for dismissal, arguing that there was no showing of severe punishment and that corporal punishment was not unacceptable according to the standards of contemporary society. This ruling was overturned by the Fifth Circuit Court of Appeals on the grounds that the punishment at the junior high school violated the Eighth Amendment's prohibition against "cruel and unusual punishment." A further appeal reversed this ruling and set the stage for a decision by the U.S. Supreme Court.

On April 19, 1977, the U.S. Supreme Court ruled that the cruel and unusual punishment clause of the Eighth Amendment does not apply to corporal punishment, nor does the due process clause of the Fourteenth Amendment require that notice be given to students before they are subjected to corporal punishment. The Court argued that corporal punishment had been the traditional means of maintaining discipline in the public schools, and that although public opinion was divided on the issue, there did not seem to be any trend to eliminate its use. The Court found no reason for extending the Eighth Amendment to the schools.

The Court felt that community pressure and common-law safeguards should be used to ensure that corporal punishment be used in a reasonable manner. This argument paralleled the lower court's argument that in this particular case, criminal charges could be brought against the junior high school principal and assistant principal. In other words, public school authorities can beat children, but the extent of the punishment must be reasonable.

Determining what is "reasonable" creates a difficult problem for courts and the community. A teacher or administrator who inflicts one or two spankings a year without causing any lasting physical damage would be considered "reasonable." But what about the teacher or principal who paddles so violently that students are left with black-and-blue marks? A principal of a Kentucky high school, in a recent lecture at my university, argued that administrators and teachers who use corporal punishment excessively exhibit behavior usually associated with child abusers.

But what if parents object to the use of corporal punishment? A decision regarding this issue was made by the Fourth Circuit Court of Appeals on May 9, 1980, in *Hall* v. *Tawney*. Thomas Flygare describes this case in the September 1980 issue of the *Phi Delta Kappan*. A West Virginia grade-school student was, in Flygare's words, "repeatedly and violently struck on the hip and thigh by a teacher using a homemade hard rubber paddle about five inches in width. She alleged that as a result of this paddling she was hospitalized for 10 days and has received the treatment of specialists for possible permanent injuries to the lower spine."

Since argument in terms of the Eighth Amendment's cruel and unusual punishment clause had failed in the *Ingraham* case, Hall's lawyers decided to use a different tactic. The lawyers argued that the paddling, as Flygare states, "violated the right of her parents to determine the means by which she could be disciplined."

The Fourth Circuit Court ruled that parents had no constitutional right to exempt their children from corporal punishment in the schools. The statement of the court raised a whole host of issues regarding the power of parents versus the power of the school. The reader is asked to reflect on the statement by the court that "the state interest in maintaining order in the schools limits the rights of particular parents unilaterally to except their children from the regime to which other children are subject."

The Language of the Schools

One of the more controversial areas of court involvement in recent years has been bilingual education. Part of the controversy stems from a lack of clarity about the intentions of the courts. Some people feel that the decisions have opened the door for primary instruction to take place in a foreign language or "black English." This is not the case. Court rulings have been quite clear that the primary task of the schools is to teach standard English, and that other languages and "black English" are to be used as a means to achieve that goal.

The landmark case was the 1974 U.S. Supreme Court decision in *Lau et al.* v. *Nichols et al.* The case was a class-action suit brought in behalf of non-English-speaking Chinese students in the San Francisco School District. The complaint was that no special instruction for learning standard English was provided to these students. The complaint did not ask for any specific instructional methods to remedy this situation. In the words of the Court decision: "Teaching English to the students of Chinese ancestry who do not speak the language is one choice. Giving instructions to this group in Chinese is another. There may be others." This point created a good deal of controversy in 1980, when the federal government issued regulations for a specific remedy to *Lau*. It was argued that specific remedies were not defined under the *Lau* decision. Those regulations were withdrawn in 1981.

The claim in *Lau* was that the lack of special instruction to help non-English-speaking students learn standard English provided unequal educational opportunity and therefore violated the Fourteenth Amendment to the Constitution. The reader will recall, from the beginning of this chapter and from Chapter 5 on school desegregation, that the Fourteenth Amendment guarantees all citizens equal protection under the laws.

The Court did not use the Fourteenth Amendment in its ruling, but relied of Title VI of the 1964 Civil Rights Act. The reader will recall that this law bans discrimination based on "race, color, or national origin" in "any program or activity receiving Federal financial assistance." The Supreme Court ruled: "It seems obvious that the Chinese-speaking minority receives fewer benefits than the English-speaking majority from respondents' school system which denies them a meaningful opportunity to participate in the educational program—all earmarks of the discrimination banned by the regulations." Although the Court did not give a specific remedy to the situation, its ruling meant that all public school systems receiving any form of federal aid must ensure that children from non-English-speaking backgrounds be given some form of special help in learning standard English so that they may have equal educational opportunity.

The problem that was not addressed in *Lau* was that of specific remedies for the situation of children from non-standard-English backgrounds. A decision regarding this issue was made by the U.S. District Court in 1979 in *Martin Luther King Junior Elementary School Children et al.* v. *Ann Arbor School*

District. The court was quite clear that the case was "not an effort on the part of the plaintiffs to require that they be taught 'black English' or that their instruction throughout their schooling be in 'black English,' or that a dual language program be provided."

As the court defined the problem, it was the ability to teach standard English to "children who, it is alleged, speak 'black English' as a matter of course at home and in their home community." The plaintiffs introduced into the case the testimony of expert witnesses who argued that attempts to teach standard English without appreciating the dialect used by the children at home and in the community could cause the children to be ashamed of their language and hinder their ability to learn standard English.

The court gave recognition to the existence of a bilingual culture within the black community, in which individuals would speak black English with peers and standard English with the larger community. In the words of the Court, the black children "retain fluency in 'black English' to maintain status in the community and they become fluent in standard English to succeed in the general society."

After reviewing the evidence and the expert testimony, the court argued that there was a possible relationship between poor reading ability and the school's not taking into account the home language of the children. This prevented children from taking full advantage of their schooling and was a denial of equal educational opportunity. This argument was based on the reasonable premise that knowing how to read was one of the most important factors in achievement in school.

The court gave a very specific remedy to the situation, a remedy that might be used as a guide in future cases. The court directed the school system to develop within 30 days a plan that would "identify children speaking 'black English' and the language spoken as a home or community language." Second, the school system was directed to "use that knowledge in teaching such students how to read standard English."

School Finances

The issue of racial segregation and equality of educational opportunity was discussed in Chapter 5. The reader will recall that equality of educational opportunity means equal access to educational institutions regardless of race. In terms of school finances, equality of educational opportunity is provided if equal amounts of public money are spent on each child's public schooling. The problem in many states is that the amount of money spent per public school student varies from one school district to another.

Resolving the problem of unequal financing of public schools does not necessarily provide complete equality of educational opportunity. As mentioned in Chapter 5, other important factors may get in the way of equality of

Table 10.1 Property Valuations in Cuyahoga School Districts

School Districts	Per Pupil Valuation 1974–75	Current Costs Per Pupil 1973–74	School Tax Rate, 1975 Collection
Cuyahoga Heights	$260,014	$2,067.76	12.0 M
Independence	66,017	1,483.04	27.8
Beachwood	44,246	1,759.94	57.2
Cleveland	22,209	1,224.50	42.2
North Royalton	20,718	954.83	52.1
Olmsted Falls	14,404	886.34	49.0

SOURCE: *Government Facts, Number 274*, May 2, 1975. Published by the Governmental Research Institute, Cleveland, Ohio.

opportunity, such as quality of teachers, type of curriculum, and instructional materials. Although these considerations are important in assessing the quality of schooling, one should not lose sight of the basic issue of justice. One can argue that it is unjust for the child of one taxpayer to have less public money spent on his or her education then is spent on the child of another taxpayer. It is unjust for the child of a taxpayer to be denied equal access to public institutions because of race. Like the issue of racial segregation, the issue of school financing is directly related to equality of educational opportunity.

There are several reasons why, in a particular state, unequal amounts of public money are spent on schoolchildren. One reason is the reliance on local property taxes to support public schools, a reliance that can vary in degree from state to state. According to Charles Tesconi and Emanuel Hurwitz in their book *Education for Whom?* in the United States about 52 percent of the financial support of schools comes from local taxes.

Reliance on local property taxes can result in unequal support of schools because of differences between school districts in the value of the property to be taxed and the amount a community is willing to tax its property. For instance, some communities have several large industries and expensive residential and commercial areas that can be taxed for support of schools. Other communities are composed of modest residential areas and do not have any large industries. Both communities might levy equal taxes. This would not result in equal revenue due to the unequal value of property in the two communities. This could mean, for instance, that a homeowner in one community could pay the same amount of taxes on a $40,000 house as a homeowner with a house of the same value in another community, but very different sums might be spent on the education of their children because of the disparity in total value of property between the two communities. Examples of these disparities can be found in Table 10.1, which covers school districts in Cuyahoga County, Ohio.

The table illustrates the differences among property values, school expenditures, and tax rates within a single county. Within this county, Cuyahoga

Heights has the lowest tax rate but spends the most per pupil ($2,067.76). The reason it is able to have a minimum property tax but generate the most income per student is because of the high property values within the community. Cuyahoga Heights is a tax haven for industrial concerns within Cuyahoga County. It is primarily composed of major industries and has only small residential areas. This is why it has a per-pupil property valuation of $260,014. On the other hand, Olmsted Falls taxes itself at more than four times the rate of Cuyahoga Heights but spends less than half as much per pupil ($886.34).

If the amount of money spent per pupil is considered to be one factor in equality of educational opportunity, then the children of Olmsted Falls and other school districts in Cuyahoga County are receiving unequal educational opportunity compared to the children of Cuyahoga Heights. Because the residential area of Cuyahoga Heights is limited, the problem cannot be resolved by everyone moving into that school district. In addition, the majority of workers in the industries in Cuyahoga Heights cannot live in the school district because of its small size and, therefore, their children cannot benefit from the high per-pupil expenditures. In other words, the industries in this community are able to pay low taxes without equally sharing the cost of education within the county with other industries and property owners.

The book that provided the basis for the original court cases against inequality of educational opportunity that is caused by the reliance upon property taxes to support education is *Private Wealth and Public Education*, by John E. Coons, William H. Clune, and Stephen Sugarman. This is a masterful study of the growth of school financing in the United States and the various attempts to solve these problems. The first part of the book presents a critical treatment of existing state aid to education plans and persuasively argues that existing attempts to equalize educational expenditures either have failed or have actually created greater inequalities. As a substitute for existing education-financing plans, the book offers a power-equalization formula that would equalize spending between school districts and between states and supposedly end inequality of educational resources between school districts. The study also presents a plan for implementing the power-equalization formula by using the judicial process to argue in court that the education of children should be considered under the Equal Protection Clause of the Fourteenth Amendment. One of the judicial techniques suggested is to compare the inequality of educational spending with those reapportionment decisions of the Supreme Court that led to the one-man, one-vote doctrine. It is the opinion of the book's authors that, in a democratic society, schooling should be considered equal in importance to voting.

The rationale given in the study for the need to support a power-equalization formula is directly related to equality of educational opportunity. The book argues that the United States is a competitive democracy in which a marketplace of talent is the prime determiner of individual success. As in other discussions about equality of opportunity, the primary concern is with assuring equal competition. The book states that "the sine qua non of a fair contest system...is equality of training. And that training is what public education is primarily about." The authors also recognize that the primary purpose of American education is preparation for a competitive job market. They state: "There are, we hope, loftier views of education that coexist, but in a competitive democracy those views represent dependent goals that can be realized only upon a foundation of training for basic competence in the market." Providing for equality in the financing of public education is necessary in order to make the operations of the marketplace fair and provide for the social mobility of the poor. The authors restate their faith in American education: "Social mobility as a value plays a potent role here, and public education must be seen in its special relation to the underclasses to whom it is the strongest hope for rising in the social scale."

The first major judicial decision dealing with school finances was made by the California Supreme Court in *Serrano* v. *Priest* (1971). This case involved the two sons of John Serrano, who lived in a poor, mainly Mexican–American, community in Los Angeles. The local school in the area had rapidly increasing class sizes and a consequent shortage of textbooks and supplies. Local school authorities told John Serrano that the financial situation in the schools would not improve. According to Charles Tesconi and Emanuel Hurwitz in their book, *Education for Whom?* the family was forced to mortgage their property and move to another community to provide a better education for the two sons.

The case presented before the California Supreme Court put the situation of the Serrano family in the following terms: "Plaintiffs contend that the school financing system classifies on the basis of wealth. We find this proposition irrefutable...." The court went on to assert that this was a direct result of the method of financing the schools. The example given by the court was of "Baldwin Park citizens, who paid a school tax of $5.48 per $100 of assessed valuation, were able to spend less than half as much on education as Beverly Hills residents, who were taxed only $2.38 per $100."

The California Supreme Court ruled in the *Serrano* case that the California school-financing system, with its dependence upon local property taxes, violated the Equal Protection Clause of the Fourteenth Amendment. The court stated: "We have determined that this funding scheme invidiously discriminates against the poor because it makes the quality of a child's education a function of the wealth of his parents and his neighbors."

Serrano was a landmark decision for action within state court systems. When the issue finally reached the U.S. Supreme Court, a major setback in the legal struggles occurred. In 1973 the Supreme Court ruled in one of the school-financing cases, *Rodriguez* v. *San Antonio Independent School District*, that the right to an education was not implicitly protected by the Fourteenth Amendment and was not entitled to constitutional protection. The Court declared: "The consideration and initiation of fundamental reforms with respect to state taxation and education are matters reserved for the legislative processes of the various states."

The *Rodriguez* decision meant that school-financing cases would have to be argued within the courts of each state in terms of state constitutions. This would mean a long struggle within each state to achieve a method of providing equal financial support to the schools. One cannot predict whether this will occur in all states in the country, but it is one important part of the attempt to achieve equality of educational opportunity in the United States.

The courts have played an essential role in protecting individual rights within the public schools. Because public schools attempt to educate a large population having a variety of backgrounds and beliefs, there is always the danger that minority rights will be lost or forgotten within the school. In addition, public schooling is a property right and in most states is compulsory. These conditions mean that some institution must exercise vigilance in the protection of rights in education. This is the important role that the courts have assumed and will continue to assume in American education.

Exercises

1. Check with a local school district about their grievance procedures for teachers and students.
2. What provisions do local school districts in your area have for protecting teacher and student rights?

Suggested Readings and Works Cited in Chapter

Coons, John, William H. Clune, and Stephen Sugarman. *Private Wealth and Public Education.* Cambridge, Mass: Harvard University Press, 1970. This is the book that provided the basic arguments for the school finance cases.

Dessem, Lawrence. "Student Due Process Rights in Academic Dismissals from the Public Schools." *Journal of Law and Education* 5, no. 3 (July 1976).

Flygare, Thomas. "Schools and the Law." *Phi Delta Kappan.* This monthly column provides one of the best guides to recent court cases related to education. It is highly recommended for any person involved in the educational system.

Grover, Alan. *Ohio's Trojan Horse: A Warning to Christian Schools Everywhere.* Greenville, S.C.: Bob Jones University Press, 1977. The book contains a description of the *Whisner* case and the arguments regarding secular humanism.

Keim, Albert N., ed. *Compulsory Education and the Amish.* Boston: Beacon, 1972. This book contains articles about the Amish and their struggle against compulsory education.

Lapati, Americo. *Education and the Federal Government.* New York: Mason/Chapter,

1975. The last section of this book reviews all the major U.S. Supreme Court cases regarding education.

Lehne, Richard. *The Quest for Justice: The Politics of School Finance Reform.* New York and London: Longman, 1978. An excellent analysis of the movement for equitably sharing the cost of school finances.

Rubin, David. *The Rights of Teachers.* New York: Avon, 1972. This is the American Civil Liberties Union handbook of teachers' rights.

Tesconi, Charles, and Emanuel Hurwitz. *Education for Whom?* New York: Dodd, Mead, 1974. This book contains essays about the school-finance cases.

Index

293